T0214102

Lecture Notes in Computer Science   12800

Christian Hochberger · Lars Bauer ·
Thilo Pionteck (Eds.)

Architecture of Computing Systems

34th International Conference, ARCS 2021
Virtual Event, June 7–8, 2021
Proceedings

 Springer

Editors
Christian Hochberger
Technische Universität Darmstadt
Darmstadt, Germany

Lars Bauer
Karlsruhe Institute of Technology
Karlsruhe, Germany

Thilo Pionteck
Otto-von-Guericke University Magdeburg
Magdeburg, Germany

ISSN 0302-9743   ISSN 1611-3349 (electronic)
Lecture Notes in Computer Science
ISBN 978-3-030-81681-0   ISBN 978-3-030-81682-7 (eBook)
https://doi.org/10.1007/978-3-030-81682-7

LNCS Sublibrary: SL1 – Theoretical Computer Science and General Issues

This Springer imprint is published by the registered company Springer Nature Switzerland AG
The registered company address is: Gewerbestrasse 11, 6330 Cham, Switzerland

Preface

The International Conference on Architecture of Computing Systems (ARCS) series has over 30 years of tradition reporting leading-edge research in computer architecture and operating systems. The conference was organized by the Special Interest Group on Architecture of Computing Systems of the GI (Gesellschaft für Informatik e.V.) and ITG (Informationstechnische Gesellschaft im VDE), which held the financial responsibility for this ARCS edition. ARCS addresses the complete spectrum from fully integrated, self-powered embedded systems up to high-performance computing systems and provides a platform covering newly emerging and cross-cutting topics, such as autonomous and ubiquitous systems, reconfigurable computing and acceleration, neural networks, and artificial intelligence, as well as outlooks on future topics such as post-Moore architectures and organic computing.

The 34th edition of the conference (ARCS 2021) was planned when we all knew that the COVID-19 pandemic would still be at large during the conference dates (June 7–8 2021). Thus, we anticipated that international travel would still be a problem and decided to organize the conference as a virtual event. Yet, this brought a number of new and previously unfamiliar problems. Should we aim for prerecorded talks and then only have a live Q&A session or should we go for live presentations? Would there be enough attendance to foster lively discussions? What type of venue would attract the most people? How should we plan the social event?

Eventually, we decided to present the talks in live sessions because we believe that this is the best basis for discussions at the conference. In addition, we chose a venue that enabled people to "walk around" and freely choose other attendees to talk to. Although this cannot fully replace the real-world networking event that ARCS has been in the past, we hoped that all guests of the ARCS conference could meet interesting people and have fruitful discussions.

The motto for ARCS 2021 was inspired by a seminal paper from John Hennessy and Dave Patterson (J.L. Hennessy and D.A. Patterson: "A New Golden Age for Computer Architecture" in Communications of the ACM 62.2 (2019), pp. 48–60). In this article, they forecast a "Cambrian explosion of novel computer architectures". We found this extremely suitable as a focus for the conference as it covers the different facets that are part of the ARCS community. Under this umbrella, all the various accelerator types that are currently explored fit as well as IoT architectures or HPC specific processor optimizations and the management of heterogeneous systems. Additionally, programming models and system concepts are well connected to the topic.

ARCS 2021 attracted 24 full submissions from authors in 10 countries worldwide, including Japan, Brazil, USA, and several European countries. Each submission was reviewed by a diverse and dedicated Program Committee. Most of the submissions got 4 or even 5 qualified reviews and 7 submissions received 3 reviews, leading to a total of 92 reviews. The Program Committee selected 12 submissions to be published in the proceedings, which corresponds to a 50% paper acceptance rate. The accepted papers cover a variety of topics from the ARCS core domains, including heterogeneous computing, memory optimizations, and system management. Thanks to our sponsor Springer, we were able to hand out a best paper and a best presentation award at the closing ceremony.

ARCS has a long tradition of hosting associated workshops. This year the 16th Workshop on Dependability and Fault Tolerance (VERFE 2021) was organized and we decided to include the accepted papers within the conference proceedings.

We thank the many individuals who contributed to ARCS 2021, in particular the members of the Program Committee and the additional external reviewers for their time and effort in carefully reviewing and judging the submissions. We further thank all authors for submitting their work to ARCS and presenting accepted papers. The workshop organization was coordinated by Carsten Trinitis, and the proceedings were compiled by Thilo Pionteck. Thanks go to these individuals and all the many other people who helped in the organization of ARCS 2021.

June 2021

Christian Hochberger
Lars Bauer
Thilo Pionteck

Organization

General Chair

Christian Hochberger   Technische Universität Darmstadt, Germany

Program Chairs

Lars Bauer   Karlsruhe Institute of Technology, Germany
Thilo Pionteck   Otto von Guericke University Magdeburg, Germany

Workshop and Tutorial Chair

Carsten Trinitis   Technical University of Munich, Germany

Publication Chair

Thilo Pionteck   Otto von Guericke University Magdeburg, Germany

Program Committee

Lars Bauer	Karlsruhe Institute of Technology, Germany
Mladen Berekovic	Universität zu Lübeck, Germany
Jürgen Brehm	Leibnitz Universität Hannover, Germany
Andre Brinkmann	Johannes Gutenberg-Universität Mainz, Germany
Uwe Brinkschulte	Goethe-Universität Frankfurt am Main, Germany
Joao Cardoso	Universidade do Porto, Portugal
Thomas Carle	Institut de Recherche en Informatique de Toulouse, France
Ahmed El-Mahdy	Egypt-Japan University of Science and Technology, Egypt
Lukas Esterle	Aarhus University, Denmark
Pierfrancesco Foglia	Università di Pisa, Italy
Roberto Giorgi	University of Siena, Italy
Daniel Gracia-Pérez	Thales Research and Technology, France
Christian Gruhl	University of Kassel, Germany
Jan Haase	Universität zu Lübeck, Germany
Joerg Haehner	University of Augsburg, Germany
Heiko Hamann	Universität zu Lübeck, Germany
Andreas Herkersdorf	Technical University of Munich, Germany
Christian Hochberger	Technische Universität Darmstadt, Germany
Gert Jervan	Tallinn University of Technology, Estonia
Wolfgang Karl	Karlsruhe Institute of Technology, Germany

Jörg Keller	FernUniversität in Hagen, Germany
Hana Kubatova	FIT CTU, Czech Republic
Erik Maehle	Universität zu Lübeck, Germany
Lena Oden	FernUniversität in Hagen, Germany
Alex Orailoglu	University of California, San Diego, USA
Thilo Pionteck	Otto-von-Guericke Universität Magdeburg, Germany
Mario Porrmann	Osnabrück University, Germany
Reza Salkhordeh	Johannes Gutenberg University Mainz, Germany
Toshinori Sato	Fukuoka University, Japan
Wolfgang Schröder-Preikschat	Friedrich-Alexander-Universität Erlangen-Nürnberg, Germany
Martin Schulz	Technical University of Munich, Germany
Leonel Sousa	Universidade de Lisboa, Portugal
Olaf Spinczyk	Osnabrück University, Germany
Benno Stabernack	Fraunhofer Institute for Telecommunications, Germany
Walter Stechele	Technical University of Munich, Germany
Anthony Stein	University of Hohenheim, Germany
Jürgen Teich	Friedrich-Alexander-Universität Erlangen-Nürnberg, Germany
Sven Tomforde	University of Kassel, Germany
Theo Ungerer	University of Augsburg, Germany
Hans Vandierendonck	Queen's University Belfast, UK
Daniel Versick	NORDAKADEMIE Hochschule der Wirtschaft, Germany
Stephane Vialle	CentraleSupélec and UMI GT-CNRS 2958, France
Klaus Waldschmidt	Goethe-Universität Frankfurt am Main, Germany
Stephan Wong	Delft University of Technology, the Netherlands

Additional Reviewers

Hannan, Abdul	University of Kassel, Germany
Aljuffri, Abdullah	Delft University of Technology, the Netherlands
Borchert, Christoph	Osnabrück University, Germany
Eichler, Christian	Friedrich-Alexander-Universität Erlangen-Nürnberg, Germany
Fieback, Moritz	Delft University of Technology, the Netherlands
Gautam, Pushpak	University of California, San Diego, USA
Handal, Dillon	University of California, San Diego, USA
Klink, Raphael	Universität zu Lübeck, Germany
Letras, Martin	Friedrich-Alexander-Universität Erlangen-Nürnberg, Germany
Lin, Hsin-Kun	Universität zu Lübeck, Germany
Marques, Diogo	Universidade de Lisboa, Portugal
Müller, Michael	Osnabrück University, Germany
Neves, Nuno	Universidade de Lisboa, Portugal
Paulino, Nuno	Universidade de Lisboa, Portugal

Procaccini, Marco	University of Siena, Italy
Sahebi, Amin	University of Siena, Italy
Schmaus, Florian	Friedrich-Alexander-Universität Erlangen-Nürnberg, Germany
Schmeißing, Jörn	University of Kassel, Germany
Schuster, Armin	Friedrich-Alexander-Universität Erlangen-Nürnberg, Germany
Witterauf, Michael	Friedrich-Alexander-Universität Erlangen-Nürnberg, Germany
Zahedi, Mahdi	Delft University of Technology, the Netherlands

16th Workshop on Dependability and Fault Tolerance (VERFE 2021)

Program Committee

Lars Bauer	Karlsruhe Institute of Technology, Germany
Fevzi Belli	University of Paderborn, Germany
Greg Bronevetsky	X, the moonshot factory, USA
Rainer Buchty	Technische Universität Braunschweig, Germany
Klaus Echtle	University of Duisburg-Essen, Germany
Wolfgang Ehrenberger	University of Fulda, Germany
Rolf Ernst	Technische Universität Braunschweig, Germany
Michael Gössel	University of Potsdam, Germany
Karl-Erwin Großpietsch	Euromicro, Germany
Jörg Henkel	Karlsruhe Institute of Technology, Germany
John Hursey	Oak Ridge National Laboratory, USA
Jörg Keller	FernUniversität in Hagen, Germany
Hans-Dieter Kochs	University of Duisburg-Essen, Germany
Miroslaw Malek	USI-Lugano, Switzerland
Erik Maehle	Universität zu Lübeck, Germany
Dimitris Nikolos	University of Patras, Greece
Francesca Saglietti	Friedrich-Alexander-Universität Erlangen-Nürnberg, Germany
Toshi Sato	University of Fukuoka, Japan
Martin Schulz	Technical University of Munich, Germany
Muhammad Shafique	TU Vienna, Austria
Janusz Sosnowski	University of Warsaw, Poland
Carsten Trinitis	Technical University of Munich, Germany
Peter Tröger	Technsiche Universität Chemnitz, Germany
Heinrich Theodor Vierhaus	Technische Universität Cottbus, Germany
Norbert Wehn	Technische Universität Kaiserslautern, Germany
Josef Weidendorfer	Technical University of Munich, Germany
Sebastian Zug	Technische Universität Bergakademie Freiberg, Germany

Keynote Talks

The Cambrian Explosion in Architecture – Are We "There" Yet?

Peter M. Kogge

University of Notre Dame, USA

Abstract. The Cambrian period of life represented a time of explosion of life forms, all driven by larger collections of cells with increased specialization. Given the recent explosion in novel architectural features, it is natural to assert that we are at least entering a similar "golden age" of computing. This talk explores this assertion, with a comparison of advances in architecture with the evolution of life, and a conclusion that no, we are not quite at the Cambrian point yet, but the diversity we see now is a sign that architecture a generation from now may look radically different than today.

The main talking point is that evolution in architecture is driven by changes in what we want to compute, coupled with limitations in the available technology. In the past we have seen at least two such "walls" (memory and power) whose vanquishing required significant advances in architecture. In this talk we will discuss evidence on the emergence of a new third wall dealing with data locality (a site of computation is "here" and data is "over there"), which is prevalent in data intensive applications where computation is dominated by memory access and movement – not flops. Such apps exhibit large sets of often persistent data, with little reuse during any single computation, no predictable regularity, significantly different scaling characteristics, and where streaming is becoming important. Further, as we move to massively parallel algorithms running in the cloud, these issues will get even worse.

Solving such problems will take a new set of innovations in architecture to overcome. In addition to data on the new wall, the talk will look at several alternatives, and relate them to changes in life evolution. One technique in particular, the concept of migrating threads, will be introduced, and related to cell functions that support various forms of mobility. The paper "Locality: The 3rd Wall and The Need for Innovation in Parallel Architectures" in the conference proceedings discusses this concept in detail, with this talk also suggesting other alternatives based on neuromorphic concepts.

Peter M. Kogge is the McCourtney Professor of Computer Science and Engineering at the University of Notre Dame, a retired IBM Fellow, and a founder of Emu Solutions, now Lucata Inc. He is a fellow of both the IEEE and AAAS. His research interests are in massively parallel computing paradigms, processing in memory, and the relationship between massive non-numeric applications, emerging technology, and computer architectures. He holds over 40 patents and is author of three books, including the first text on pipelining and an upcoming text on models of computing. His Ph.D. thesis led to the Kogge-Stone adder used in many microprocessors. Other projects included the IOP - the world's second multi-threaded parallel processor which flew on every Space

Shuttle, the IBM 3838 Array processor which was for a time the fastest floating point machine marketed by IBM, RTAIS and PIM Lite - systems with significant non-numeric computation built into a memory controller, and EXECUBE - probably the world's first multi-core processor and first processor fabbed on a DRAM chip. In 2008, he led DARPA's Exascale technology study group, which resulted in a widely referenced report on technologies and architectures for exascale computing. His startup, Emu Solutions, has demonstrated the first scalable system that utilizes mobile threads to attack large-scale big data and big graph problems. Dr. Kogge has received the Daniel Slotnick best paper award (1994), the IEEE/ACM Seymour Cray award for high performance computer engineering (2012), the IEEE Charles Babbage award for contributions to the evolution of massively parallel processing architectures (2014), the Gauss best paper award for high performance computers (Int. Supercomputing Conf. 2015), and the IEEE Computer Pioneer award (2015) (Highest award from IEEE Computer Society).

Brain Inspired Computing

Johannes Schemmel

Heidelberg University, Germany

Abstract. Brain Inspired or Neuromorphic Computing, as a realization of Non-Turing, in-memory, event-based computing, will allow us to overcome the power wall our CPU-centric CMOS technology is facing. But that does not mean that the era of Turing-based computing will come to an end soon, or that Turing-based computing does not have its place in the neuromorphic world. This talk will summarize how the Heidelberg BrainScaleS-2 accelerated analog neuromorphic architecture balances Turing and Non-Turing computing to combine power efficiency with the necessary flexibility and programmability, thereby reducing the resource requirements of AI and extending it by recent insights from neuroscience. These bio-inspired AI technologies may be beneficial for the data challenges the next generation of science instrumentation is facing. Possible applications of the BrainScaleS technology in the area of edge computing will be presented.

Johannes Schemmel I is is head if the Electronc Vision(s) research group at Heidelberg University. Since 2018 he acts as interim professor at the chair of neuromorphic computing. His core research interests are massively parallel analog, in-memory, neuromorphic computing technologies for brain-inspired artificial intelligence. He is the lead architect of the BrainScaleS neuromorphic system.

Contents

Organic Computing

Low Power Design

VEFRE Workshop

Memory Organization

Locality: The 3rd Wall and the Need for Innovation in Parallel Architectures

Peter M. Kogge[✉] and Brian A. Page

University of Notre Dame, Notre Dame, IN 46556, USA
{kogge,bpage1}@nd.edu

Abstract. In the past we have seen two major "walls" (memory and power) whose vanquishing required significant advances in architecture. This paper discusses evidence of a third wall dealing with data locality, which is prevalent in data intensive applications where computation is dominated by memory access and movement – not flops, Such apps exhibit large sets of often persistent data, with little reuse during computation, no predictable regularity, significantly different scaling characteristics, and where streaming is becoming important. Further, as we move to highly parallel algorithms (as in running in the cloud), these issues will get even worse. Solving such problems will take a new set of innovations in architecture. In addition to data on the new wall, this paper will look at one possible technique: the concept of migrating threads, and give evidence of its potential value based on several benchmarks that have scaling difficulties on conventional architectures.

Keywords: Architecture · Parallelism · Multi-threading

1 Introduction

The Cambrian explosion started about 540 million years ago, and represented the jump from simple multi-cell colonies to complex multi-cell organisms, both plant and animal, with rich internal structures and optimized for a wild variety of environments. In their 2018 Turing Lecture [16], Hennessey and Patterson suggested that we are reaching a similar threshold in computer architecture. We have gone from simple single "cell" cores, through clustered "colonies" of such cells, to the point where we are beginning to see specialized "organs" implemented by accelerators for different functions. While the efficiency and scalability of such systems are often quite good for problems with dense data that is accessed in a regular pattern, this is not so true for "newly evolving" problems that are sparse and irregular in their access patterns.

The thesis of this paper is that the problem is **locality**, which as typically defined can come in several forms. In **temporal locality**, if some memory location is accessed once, there is a high probability that the same location will be accessed again within a short period of time. In **spatial locality**, if one location is accessed, then there is a high probability that nearby locations will be

© Springer Nature Switzerland AG 2021
C. Hochberger et al. (Eds.): ARCS 2021, LNCS 12800, pp. 3–18, 2021.
https://doi.org/10.1007/978-3-030-81682-7_1

Table 1. Eras in parallel architectures

Era	Slime Mold		Fungi		Moss	
	Prehistory	Archaic	Yesteryear	Last Month	Yesterday	Today
App	3D Mesh-like	Ax=b, A dense $n \times n$ matrix			Ax=b sparse, BFS	ML, Analytics
Time Frame	1980s	1990s	2004	2008	2013	
Computation	$O(n^3)$	$O(n^3)$	$O(n^3)$	$O(n^3)$	$O(n)$	$O(n^?)$
Memory	$O(n^3)$	$O(n^2)$	$O(n^2)$	$O(n^2)$	$O(n)$	$O(n^?)$
I/O	$O(n^2)$	$O(n)$	$O(n)$	$O(n)$	$O(n^{2/3})$	$O(n^?)$
Issue	Basic Scaling	Memory Bandwidth	Socket Power	Power Efficiency	Low App Intensity	Locality
New Advances	2D topology Moore's Law	Caches Clock	Multi-core Flat Clock SOC	Heterogeneous Hybrid Fat Tree Low precision	GPUs, Hybrid Many Core Hi-degree N/W Proc. In/Near Mem	Massive core Smart NICs

accessed within a short period of time. In parallel systems we also have **physical locality** where it matters whether or not data is in a locally accessible memory.

This paper is organized as follows. Section 2 walks briefly through the historical changes. Sections 3 and 4 provide evidence of this new wall. Section 5 discusses one possible approach to solve these issues by allowing threads to migrate. Section 6 provides examples of its effectiveness. Section 7 concludes.

2 Parallel Architectural Archaeology

To understand more fully the forces driving the need for changes in parallel architectures, it is instructive to review briefly the historical record. In analogy with biological evolution, the Proterozoic Eon saw the rise of the first cells with organelles, which in computing terms corresponds to simple single core computers with basic function units. The Phanerozoic Eon saw the growth of multi-cell organisms, or, in computing terms, systems with multiple cores. While parallel function units date back to the Illiac IV (1972), and small-scale shared memory machines date back almost as far, the first highly parallel machines really appeared only in the mid 1980s (the Caltech Cosmic Cube). From then to now we have seen three major eras in parallel systems:

- **Slime Mold era**: In biology, this early era was dominated by loose colonies of simple single-cell organisms. The parallel architecture equivalent was the early systems that had simple single core nodes with simple interconnects.
- **Fungi era**: In biology, this era represented a change to colonies of multi-cell organisms, but where the cells are still mostly undifferentiated. The parallel architecture equivalent was the appearance of multi-core processor chips.
- **Moss era**: In biology, this era began the evolution to organisms with multiple types of cells. The parallel architecture equivalent was the introduction of hybrid nodes with different types of cores and smart network interfaces.

In evolutionary terms, there have been major "extinction events" that caused die-offs of lifeforms, and the emergence of newer ones that were better suited. The same thing has happened with parallel architectures, driven by either technology ("walls") or changes in application needs. Table 1 summarizes how such events have bifurcated the above three eras further into six periods.

Prehistory - The Start of the Slime Mold Era: The first wave of parallel computers were designed to solve 3D problems that were decomposable into relatively independent sub-cubes that could be solved largely separately, such as 3D mesh equations and N-body problems, where "surfaces" of sub-cubes were exchanged with nearest neighbors. Architecturally, nodes in such systems were simple single cores. The major issue was simply getting enough parallel nodes. The major technology advance was using Moore's Law to move to single-chip cores and scale the clock, with simple 2D or 3D hypercube interconnect topology.

Archaic: The Memory Wall. The second period emerged when processors had accelerated clock speeds to the level where now memory bandwidth was the major impediment. This triggered a shift from mesh-like simulation to the solution of large linear equations of the form $Ax = b$ where A is a large dense matrix. Packages such as LAPACK became quite efficient and easily parallelizable, and led to **HPL** - the benchmark used for the semi-annual TOP500 rankings of supercomputers. An advantage of these algorithms was that these large matrices could be partitioned into smaller sub-matrices, such that a sub-matrix of $O(m^2)$ values could be read into a core once, and $O(m^3)$ operations could be performed on them, for the equivalent of m flops for each value read from memory. This results in high locality, and with a sufficient-sized cache, a core could use nearly all its capability. Moore's Law provided the transistors to do this.

Yesteryear: The Power Wall. For a long time "Dennard scaling" allowed us to reduce the size of transistors, increase the clock, and decrease the supply voltage, all while keeping chip power density relatively constant. This meant faster cores with bigger caches and enhanced ILP. Improving fabrication technology allowed larger die to be produced, resulting in power that was linear in die size, but independent of clock or computational features. Around 2004, however, our ability to scale voltage down slowed tremendously, and chip power dissipation sykrocketed. This forced a major change in architecture. Maximum clock speeds flattened to around 2–3 GHz, and processor chips went from holding single complex cores to multiple simpler cores that were more power efficient. Caches continued to grow in size, with additional levels of caching introduced to serve the multiple on-chip cores. Systems-on-a-chip that integrated multi-core processing and networking became practical, such as IBM Blue Gene [11].

Last Month: Energy Efficiency. Even with multi-core processing chips with simple cores, it became obvious that additional energy efficiencies would have to be developed to allow cracking the petaflops (10^{15} flops/sec.) barrier at acceptable power levels. The first such system to do so in 2008, Roadrunner [1], had several unique architectural features, and was a precursor for what became standard in the following decade. First, it employed a **heterogeneous** architecture with two distinct types of processing chips, a conventional chip and one adapted for specialized computation. Further, the accelerator chip was itself a **hybrid** multi-core, where there were two types of cores that shared the same memory space. Finally, the topology of the network changed from a mesh or torus to a switched fat-tree that provided better non-nearest neighbor communication.

At the same time it became obvious that to get the next 1000x ("exascale") at acceptable power and in a reasonable period of time would need even more architectural advances. A major study [21] performed an in-depth projection that determined energy efficiency was the major problem, with memory and interconnect, not computation, as the major culprits. The proposed architecture featured not multi-core but **many-core** chips with hundreds of cores, 3D **stacked memory** with substrate-level chip-to-chip connectivity to the processor cores, on-chip integrated network interfaces, and high-radix interconnect topologies that do not use external switches. Even with all this, the projection for a 2015 exascale machine was 3X over the power goal, and to run at high efficiency for dense problems could not provide anywhere near the relative memory or network bandwidth found in then current machines. In addition, with millions of cores, programming would have to deal with perhaps up to one billion threads.

Finally, this era also saw the rise of "Big Data" with analysis on large data sets that were too unstructured for conventional databases. New parallel execution models like MapReduce staged data partitioned across many nodes through various processing and merge steps. Architecturally, the workload presented by such apps was dramatically different than their original design point (cf. [18]).

Yesterday: Sparsity. By the mid 2010s it became obvious that real algorithms were not performing at anywhere near the floating point rates that HPL achieved on the then top supercomputers. The percentage of non-floating point operations had grown dramatically. Sparsity in data sets required significantly more memory accesses that were not cacheable, and added to memory bandwidth needs. Inter-node communication could no longer be fully overlapped with computation, and thus became significant to compute times. Short point-to-point messages with remote atomic operations were important for collectives that controlled the overall flow of parallel computations. To shed light on these issues, two new benchmarks were introduced. The first, Graph500, (2010) performs a breadth-first search (BFS) through very large random graphs, and emphasizes memory performance, short messages to random targets, and remote atomic operations. Performance is in **Traversed Edges Per Second** (**TEPS**). The second, High Performance Conjugate Gradient (**HPCG**) [17], is the solution of $Ax = b$, but where A is very sparse, and integrated a local sparse matrix-vector product with an iterative algorithm where the full matrix was partitioned across a large number of nodes. Communication between nodes is regular and a secondary performance gate. As with HPL, performance is in flops. Unlike HPL, where floating point efficiencies 80% and above are common, HPCG delivers at best low single digits. The issue is the extra memory accesses to handle the sparsity in the local matrix [23].

This era saw an explosive growth in heterogeneous architectures with the coupling of conventional many-core processors to **GPGPUs** that themselves are hybrid processors capable of running hundreds' to thousands' of threads. At least one system (TaihuLight [10]) had only hybrid chips, each with literally hundreds of cores. While highly efficient for traditional dense applications, these features offered little for the newer sparse applications. However, given their origins in graphics applications needing less than 64-bit precision, they included capabilities of performing multiple reduced-precision functions in the same time as single 64-bit floating point operations.

Coupled with this were significant changes to the memory hierarchy. Three levels of caching became commonplace. "Scratchpad" memory emerged that was not cache but directly accessible, especially in many-core hybrid chips. 3D memory stacks offered more memory channels and much higher bandwidths. Persistent memory that does not lose contents on power down is blurring the line between main memory and file systems, and led to the term **storage class memory**. Another trend has been to push intelligence out into the network. "Smart NICs" reduced the overhead of message management by performing such functions in hardware at either endpoints or in network switches.

Today: The Locality Wall. In the last few years we have seen a sea-change in the applications driving high end parallel systems, with machine learning (**ML**) leading the way. The emergence of the Internet of Things (**IoT**) has pushed computation out to huge numbers of endpoints. The need to extract and recognize complex connections in such massive, irregular, real-time, and growingly sparse, data sets has become critical to both science and business.

The bulk of today's AI applications take two forms: training and inference. The former takes large data sets and tries to deduce a model. The latter apply such models to real data to make predictions about the data. Architecturally, such apps have triggered a growth in non-traditional parallel accelerators. Nvidia, for example, markets a "DGX^{tm} SuperPOD" that networks over 1500 GPUs. Google is even more application-specific with systems of thousands of Tensor Processing Unit (**TPUs**) chips [19] that have up to 32,000 multiplier-adders on a chip to accelerate matrix-vector products. Wafer-scale integration as in the Cerebus chip now allows over 400,000 AI-tuned cores to be placed on a huge chip with over 1 trillion transistors [15]. Such systems have several common features. First is a use of short floating point to greatly reduce the hardware needed to perform computations. Second is the use of 3D stacked memory to provide sufficient bandwidth to keep these huge numbers of function units fed.

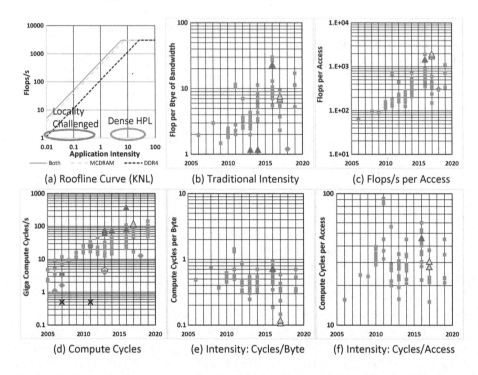

Fig. 1. Today's architectures in terms of ridge point intensity. The different color points represent different classes of chip architectures.

Given the importance of lower precision arithmetic in such ML applications, a new benchmark **HPL-AI** has been developed to continue attacking the $Ax = b$ problem on conventional computers, but using lower than 64-bit precision for the bulk of the computation. Limited results to date indicate a speedup of between 2.5 and 4.5× on the same hardware over native 64-bit performance.

Also there are indications that the old idea of "Processing Near Memory" (PNM) or "Processing/Computing In Memory" (PIM/CIM) may finally demonstrate real advantages, both for increased peak intensity for specialized apps and for lowered energy. IBM's TrueNorth chip [7] mirrors parallel functions found in the human brain. Other chips, c.f. [35], implement low precision linear algebra within a novel memory structure at extraordinarily low levels of energy.

3   Evidence of a New Wall - Low Intensity Apps

The **roofline** model [36] is a useful visualization of multiple performance bounds, and how close a particular code is to reaching those bounds for a particular architecture. In such charts, the y-axis is a measure of predicted performance in terms of some basic operation count per second (such as flops/s), and the x-axis a measure of "operational intensity," the ratio of the number of such operations performed in the algorithm divided by the minimum traffic from some level of memory needed to support them. The numerator is a property of the program being run, and the denominator a property of the memory hierarchy. A bounding curve for such a chart is a line that represents the maximum performance possible out of a particular system when running a code with a particular intensity.

Figure 1(a) is an example of a bounding curve for a system using an Intel Knight's Landing many-core chip. In terms of bandwidth between memory and the processor chip there are three possibilities: all data transfers are from the main DDR4 memory, all is from the 3D stacked MCDRAM memory, or data can come from either one at the same time. Each bounding curve consists of two intersecting lines. The upper flat line is the peak performance possible from the system if the computational units in the cores can run at 100%. The sloping line is a bandwidth constraining bound with a slope equalling the bandwidth of the memory in bytes/sec. The "ridge point" where the two lines intersect is when the peak bandwidth times the application's peak intensity equals the peak system performance. Alternatively, this ridge point is when a code's operational intensity equals the ratio of the processor's peak computational performance divided by the processor's peak memory bandwidth. This ridge point is thus an important characteristic of a processor. Figure 1(b) charts how such a metric has changed with time when flops is the metric. Modern designs have values of 10 or more, meaning that to utilize all their computational capability, a code must continually find 10 or more flops to perform in the time required to transfer a single byte from memory. This is the direct result of optimizing for dense HPL.

As some real examples, the **SKA** project is a massive radio-telescope project with real-time computation at its core. An estimate of the Science Data Processing chain is that it needs 250 pflops/s peak with a memory bandwidth of 200 pB/s [5,32]. This is an intensity of only 1.25 flops/byte. Further, the HPCG sparse benchmark has an intensity of about 0.2 - even further below modern systems. Also, the Sparse Matrix Dense Vector (SpMV) kernel that is central to HPCG is even lower, at about 0.1 flops/byte. As another example, an ML kernel using Stochastic Gradient Descent to compute a Support Vector Machine model employs a loop involving an inner product and a vector-vector like operation where one of the vectors (the model) has some temporal locality but the other does not. The intensity varies between 0.01 and 0.4 depending on sparsity.

A variant of this is to use access rate as the denominator. Today's architectures are designed to deliver 64 or more bytes per access, regardless of how much is used. This is fine for dense HPL where there is significant spatial locality, but for applications with little such, much of the accessed data is never used, and represents wasted bandwidth. Figure 1(c) charts this variation of intensity for the same processors as Fig. 1(b). For a modern processor to run at maximum efficiency, it must execute 1,000 or more flops for each memory access it makes.

Looking further, many of the newer locality-sensitive apps are not flop-intensive, so the traditional flop intensity metric does not make sense. An alternative to flops/s might be simply "compute cycles" - clock rate times number of cores. If "operations" are measured as some number of instructions, and each

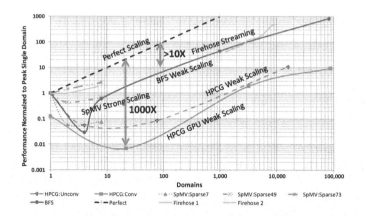

Fig. 2. Some traditional scaling results. BFS comes from www.graph500.org; HPCG from www.hpcg-benchmark.org; SpMV from [4]; Firehose from firehose.sandia.gov.

core may have some CPI up to a maximum of its issue width, then such a metric is a decent approximation. Figure 1(d) diagrams aggregate compute cycles per processor over time, and Figs. 1(e) and (f) diagram equivalent intensity values for both bandwidth and access rates. As can be seen, if apps have high locality then it is easy to stay compute bound. However, with low locality, an app would need 10s to 100s of instructions per operation to not be memory-bound.

An example is the BFS from the Graph500. Dividing the peak TEPS rating for a typical processor by its memory bandwidth yields an intensity of about 0.03 TEPS/byte. The **Firehose** [2] kernel takes streams of internet packets of data containing IP addresses and a payload, correlates them via a huge hash table, and looks for "events" based on the aggregate payloads. The metric is "Datums per second," with an intensity of about 0.01 Datums/byte.

In terms of PIM-like architectures, a recent study [12] looked at a variety of challenges associated with when to use such concepts and the integration with conventional systems. Such issues included many of the same ones mentioned, especially how to integrate into a larger memory system, handle cache coherency, and support a programming model that allows asynchronous executions.

The key take-away is that in many emerging cases the app intensity is at least an order of magnitude less than the peak capability of a modern core, meaning that performance is dominated by memory not processor architecture.

4   Further Evidence of a New Wall - Poor Scaling

The prior section gave evidence that memory has once again become a gating issue, but there is additional evidence that it is more than just a return to the Memory Wall. Figure 2 diagrams speedup for several sparse or irregular benchmarks over a wide range of scaling and many different multi-node parallel architectures. Each line represents a different benchmark for which years of

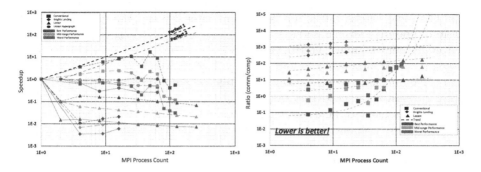

Fig. 3. SpMV strong scaling (from [30]).

reports are available. The x-axis is the number of nodes that have been reported for the same benchmark. The y-axis is the best relative speedup that some system exhibited over the performance reported for the best case of a single node. For each benchmark, the performance at (1,1) is the best reported for a single node (this is often from a multi-threaded algorithm running on a multi-core chip where memory is shared). The curves all have similar characteristics. Going from 1 to multiple nodes causes an immediate performance <u>loss</u> of sometimes 10× or more. While in most cases decent linearity in the scaling is eventually obtained, 10 to 100 nodes are needed to regain the best performance of a single node, and even then there is still significant performance loss over perfect scaling.

To provide even more insight, Fig. 3(a) (from [30]) diagrams SpMV strong scaling results from three different architectures for a variety of matrices of varying sizes and sparsity. The architectures include a conventional cluster, a cluster of Knight's Landing nodes, and Lassen (a smaller version of Sierra with dual socket IBM POWER9 chips and multiple GPUs). The three curves for each included the best results from any matrix in the suite, the worst results, and the median results. For all but the densest matrices, the conventional cluster was the only one to actually achieve even slightly positive speedup. Looking closer, Fig. 3(b) shows why. For most cases, the ratio of the communication time to computation time exceeds 1 and increases as the parallelism increases, meaning that as the computational power of the nodes increases the computation time drops but communication time does not. Making this even worse, as the level of parallelism increases, the size of the local problem also decreases. Only for the conventional case is the ratio ever less than 1, namely because this architecture has relatively less computation capability than KNL or Lassen. Communications delays increase with parallelism and dominates overall execution time. This is true even for the second Lassen case where an expensive hypergraph partitioner was used to optimize data placement to reduce communication by up to 90%.

Another example can be seen in the Firehose data in Fig. 2, especially the leftmost part of the curve where the parallelism involves multiple cores on the same node. Going from 1 to 7 cores increased performance by less than a factor of 2. The issue here is a combination of low intensity and the need to employ multiple expensive atomic updates to non-local hash table entries.

Yet another example is an HogWild!-style algorithm for a parallel ML trainer for sparse SVM problems. Before HogWild! [25], attempts to parallelize via multi-threading suffered from memory contention and excessive cache coherency traffic. HogWild! attacked this by noticing that for sparse problems different trainers are unlikely to be updating the same features at the same time, and as long as individual updates are done atomically, coherency issues are minimized. While this was relatively successful for low levels of parallelism and moderate sparsity, after that the speedup plummeted much as for SpMV. A variant, Hog-Wild++ [38], had each socket in a node operating separately, and used a token-passing mechanism to perform inter-socket updates. This worked relatively well for up to 40 cores except for very sparse data sets. In one case, the *news20* data set with 1.5 million features per sample, but only on average 460 of them non-zero, only achieved a speedup of about 9.5 in a 40 core system. Once again a combination of sparsity and inter-socket communication caused the scalability issues.

Finally, even experimental CIM/PIM chips such as [35], have scaling issues, as the energy needed to combine two or more memory blocks far exceeds the energy to perform a parallel operation within them, even if on the same chip.

The net effects is that such applications cause memory access issues "in the small" by low intensity within a single (perhaps multi-threaded) node, AND access issues "in the large" where accessing data on remote nodes becomes dominant. Together, these issues form what we claim is the new Locality Wall.

5   An Alternative Architecture - Migrating Threads

As an alternative, instead of keeping the site of a computation stationary at some core and moving copies of data as needed to it (and thus causing locality problems), we might consider what happens if instead we allow the state of a thread to *migrate* as needed to different computational sites. This has been implemented for years in software, from actors and SmallTalk [14], active messages [9], to autonomous objects [3] and messengers [13]. All have been conceptually attractive, but suffered from significant software overhead and scalability.

Limited hardware implementations have been demonstrated, such as the J-machine [26], but only for primarily remote procedure calls. A more complete model would handle all remote memory references in hardware, without any explicit software involvement. When a thread executing on some core tries to access a location not found in a memory to which the core is associated, the hardware suspends the thread from execution, its state is packaged, sent to the appropriate node, unpackaged, and restarted on a more appropriate core - all without any explicit software or additional memory references. Thus all memory references are local, and if any caching is memory and not core correlated, without any coherency traffic. Further, to allow such migrations, all memory must be in a common logical address space. Figure 4 diagrams such an architecture.

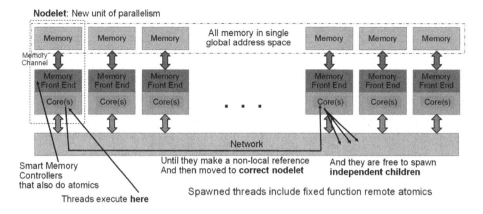

Fig. 4. A migrating thread architecture (from [20]).

There are at least two reasons why this concept might be an aid to overcoming locality issues. First, while migrating an execution doesn't change the intensity of an application, it does eliminate all the cache coherency traffic required to track the *copies* of data that are shared among traditional threads in a classical shared memory node. Second. and of more impact, it eliminates the entire software stack needed to communicate between nodes in a traditional distributed memory cluster. In most of the above apps with scaling problems, the inter-node communication is usually to request that some small amount of data be shipped to another node and some rather simple set of operations performed there. An example is a remote atomic operation on some memory location, such as a partial sum accumulation. Today, with MPI, SHMEM, or the like, software must copy the data to a buffer, assemble a message around it, read out the message into the sending NIC, write the message back to a buffer on the receiving side, and trigger a thread to interpret and execute the required action. An acknowledgement requires a similar path. When we add in the memory references needed to save and restore registers at both procedure call/returns and interrupt handling, it should be clear that we have added a huge number of memory references to support what should be a simple operation. With today's architectures we have also idled the core on the sending side and interfered with the core on the receiving side. This is a performance and energy hit.

There are several obvious enhancements. First is to make the cores multi-threaded so that arriving and departing threads can be scheduled for execution at the hardware level, and with sufficient threads at each core, the cores can be kept fully utilized. Second is enhancing the memory controllers at each channel to perform **atomic operations** directly on memory, with an absolute guarantee of atomicity in terms of other threads. Next, adding lightweight mechanisms to allow a thread to spawn additional threads provides cheap mechanisms for ad hoc parallelism. Finally, allowing this mechanism to spawn not just full threads but even lighter weight threads with limited functionality (such as perform a remote atomic add) can reduce even further the cost of remote operations.

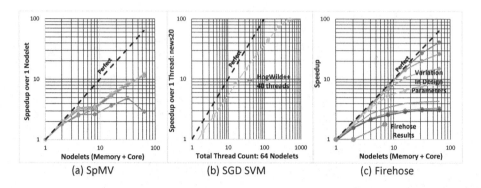

Fig. 5. Speedup results on the CRNCH system.

6   A Real Example

One such machine [8] was designed by Lucata Inc. and is housed at Georgia Tech's CRNCH center[1]. It consists of 64 memory channels, each with a multi-threaded core capable of holding 64 active thread states, and interconnected with a RapidIO network designed to transport the register set of a thread between cores without software. Each memory channel holds 8 GB and returns only 8 bytes per access, minimizing unused spatial locality. All memory is in a single common logical address space. The memory channel/core combination is packaged 8 to a board, with 8 boards in a hypercube topology. The current implementation is in an FPGA with programs written in Cilk. Each board also houses a conventional dual-core processor that runs Linux, hosts a local SSD, and can interface to a PCIe adapter for communication with the outside world. Applications are launched from a Linux process into the system as a single master thread, which then spawns threads on each nodelet to perform localized initialization and then spawn additional worker threads to perform the parallel computations. At completion, the parent Linux process is signaled.

A variety of demonstration benchmarks have been developed and run on this machine. Figure 5 diagrams summary speedup for three of them. The SpMV results [28], Fig. 5(a), should be compared to Fig. 3(a). Both use the same set of matrices, and while none of the conventional architectures had good scaling for all cases, the migrating thread system was positive not only for the best cases, but even the worse cases. The key feature used was the ability to launch very light weight threads to perform remote atomic memory operations.

Figure 5(b) diagrams some results for the migrating thread version ([27] Chap. 4) of the HogWild! style algorithms. The data set is the sparse news20, which achieved only a speedup of 9.5 on a 4-socket 40 core system. The code was similar in that one nodelet corresponded to a single multi-threaded training process. The inter-process algorithm, however, was optimized to use the features

---

[1] https://crnch.gatech.edu/rogues-emu.

of the migrating thread architecture. At 40 threads, the migrating threads version exceeded the classical reported speedup by a factor of 2, and continues to increase.

Finally, Fig. 5(c) diagrams an implementation of the Firehose streaming benchmark for which today's architectures have scaling issues. There are three versions of the benchmark, in increasing complexity, with a metric of datums processed per second. For the simplest version the migrating thread architecture [29] not only had better speedup, but actually beat the conventional architectures in datums/s by a large factor, even though the classical cores had a 20× higher clock. For the intermediate version, [31], the conventional 7 core version achieved a measly 1.8× speedup while an 8 nodelet migrating version achieved near perfect 6.6×. Other examples of benchmarking for this machine include radix sort [24], machine learning using the Random Forest algorithm [34], sparse linear algorithm kernels [22], pointer chasing [37], approaches to handling sparsity [33], and new compilation techniques [6].

7   Conclusions

In evolutionary terms, parallel architectures have grown from colonies of simple cells to simple plants with a few cell types performing different functions, but with all "life activities" occurring within some limited region. Explicit messaging across an interface is needed to affect computation being performed elsewhere. This paper has presented evidence that today's architectures are highly inefficient at supporting many emerging apps. The paper then suggests that the introduction of primitive "animals" in the form of migrating threads that can move freely around a system can provide better efficiency.

Also, given the current implementation of the prototype migrating thread system in a FPGA, there are some interesting caveats to some of the currently demonstrated benchmarks. First, the core is a single issue design running at 175 MHz, vs multi-issue 2–3 GHz classical cores. Then each classical socket has 3–4 memory channels for a combined memory bandwidth of 30–50 GB/s. This is about 5–6 GB/s per core. The migrating thread implementation has only 1.2 GB/s per core. Thus on a per core basis the FPGA cores are significantly less capable than a classical core. This makes many of the migrating thread results especially striking, especially the throughput numbers for Firehose. It will be interesting to see what happens when faster and larger migrating thread systems become available.

Looking further, the marriage of migrating threads with PIM/CIM and PNM processors placed on the bottom of 3D stacks of memory may usher in an era where computing is done in a sea of "plant-like" stacks, with "animal" threads moving naturally and freely throughout them to manage computation.

Acknowledgements. This work was supported in part by NSF grant CCF-1642280, and in part by the University of Notre Dame. We would also like to acknowledge the CRNCH Center at Georgia Tech for allowing us to use the Emu system there.

References

1. Barker, K., Davis, K., Hoisie, A., et al.: Entering the petaflop era: the architecture and performance of roadrunner. In: 2008 SC - International Conference on High Performance Computing, Networking, Storage and Analysis, SC 2008, p. 1, November 2008
2. Berry, J., Porter, A.: Stateful streaming in distributed memory supercomputers. In: Chesapeake Large Scale Data Analytics Conference (2016)
3. Bic, L.: Distributed computing using autonomous objects. In: Proceedings of 5th IEEE Workshop on Future Trends of Distributed Computing Systems, pp. 160–168 (1995)
4. Bylina, B., Bylina, J., Stpiczynski, P., Szalkowski, D.: Performance analysis of multicore and multinodal implementation of SpMV operation. In: 2014 Federated Conference on Computer Science and Information Systems, pp. 569–576, September 2014
5. Chan, T., Brown, A., Ensor, A.: SDP memo 54: compute node pipeline efficiency assessment framework. Technical report, SKA Square Kilometre Array, August 2018
6. Chatarasi, P., Sarkar, V.: A preliminary study of compiler transformations for graph applications on the EMU system. In: Proceedings Workshop on Memory Centric High Performance Computing, MCHPC 2018, pp. 37–44. Association for Computing Machinery, New York (2018)
7. Cheng, H., Wen, W., Wu, C., Li, S., Li, H.H., Chen, Y.: Understanding the design of IBM neurosynaptic system and its tradeoffs: a user perspective. In: Design, Automation Test in Europe Conference Exhibition (DATE), 2017, pp. 139–144 (2017)
8. Dysart, T., Kogge, P.M., Deneroff, M., et al.: Highly scalable near memory processing with migrating threads on the EMU system architecture. In: Proceedings of 6th Workshop on Irregular Applications: Architectures and Algorithms, IA3 2016, pp. 2–9. IEEE Press, Piscataway, November 2016
9. von Eicken, T., Culler, D.E., Goldstein, S.C., Schauser, K.E.: Active messages: a mechanism for integrated communication and computation. In: Proceedings of 19th International Symposium on Computer Architecture, ISCA 1992, pp. 256–266. ACM, New York (1992). http://doi.acm.org/10.1145/139669.140382
10. Fu, H., Liao, J., Yang, J., et al.: The Sunway TaihuLight supercomputer: system and applications. Sci. China Inf. Sci. **59**, 072001:1–072001:16 (2016)
11. Gara, A., Blumrich, M.A., Chen, D., et al.: Overview of the Blue Gene/L system architecture. IBM J. R&D **49**(2.3), 195–212 (2005)
12. Ghose, S., Boroumand, A., Kim, J.S., Gómez-Luna, J., Mutlu, O.: Processing-in-memory: a workload-driven perspective. IBM J. R&D **63**(6), 3:1–3:19 (2019)
13. Gmelin, M., Kreuzinger, J., Pfeffer, M., Ungerer, T.: Agent-based distributed computing with JMessengers. In: Böhme, T., Unger, H. (eds.) IICS 2001. LNCS, vol. 2060, pp. 134–145. Springer, Heidelberg (2001). https://doi.org/10.1007/3-540-48206-7_12
14. Goldberg, A.: SMALLTALK-80: The Interactive Programming Environment. Addison-Wesley Longman Publishing Co. Inc., Boston (1984)
15. Groeneveld, P.: Wafer scale interconnect and pathfinding for machine learning hardware. In: Proceedings of the Workshop on System-Level Interconnect: Problems and Pathfinding Workshop. SLIP 2020, Association for Computing Machinery, New York (2020)

16. Hennessy, J.L., Patterson, D.A.: A new golden age for computer architecture. Comm. ACM **62**(2), 48–60 (2019)
17. Heroux, M.A., Dongarra, J.: Toward a new metric for ranking high performance computing systems. Sandia Report SAND2013 4744, June 2013
18. Jia, Z., Zhan, J., Wang, L., et al.: Understanding big data analytics workloads on modern processors. IEEE Trans. Parallel Distrib. Syst. **28**(6), 1797–1810 (2017)
19. Jouppi, N.P., Yoon, D.H., et al.: A domain-specific supercomputer for training deep neural networks. Comm. ACM **63**(7), 67–78 (2020)
20. Kogge, P.M.: Unifying threading paradigms for highly scalable PGAS systems with mobile threads. In: International Conference on High Performance Computing and Simulation (HPCS), July 2019
21. Kogge, P.M., Bergman, K., Borkar, S., et al.: ExaScale computing study: technology challenges in achieving exascale systems. Technical Report CSE 2008-13, University of Notre Dame, September 2008. http://www.cse.nd.edu/Reports/2008/TR-2008-13.pdf
22. Krawezik, G.P., Kuntz, S.K., Kogge, P.M.: Implementing sparse linear algebra kernels on the Lucata Pathfinder-a computer. In: IEEE High Performance Extreme Computing Conference (HPEC), September 2020
23. Marjanović, V., Gracia, J., Glass, C.W.: Performance modeling of the HPCG benchmark. In: Jarvis, S.A., Wright, S.A., Hammond, S.D. (eds.) PMBS 2014. LNCS, vol. 8966, pp. 172–192. Springer, Cham (2015). https://doi.org/10.1007/978-3-319-17248-4_9
24. Minutoli, M., Kuntz, S., Tumeo, A., Kogge, P.M.: Implementing radix sort on EMU 1. In: 3rd Workshop on Near-Data Processing in Conjunction with 48th IEEE/ACM International Symposium on Microarchitecture (MICRO-48), December 2015
25. Niu, F., Recht, B., Re, C., Wright, S.J.: HOGWILD!: a lock-free approach to parallelizing stochastic gradient descent. In: Proceedings of the 24th International Conference on Neural Information Processing Systems, NIPS 2011. pp. 693–701. Curran Associates Inc., USA (2011)
26. Noakes, M.D., Wallach, D.A., Dally, W.J.: The J-machine multicomputer: an architectural evaluation. In: Proceedings 20th International Symposium on Computer Architecture, ISCA 1993, pp. 224–235. ACM, New York (1993)
27. Page, B.A.: Scalability of irregular problems. Ph.D. thesis, University of Notre Dame, USA, October 2020
28. Page, B.A., Kogge, P.M.: Scalability of sparse matrix dense vector multiply (SpMV) on a migrating thread architecture. In: Tenth International Workshop on Accelerators and Hybrid Exascale Systems (AsHES) held in conjunction with 34th IEEE International Parallel and Distributed Processing Symposium, May 2020
29. Page, B.A., Kogge, P.M.: Scalability of streaming on migrating threads. In: IEEE High Performance Extreme Computing Conference Extreme Computing Conference (HPEC), September 2020
30. Page, B.A., Kogge, P.M.: Scalability of hybrid SpMV with hypergraph partitioning and vertex delegation for communication avoidance. In: International Conference on High Performance Computing and Simulation (HPCS 2020), March 2021
31. Page, B.A., Kogge, P.M.: Scalability of streaming anomaly detection in an unbounded key space on migrating threads. In: 2021 IEEE International Symposium on Parallel Distributed Processing (2021)
32. Rees, N.: SKA and its computing challenges. Technical report, SKA Square Kilometre Array, May 2017. https://indico.cern.ch/event/638811/attachments/1460553/2255823/SKA_Computing_Challenges-20170516.pdf/

33. Rolinger, T.B., Krieger, C.D.: Impact of traditional sparse optimizations on a migratory thread architecture. In: 2018 IEEE/ACM 8th Workshop on Irregular Applications: Architectures and Algorithms (IA3), pp. 45–52 (2018)
34. Springer, P.L., Schibler, T., Krawezik, G., Lightholder, J., Kogge, P.M.: Machine learning algorithm performance on the Lucata computer. In: IEEE High Performance Extreme Computing Conference (HPEC), September 2020
35. Wan, W., Kubendran, R., Eryilmaz, S.B., et al.: 33.1 A 74 TMACS/W CMOS-RRAM neurosynaptic core with dynamically reconfigurable dataflow and in-situ transposable weights for probabilistic graphical models. In: 2020 IEEE International Solid-State Circuits Conference (ISSCC), pp. 498–500 (2020)
36. Williams, S., Waterman, A., Patterson, D.: Roofline: an insightful visual performance model for multicore architectures. Commun. ACM **52**(4), 65–76 (2009)
37. Young, J., Hein, E.R., Eswar, S., et al.: A microbenchmark characterization of the EMU chick. CoRR abs/1809.07696 (2018)
38. Zhang, H., Hsieh, C.J., Akella, V.: HogWild++: a new mechanism for decentralized asynchronous stochastic gradient descent. In: 2016 IEEE 16th International Conference on Data Mining (ICDM), pp. 629–638, December 2016

Static Extraction of Memory Access Profiles for Multi-core Interference Analysis of Real-Time Tasks

Thomas Carle$^{(\boxtimes)}$ ⓘ and Hugues Cassé

Université Paul Sabatier, IRIT, CNRS, Toulouse, France
{thomas.carle,hugues.casse}@irit.fr

Abstract. We present a static analysis framework for real-time task systems running on multi-core processors. Our method analyzes tasks in isolation at the binary level and generates worst-case timing and memory access profiles. These profiles can then be combined to perform an interference analysis at the task system level, as part of a multi-core Worst-Case Response Time (WCRT) analysis. In this paper we introduce a formal description of the models and algorithmic building blocks composing our framework. We also discuss how the memory access profiles generated by our method could be used to feed existing state-of-the-art WCRT frameworks. To the best of our knowledge, it is the first time that a method is documented on how to produce sound, safe and precise inputs for interference analysis methods.

Keywords: Multicore architectures · Worst-Case Execution Time · Static analysis

1 Introduction

Worst-Case Execution Time (WCET) and Response Time (WCRT) analysis methods have existed for decades and are currently being used in the industry to provide static guarantees that tasks running in real-time systems will respect their deadlines. Such methods have been improved over the years in order to integrate the effects of complex hardware [1,3] (e.g. pipelines, caches, branch predictors) and software [2] (e.g. preemption, mutual exclusion) mechanisms, but have mainly targeted single-core processors. The ongoing adoption of multi-core architectures for the implementation of hard real-time systems raises new challenges for the research community. Indeed previously unseen phenomena appear in such architectures, which can have a significant impact on the execution time of the tasks that run in parallel. This so-called timing interference stems from the fact that while tasks run in parallel on separate cores, they share some hardware resources such as memories and interconnects. Classical timing analysis methods make the hypothesis that tasks run in isolation (either on completely isolated hardware or on the same core but at separate times). When tasks

© Springer Nature Switzerland AG 2021
C. Hochberger et al. (Eds.): ARCS 2021, LNCS 12800, pp. 19–34, 2021.
https://doi.org/10.1007/978-3-030-81682-7_2

run in parallel, this hypothesis no longer holds, and some additional delay can be experienced if they try to access a shared resource simultaneously. As a result their actual execution time may exceed the WCET computed in isolation, thus voiding all timing guarantees.

Different methods have been developed to handle this phenomenon, such as predictable hardware components [10,12,19], extensions of previously existing WCRT analysis [5,17] and interference-free execution models enforced through careful static scheduling and synchronization [8]. In this paper we focus on a mixed analysis/compilation framework based on the notion of Time Interest Points (TIPs), which was first introduced in [4]. In this framework, tasks are initially analyzed in isolation in order to pinpoint the instructions which may cause or suffer from interference at runtime (the TIPs). The result of this first phase is a representation of the worst case memory access profiles of the tasks in time, under the form of timed execution traces. This information is then abstracted as sequences of segments (one sequence per task) characterized by a worst-case duration and a worst-case number of memory accesses, to be combined in a static scheduling phase in which an interference analysis is performed. Finally, synchronizations are automatically injected in the code in order to enforce the schedule/response-time computed in the second phase. The main advantages of this method are:

- It is applicable to a wide range of Commercial Off The Shelf (COTS) processors. Some restrictions apply, but are not as strict as the ones imposed in predictable hardware components,
- It is applicable to legacy code, with minimal automatic code modifications, where existing methods based on static scheduling require heavy transformations of the source code of the tasks to make it comply with the execution model,
- The byproducts of the analyses of the first phase (traces and segments) can be used to feed state-of-the-art WCRT and Real-Time calculus [5,17] analyses rather than a static scheduling back-end, in order to allow more dynamic implementations of the system, with minimal code adjustment (time-triggered or lock-based synchronizations, or thread yielding mechanisms and scheduler configuration).

In this paper we focus on architectures where all cores have a private scratchpad memory in which their code is loaded and are equipped with private L1 data caches and a shared memory bus implementing a greedy first-come first-served policy. In this context we provide a formal description of the models and algorithms which allow the abstraction of tasks binary code into time and memory access profiles, and discuss how these profiles can be fed to state-of-the-art analysis techniques for which, to the best of our knowledge, no method was yet provided to produce inputs.

2   Related Works

The real-time systems community has been working on the problem of multi-core interference for nearly two decades now. A comprehensive survey on the topic has been published in [14]. In this section we position our work within the state-of-the-art, and focus on two existing analysis frameworks for which our results can be particularly useful.

Reduction of Interference Through Predictable Execution: The framework we present here can be seen as a generalization of the PRedictable Execution Model (PREM) [16] for multi-core architectures, or as a relaxation of the constraints of the Acquisition-Execution-Restitution (AER) [8,18] execution model. The original idea of PREM was to avoid interference between memory accesses and asynchronous I/O traffic on a bus by carefully scheduling and enforcing the execution of tasks so that it does not occur in parallel with I/O interrupts or DMA transfers. The TIPs framework leverages this idea to the problem of multi-core interference analysis: the primary objective is to generate timing and memory access profiles of real-time tasks in order to statically schedule them on multi-core processors in a way that carefully accounts for, and possibly reduces the interference between them. The AER execution model aims at suppressing all interference by construction. The idea is to separate the execution of each task into three consecutive parts: the acquisition (A) of code and data for the task, the execution (E) of the task, and the restitution (R) of the outputs of the task to the shared memory. This separation is ensured either by the programmer or by the compiler [15]. Then the tasks are statically scheduled in a way that ensures that the A and R parts of the different tasks never occur in parallel. The TIPs framework implements the same idea, but the granularity at which it works (single memory accesses) is much finer, and it does not require to compile the task as three separate parts. This has multiple advantages such as the possibility to analyse and deploy legacy code with only small, automatic modifications (for synchronizations), and the limitation of the memory overhead due to static reservation in the AER model. Another difference is that TIPs allow the construction of programs in which some amount of interference can be tolerated (and statically quantified for compositionable processors [9]).

WCRT Analysis Frameworks: In [5] the authors present a WCRT analysis framework for sporadic task systems scheduled on multi-core processors using a preemptive fixed priority algorithm (and static partitioning of tasks on the cores). The authors consider that each possible execution trace of each task in the system is available for analysis, and from this set provide precise formulas to quantify the effect of interference between tasks on the shared elements of the target processor (memories, busses, processor time). This work extends classical WCRT analyses [11] by introducing new interference terms to cover the particularities of multi-core processors, and by making it possible to precisely account for the execution context of the tasks (i.e. which other tasks are running on the same core, or in parallel). These terms are computed by extracting worst-case information for any time interval of any given size on the execution traces of tasks. In [5] the authors discuss the empirical complexity of obtaining and manipulating the entirety of the execution traces for a task system corresponding to an industrial application. Their conclusion is that traces are a desirable abstraction of the tasks execution behavior since they can be easily manipulated and they express precisely the relation between the task and the shared resources. In particular they emphasize the fact that the worst case behavior of a task depends on its execution context, and that traces allow to exploit this. They conclude that although working on all execution traces is unfeasible for arbitrary applications, it is possible to feed the framework with a set of abstract traces which overestimate the worst case behaviors of the tasks. However nothing is said on how to obtain such an abstraction, nor on the potential costs of the various abstraction methods that could be used.

In [17] the authors provide a method close to real-time calculus [20] in order to compute the WCRT of a task system on a multi-core processor. Each task is represented as a sequence of time intervals, and for each time interval, a bound on the worst case number of memory accesses performed by the task is assumed to be known. Using this information, memory access arrival curves are derived and then combined to upper-bound the interference effect in time. A method is briefly sketched to derive the time intervals, which assumes precise knowledge on the tasks behavior (in particular local best and worst case execution times), but nothing is said on how this knowledge can be acquired in practice, nor on the abstraction cost of building the time intervals this way.

In Sect. 4 we discuss how the worst-case traces and the temporal segments that are generated by the TIPs framework could be good candidates to feed the analyses of [5] and [17]. This discussion is preceded by a precise description of these models, how they can be generated, and on the various optimization objectives that can be used to tune the analysis and their potential impact on the precision of the abstracted representations of the tasks.

3   Static Analysis Framework

In this section we first provide an overview of the TIPs static analysis framework, and then focus on each of the separate transformations that compose it.

3.1   Overview of the Method and Models

The TIPs static analysis framework processes a real-time task system by a sequence of analyzes and transformations, which are detailed in the next sections:

- In a first step (Sect. 3.2), each task is analyzed in isolation. Starting from the disassembled binary of a task, a Control Flow Graph (CFG) is constructed. The CFG is analyzed in order to extract TIPs, that is to say instructions which can produce or suffer from interference. In our current implementations, we focus on instructions which may generate traffic on the memory bus due to a data cache miss, but the method could be easily extended to misses from instruction caches. Other potential sources of interference such as shared L2 caches or effects from cache coherence protocols can also be modeled in the same framework, but are left for future work.

- Once the TIPs have been obtained, the CFG is transformed into a TIPs-Graph (Sect. 3.2 as well): a simplified control flow graph where the nodes correspond to the TIPs of the task, and the edges represent the possible control flow between the TIPs, in an abstract version. Nodes are labelled with the number of memory accesses made by the corresponding TIP, and edges are labelled with the worst case execution time of any execution paths linking the source TIP and the destination TIP of the edge. This representation is TIP-centered, and simplifies the CFG while allowing the following analyses and transformations to remain conservative.
- The TIPsGraph is then used to enumerate execution traces using a working list algorithm (Sect. 3.3). The enumerated traces exhibit the occurrence of the TIPs in all possible executions of the task. For each trace, the TIPs execution dates are a worst-case approximations. The enumerated traces can be used as timed memory access profiles for the tasks in WCRT analyses, but may remain too complex to be used in practice for other methods (such as static scheduling).
- For uses for which the enumerated traces are too complex to be exploited, the traces for each task are then transformed into a sequence of so-called "time segments" (Sect. 3.4): each segment has a duration and a worst case number of memory accesses, and the sequence of segments represents an over-approximation of the number of memory accesses that can be performed by the task in the corresponding time windows.
- In the TIPs framework, the tasks of the system are then subjected to static scheduling, using their representation as sequences of segments (Sect. 4). During this step, an interference analysis is performed, which assumes that the processor architecture is time-compositionable [9], and its results are included in the schedule. Once an acceptable schedule (i.e. which respects all real-time constraints) has been found for the whole tasks system, synchronizations are automatically inserted in the binary code of the tasks to enforce the schedule.

In the remainder of this section we will provide more details and a formal representation for each of the aforementioned steps and models.

3.2 Extracting a TIPsGraph from a CFG

The analysis of each task τ in isolation starts working on the CFG $CFG_\tau = \{\mathcal{N}, \mathcal{E}\}$ of τ, where $\mathcal{N}$ is the set of nodes called Basic Blocks (BBs) of the graph, and $\mathcal{E}$ is the set of edges $e \in \mathcal{N} \times \mathcal{N}$ which represent the control flow of the application. In this model BBs are sequences of instructions $i_0, i_1, ..., i_n \in \mathcal{I}$ with a single entry point and a single exit point. Using MUST and MAY cache

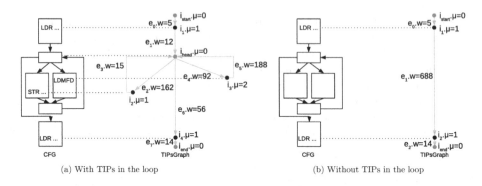

(a) With TIPs in the loop   (b) Without TIPs in the loop

Fig. 1. Example of CFGs and their corresponding TIPsGraphs

analyses [13], TIPs are pinpointed from the rest of the instructions. As stated before, a TIP is an instruction which may create or suffer from interference. Recall that in the scope of this paper we focus on multi-core architectures in which each core has a private L1 data cache, a private scratchpad holding the code to execute and all cores share a memory bus. In this context TIPs are the memory instructions which cannot be statically determined to always result in a hit (called in short Always Hit - AH) in the L1 data cache of the core which executes them. The objective of the first step of the analysis is to build for each task τ a TIPsGraph $TG_\tau = \{T, \mathcal{E}_{TG}\}$ where $T \subseteq \mathcal{I} \times \mathbb{N}$ is the set of TIPs of the task and $\mathcal{E}_{TG} \subseteq T \times T \times \mathbb{N}$ is the set of edges representing the control flow between TIPs. Each TIP $t \in T$ is composed of an instruction $t.i$ and of the worst case number of memory accesses that this instruction may perform when executed $t.\mu$. Each edge $e \in \mathcal{E}_{TG}$ is composed of a couple of TIPs $(e.src, e.dst)$, as well as a conservative approximation of the worst case execution time $(e.w)$ of the code portions between $e.src.i$ and $e.dst.i$.

Property 1: $\forall e \in \mathcal{E}_{TG}, e = (i_j, i_k, e.w), \forall p \in PATHS(i_j, i_k),$

$$e.w \geq WCET(p),$$

where $PATHS(i_j, i_k)$ is the set of possible execution paths between instructions $i_j.i$ and $i_k.i$, and $WCET(p)$ is a conservative approximation of the WCET of the code portion composed of the instructions of p, which can be computed using a static analysis tool.

To ensure that a TIPsGraph covers the possible executions of the whole task it represents, we add two fictive nodes i_{start} and i_{end} which represent the entry and exit points of the task. Both $i_{start}.\mu$ and $i_{end}.\mu$ are equal to 0. Figure 1a shows a TIPsGraph along with the CFG from which it was extracted. The TIPs-Graph starts with node i_{start} and ends with node i_{end}. The rest of the nodes composing the TIPsGraph is extracted from the CFG: in this example we assume that four memory instructions may access the bus (the cache analysis did not result in AH for these). Each of them is represented in the TIPsGraph, as well as the possible control flow between them. Each arc records such a possible transition, and is labelled with the WCET of the portion(s) of code that are executed between the TIP instructions.

In order to correctly handle loops, a TIP i_{head}, with $i_{head}.\mu = 0$ is also created to represent the loop header BB, if and only if there exists at least a TIP i inside the loop with $i.\mu > 0$. When there is no TIP inside the loop, the loop gets abstracted in the TIPsGraph, like illustrated in Fig. 1b: the control flow of the loop is no longer detailed in the TIPsGraph, but the edge representing the transition between the last TIP before the loop and the first TIP after the loop accounts for the worst case loop duration.

3.3 Enumeration of Timed Execution Traces

The next step of the analysis is to enumerate execution traces from the TIPs-Graph. The result of this enumeration is an abstract representation of the possible execution traces of the task, with two interesting properties for our analysis purposes:

- It is centered around memory accesses: only memory access instructions are represented (and loop headers, when the loop body contains memory access instructions) in the traces. In particular, control flow divergence which does not lead to memory accesses is abstracted away, and accounted for in the WCETs between TIPs. This reduces the empirical complexity of the subsequent analyses.
- All transitions between TIPs are labelled with local WCETs. This guarantees that the abstraction used to represent the tasks execution is conservative: although not all actual execution traces are detailed in the analysis, the subset on which we work is a sound conservative approximation for WCET analysis. Moreover, in combination with the following steps (static scheduling, interference analysis, injection of synchronizations), this model is also sound for the analysis of interference.

We define a trace tr as a sequence of couples $(t, d) \in \mathcal{T} \times \mathbb{N}$, where t is a TIP and d is a conservative approximation of the worst case execution date of $t.i$ in trace tr. For a trace $tr = [p_0, p_1, ..., p_n]$ with $\forall i \in [|0, n|], p_i = (t_i, d_i)$, we denote by $last(tr)$ the element p_n. We also use $tr :: p_{k+1}$ to denote the trace obtained by concatenating trace tr with element p_{k+1}.

A basic enumeration algorithm is described in Algorithm 1. It is a working list algorithm which performs a depth-first traversal of the TIPsGraph of a task. The working list contains triplets composed of a trace currently under construction, a TIPsGraph edge and a stack containing information regarding the current iteration of loops that are being traversed. The algorithm iteratively builds the set $Traces$ of the enumerated traces. Initially, WL and $Traces$ are empty. At each step of the process, the algorithm gets a trace under construction from WL, along with an edge from the TIPsGraph whose source node is the current last node of the trace, and the corresponding loop iteration context. From this, the

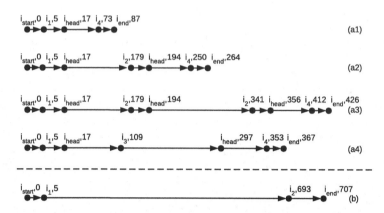

Fig. 2. Examples of enumerated traces from the TIPsGraphs of Fig. 1

trace is extended with the destination instruction of the edge, and pushes this new state on WL, along with all possible successor edges of the new last node of the trace. One trace is completed and thus added to the $Traces$ set when the node i_{end} has been reached.

The tricky cases concern loop headers (**L.8** to **L.26**): in order for the algorithm to finish, it is mandatory for the number of iterations of each loop of the task to be bounded (which is a basic requirement for WCET computation). When the trace enumeration reaches an edge whose destination node corresponds to a loop header (**L.10**), the algorithm checks (**L.11**) whether the arc in question is a return arc from inside the loop (marking the end of an iteration of the loop), or not (meaning the enumeration is entering the loop for the first iteration). If the enumeration just enters the loop, a new loop iteration context is created by pushing 0 (corresponding to the first iteration of the loop) on the *context* stack (**L.18**). The algorithm uses a stack so it can handle nested loops. If on the other hand, the current arc is a return arc, the algorithm checks if the current iteration corresponds to a valid execution : it must not exceed the maximum iteration bound for the loop. If the execution is invalid, the current trace is simply discarded (**L.13**), and the algorithm pops a new element from WL. In order to work, the algorithm must also be able to pop an element from the context stack when exiting a loop. This is done by detecting that the current edge exits from the loop (**L.21**), and by checking that the minimum iteration bound has been reached in the current stack (**L.22**). This minimum iteration bound is set to 0 by default, but the more precise it is, the better the outcome of the analysis.

Figure 2 displays 5 traces enumerated from the TIPsGraphs of Fig. 1. The last trace (at the bottom), labelled (b) is the only trace that can be enumerated from the TIPsGraph of Fig. 1b. The first element of the trace, i_{start}, corresponds to the start of the execution of the task at date 0. The next elements are the execution of $i_1.i$ at date 5, the execution of $i_2.i$ at date 693 and finally the end of the task at date 707. Traces (a1) to (a4) are a subset of all possible enumerated traces from the TIPsGraph of Fig. 1a. In order to enumerate them, we assumed

Algorithm 1. Basic trace enumeration

1: $Traces \leftarrow \emptyset$
2: $tr \leftarrow (i_{start}, 0)$
3: $WL \leftarrow \{(tr, e, []) \mid e \in \mathcal{E}_{TG} \wedge e.src = i_{start}\}$
4: **while** $WL \neq []$ **do**
5:     $(tr, e, context) \leftarrow pop(WL)$
6:     $(i_{last}, d) \leftarrow last(tr)$
7:     ▷ *Dealing with loops*
8:     $iteration \leftarrow pop(context)$
9:     **if** $is\_loop\_head(e.dst)$ **then**
10:         **if** $is\_return\_arc(e)$ **then**
11:             **if** $iteration = max\_bound(loop(e))$ **then**
12:                 **continue**   ▷ *Not a valid trace: dump it*
13:             **else**
14:                 $push(context, iteration + 1)$ ▷ *Advance iteration counter*
15:             **end if**
16:         **else**
17:             $push(context, 0)$ ▷ *Entering a new loop*
18:         **end if**
19:     **else**
20:         **if** $is\_loop\_exit(e)$ **then**
21:             **if** $iteration < min\_bound(loop(e))$ **then**
22:                 **continue**   ▷ *Not a valid trace: dump it*
23:             **end if**
24:         **end if**
25:     **end if**
26:     ▷ *Adding a new element to the trace*
27:     $tr \leftarrow tr :: (e.dst, d + e.w)$
28:     **if** $e.dst = i_{end}$ **then**
29:         $Traces \leftarrow Traces \cup \{tr\}$
30:     **else**
31:         $WL \leftarrow WL \cup \{(tr, e_n, context) \mid e_n \in \mathcal{E}_{TG} \wedge e_n.src = e.dst\}$
32:     **end if**
33: **end while**

---

that the number of loop iterations varied at least between 0 iteration (trace (a1)) and 2 iterations (trace (a3)). Trace (a1) corresponds to the execution of the task when the loop is not executed. Traces (a2) and (a3) correspond to the execution of the task when the left branch of the loop is taken respectively once and twice before exiting the loop. Trace (a4) corresponds to the execution of the task when the right branch of the loop is taken once before exiting. Notice that the dates for each element of these traces are worst case dates, meaning that the corresponding instructions can in practice execute before that date, but are guaranteed to never execute after. This means that any such trace covers multiple execution patterns, which reduces the empirical complexity of the next steps of the analysis (regardless of the analysis framework). However, three important issues must be raised at this point:

– Knowing only a worst case date for the memory accesses may increase the imprecision of the interference analysis, since it must consider that an access can occur at any time before the worst case date. One way to mitigate this issue is to inject synchronizations inside the code of the tasks to reduce the size of the time intervals during which accesses may occur.
– As illustrated by the 4 traces (a1) to (a4), the same instruction can have a different worst case date in different traces (e.g. $i_4.i$), which can also lead to imprecision in the interference analysis. Methods must be found to mitigate this issue, either at the code generation level (once again, synchronizations) or at the analysis level (careful accounting of the worst case number of memory access of the task on a given time interval).
– Enumerating traces when a loop has a different minimum and maximum iteration bounds dramatically increases the empirical complexity of the enumeration algorithm: the enumeration of all possible sub-traces after the exit of the loop must be performed entirely as many times as there are ways to exit the loop (i.e. for each iteration between the minimum and maximum loop bound), even though the enumeration of these sub-traces is exactly the same each time, since they correspond to exactly the same portion of the TIPs-Graph (when infeasible paths are not considered). In the given example, the portion of the TIPsGraph located after the loop is very small, but in practice we have noticed that it is not the case for arbitrary applications, and that the enumeration may become infeasible in acceptable time when the min and max bounds for a loop differ too much.

The enumerated traces are a first, rather raw representation of the timing and memory access profile of the tasks of the analyzed system. They can be used to perform a WCRT analysis following the method described in [5], even though caution must be taken: these are not real execution traces, but worst-case approximations of execution traces. This means that the method of [5] will have to be adapted to take into account this specificity, or that synchronizations will have to be added to the task code in order to enforce some of the worst case dates for the memory accesses.

In the TIPs framework however, the objective is to perform static scheduling, in order to analyze and try to limit the interference between tasks. To do so, we need to transform the enumerated traces into entities that will be practical to schedule, such as temporal segments.

3.4   Temporal Segments

We now present the kind of temporal segments that are used in the TIPs framework in order to represent the time and memory access profile of tasks and to statically schedule them. A temporal segment s_i is a triplet $(s_i.start, s_i.dur, s_i.\mu)$ where $s_i.start$ is the start date of the segment, $s_i.dur$ is its duration, and $s_i.\mu$ is a map which contains the number of memory accesses that can happen on the time interval $[s_i.start, s_i.start + s_i.dur]$ for each trace. In the following, we also denote by $s_i.end = s_i.start + s_i.dur$ the end date of segment s_i.

Any task τ (resp. any enumerated trace $tr \in Traces(\tau)$) can be abstracted using a sequence of segments $Segs_\tau = [s_0(\tau), ..., s_n(\tau)]$ (resp. $Segs_{tr} = [s_0(tr), ..., s_k(tr)]$), with the property that segments of a sequence do not overlap and the first segment starts at date 0 i.e. $s_0(\tau).start = 0$ and $\forall i \in [|1, n|], s_i(\tau).start \geq s_{i-1}(\tau).end$.

The shape of the segments sequence of each task will have an impact on the scheduling and interference analysis phase. A trade-off must be found between:

- The number of segments for each task. Scheduling elements (tasks, or segments) on a multi-core target is a NP-hard problem, so increasing the number of segments to schedule can increase the time it takes to build a schedule, potentially to a point where it is no longer feasible in practice.
- The length of the segments. During the interference analysis, any two segments from different tasks scheduled on overlapping time intervals on different cores will be considered as being in interference. By definition, smaller segments occupy a core for less time than larger segments, and are thus less exposed to interference from other cores. Moreover, smaller segments offer more flexibility to the scheduler to reduce the impact of interference.
- The worst case number of memory accesses on each segment. The length of the segments and the number and position of the synchronizations used to enforce them have an impact on the number of memory accesses attributed to each segment. This number must be conservative for each segment, so a memory access from a single instruction can be counted in multiple segments if the execution date of the instruction cannot be proven to happen in the time interval of only one segment. This can increase the imprecision of the method if one is not careful when shaping the segments and selecting the synchronization points.
- The number of synchronizations that will be required to guarantee that the code corresponding to the segments does not start before it is intended to. Each synchronization corresponds to additional code for the task, so their number must remain limited. Without optimization, code must be added (automatically) to the task code to ensure that in each execution trace a synchronization will be executed to enforce the start date of each segment.

In the remainder of this section, we provide algorithms that enable the extraction of valid segment representations for tasks. These are baseline algorithms which do not perform any optimization with regard to the aforementioned trade-offs. In the description of the algorithms we use the empty sequence ($[]$) and concatenation of an element e at the right-end of a sequence seq (::).

These algorithms rely on the *Intersect* operator which is defined in Definition 1. This operator computes the intersection of two segments: if the segments correspond to non-overlapping time intervals, the return value is empty. Otherwise, the operator returns a segment whose time interval is the intersection of the time intervals of the two input segments, and its summary of worst case number of memory accesses is the union of the summaries of worst case memory accesses of the input segments. Our algorithms also use the *Segments* procedure described in Algorithm 3. This procedure transforms a trace tr of a task τ into a sequence of segments in the following manner: for each node n in the trace, it creates two segments: s_1 which starts at the date of the node, spans the worst case duration of the accesses of this node and has $s_1.\mu = \{tr : n.\mu\}$ (marking that on this time interval trace tr makes at most $n.\mu$ accesses), and s_2 which starts just after and spans until the date of the next node and has $s_2.\mu = \{tr : 0\}$. The procedure is also called with parameter d_{max} which is the maximum of the dates of the last nodes of all traces of τ (i.e. the WCET of τ in the absence of interference). This is used to extend the last segment so that it spans until d_{max}.

Definition 1. $\forall s_i, s_j \in Segs,\ Intersect(s_i, s_j) =$

$$
\begin{cases}
\emptyset & if\ s_i.start \geq s_j.end \vee s_j.start \geq s_i.end \\
(s_i.start, s_i.dur, s_i.\mu \cup s_j.\mu) & if\ s_i.start \geq s_j.start \wedge s_j.end \geq s_i.end \\
(s_i.start, s_j.end - s_i.start, s_i.\mu \cup s_j.\mu) & if\ s_i.start \geq s_j.start \wedge s_i.end \geq s_j.end \\
(s_j.start, s_i.end - s_j.start, s_i.\mu \cup s_j.\mu) & if\ s_i.start < s_j.start \wedge s_i.end \leq s_j.end \\
(s_j.start, s_j.dur, s_i.\mu \cup s_j.\mu) & if\ s_i.start < s_j.start \wedge s_i.end > s_j.end
\end{cases}
$$

The top-level algorithm is described in Algorithm 2: starting with an arbitrary trace tr_1 from the set of traces of τ, it transforms tr_1 into a segments representation using procedure $Segments$ (described in Algorithm 3): $Segs_\tau$. Then each other trace tr_i of τ is transformed into a sequence of segments, and $Segs_\tau$ is updated with the intersection of the current segments of $Segs_\tau$ and the segments that represent tr_i. When this is done, a procedure tries to reduce the number of segments using a minimum size Δ, by :

- preserving all segments s with $max\_access(s) = 0$ and $s.dur \geq \Delta$,
- for all other segments, fusing consecutive segments until the result of the fusion has a length of at least Δ or there is no more available segment to fuse. When fusing segments, the information about the worst case number of memory accesses is combined trace-wise instead of blindly summed in order to limit over-approximations.

We illustrate this algorithm in the examples of Fig. 3. Segment sequences (S_{a1}) and (S_{a2}) are extracted directly from traces (a1) and (a2) of Fig. 2 using

---

Algorithm 2. Segments creation for a task

Require: $Traces(\tau)$, $tr_1 \in Traces(\tau)$, $\Delta \in \mathbb{N}$, $d_{max} \in \mathbb{N}$
Ensure: $Segs_\tau$
1: $Segs_\tau = Segments(tr_1, d_{max})$
2: **for all** $tr_i \in Traces(\tau)$, $tr_i \neq tr_1$ **do**
3:     $Segs_\tau \leftarrow Intersect(Segs_\tau, Segments(tr_i, d_{max}))$
4: **end for**
5: $Segs_\tau \leftarrow Fusion(Segs_\tau, \Delta)$
6: **return** $Segs_\tau$

Algorithm 3. The result of their intersection is provided as (S_{a1+a2}). In this sequence, the first access is displayed in gray to show that this segment corresponds to either one access from trace (a1) or one access from trace (a2). The sequence labelled (S_a) is obtained by iterating the intersection of the traces (a1), (a2), (a3) and (a4). Different colors mean that accesses from different traces may occur. Finally trace (S'_a) is obtained by fusing together the smaller segments and preserving large segments which are guaranteed to not perform any memory access.

Algorithm 3. Extract a segments representation for a single trace

---

Require: $tr_1 \in Traces(\tau), tr_1 = (i_0, d_0), (i_1, d_1), ..., (i_n, d_n); d_{max}$
Ensure: $Segs_{tr_1}$
 1: $Segs_{tr_1} = []$
 2: **for all** $k \in [|0, n-2|]$ **do**
 3:     $acc\_end \leftarrow d_k + i_k.\mu \times access\_time$
 4:     $Segs_{tr_1} \leftarrow Segs_{tr_1} :: (d_k, acc\_end, \{tr_1 : i_k.\mu\}) :: (acc\_end, d_{k+1} - acc\_end, \{tr_1 : 0\})$
 5: **end for**
 6: $acc\_end \leftarrow d_{n-1} + i_{n-1}.\mu \times access\_time$
 7: $Segs_{tr_1} \leftarrow Segs_{tr_1} :: (d_n - 1, acc\_end, \{tr_1 : i_k.\mu\})$
 8: $Segs_{tr_1} \leftarrow Segs_{tr_1} :: (acc\_end, d_{max} - acc\_end, 0)$
 9: **return** $Segs_{tr_1}$

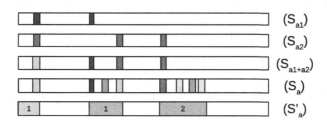

Fig. 3. Examples of memory access profiles obtained from the traces of Fig. 2

4   Exploitation of the Memory Access Profiles

In this section we conclude the description of the TIPs framework by a quick discussion about the uses that can be made of the enumerated traces and segments in order to perform an interference-aware analysis of the task system. We thus discuss how the enumerated traces and segments representations can be fed to various "back-ends" such as static schedulers or the WCRT analysis frameworks described in Sect. 2.

4.1   Interference Analysis for Static Scheduling

Regardless of the task model (single period, sporadic, multi-periodic, dependent or independent tasks) any existing static scheduling method can be adapted to the TIPs model: instead of scheduling one time interval for a task as in classical models, all segments for a task are scheduled in order. The potential interference is computed using the information contained in the segments, and must reflect the bus arbitration policy. Only segments scheduled on separate cores and whose time intervals overlap are considered to interfere. The potential interference is accounted for either by increasing the size of the segments on-the-fly (e.g. [4,7]), or by consuming an interference budget which can be added to the tasks' WCET prior to scheduling [6] (e.g. a 10% overhead on the computed WCET for interference tolerance).

4.2   Multi-core WCRT Analysis Techniques

In order to use the interference formulas presented in [5] (at least for the part regarding interference on the buses and memories), an upper bound on the number of accesses that can be made in any time-interval of any size must be found for each task. In the TIPs framework, this information is available at 2 different abstraction levels: the enumerated worst-case traces (Sect. 3.3) which offer a finer level of granularity, and thus can lead to more precise bounds at the cost of a more complex computation, and the segments (Sect. 3.4) which represent the memory access profiles at a higher level of abstraction. In both cases, since the timings obtained in the TIPs framework are worst-case dates, synchronizations must be added to the code to be able to lower-bound with certainty the occurrence of accesses in time. The same is true for the real-time calculus method of [17], for which the segment representation obtained through the TIPs framework is a natural input format.

5   Conclusion and Future Works

We presented the TIPs framework: a collection of models and algorithms for the extraction of precise timing and memory access profiles of real-time tasks. For each level of abstraction, we provided a formalization of the corresponding models and algorithms, as well as a discussion on the cost of the presented abstractions. We finally discussed how the obtained memory access profiles could be used as inputs for existing state-of-the-art analysis frameworks and tools. In the future, we will work on optimizations and the evaluation of their impact on the different "back-ends". In particular, we are currently working on a multi-criterion optimization of the transformation of enumerated traces into segments, trying to minimize the overestimation of the number of accesses in each segment and the number of synchronizations to add to the tasks' code.

References

1. absInt aiT. https://www.absint.com/ait/index.htm
2. Altmeyer, S., Maiza, C.: Cache-related preemption delay via useful cache blocks: survey and redefinition. J. Syst. Arch. Embed. Syst. Design **57**, 707–719 (2011)
3. Ballabriga, C., Cassé, H., Rochange, C., Sainrat, P.: OTAWA: an open toolbox for adaptive WCET analysis (regular paper). In: IFIP Workshop on Software Technologies for Future Embedded and Ubiquitous Systems (SEUS) (2010)
4. Carle, T., Cassé, H.: Reducing timing interferences in real-time applications running on multicore architectures. In: 18th International Workshop on Worst-Case Execution Time Analysis (WCET 2018) (2018)
5. Davis, R.I., Altmeyer, S., Indrusiak, L.S., Maiza, C., Nelis, V., Reineke, J.: An extensible framework for multicore response time analysis. Real Time Syst. **54**(3), 607–661 (2017). https://doi.org/10.1007/s11241-017-9285-4
6. Didier, K., et al.: Correct-by-construction parallelization of hard real-time avionics applications on off-the-shelf predictable hardware (2019)
7. Dupont de Dinechin, M., Schuh, M., Moy, M., Maiza, C.: Scaling up the memory interference analysis for hard real-time many-core systems. In: 2020 Design, Automation Test in Europe Conference Exhibition (DATE) (2020)
8. Durrieu, G., Faugère, M., Girbal, S., Gracia Pérez, D., Pagetti, C., Puffitsch, W.: Predictable flight management system implementation on a multicore processor. In: ERTS 2014 (2014)
9. Hahn, S., Jacobs, M., Reineke, J.: Enabling compositionality for multicore timing analysis. In: Proceedings of the 24th International Conference on Real-Time Networks and Systems, RTNS 2016 (2016)
10. Hahn, S., Reineke, J.: Design and analysis of SIC: a provably timing-predictable pipelined processor core. Real-Time Syst. **56**(2), 207–245 (2019). https://doi.org/10.1007/s11241-019-09341-z
11. Joseph, M., Pandya, P.: Finding response times in a real-time system. Comput. J. **29**, 390–395 (1986)
12. Liu, I., Reineke, J., Lee, E.A.: A PRET architecture supporting concurrent programs with composable timing properties. In: 2010 Conference Record of the Forty-Four Asilomar Conference on Signals, Systems and Computers (2010)
13. Lv, M., Guan, N., Reineke, J., Wilhelm, R., Yi, W.: A survey on static cache analysis for real-time systems. Leibniz Trans. Embed. Syst. (2016)
14. Maiza, C., Rihani, H., Rivas, J.H., Goossens, J., Altmeyer, S., Davis, R.: A survey of timing verification techniques for multi-core real-time systems. ACM Comput. Surv. **52**, 1–38 (2019)
15. Pagetti, C., Forget, J., Falk, H., Oehlert, D., Luppold, A.: Automated generation of time-predictable executables on multicore. In: Proceedings of the 26th International Conference on Real-Time Networks and Systems (RTNS 2018) (2018)
16. Pellizzoni, R., et al.: A predictable execution model for cots-based embedded systems. In: RTAS (2011)
17. Pellizzoni, R., Schranzhofer, A., Caccamo, M., Thiele, L.: Worst case delay analysis for memory interference in multicore systems. In: 2010 Design, Automation Test in Europe Conference Exhibition (DATE 2010), pp. 741–746 (2010)
18. Rouxel, B., Skalistis, S., Derrien, S., Puaut, I.: Hiding communication delays in contention-free execution for SPM-based multi-core architectures. In: 31st Euromicro Conference on Real-Time Systems (ECRTS 2019) (2019)

19. Schoeberl, M., et al.: T-CREST: time-predictable multi-core architecture for embedded systems. J. Syst. Archit. (2015)
20. Thiele, L., Chakraborty, S., Naedele, M.: Real-time calculus for scheduling hard real-time systems. In: ISCAS (2000)

Transparent Resilience for Approximate DRAM

João Fabrício Filho[1,2]([✉]), Isaías Felzmann[2], and Lucas Wanner[2]

[1] Federal University of Technology - Paraná, Campo Mourão, PR, Brazil
joaof@utfpr.edu.br
[2] Institute of Computing, University of Campinas, Campinas, SP, Brazil
{isaias.felzmann,lucas}@ic.unicamp.br

Abstract. Approximate DRAM can reduce energy consumption by exposing application data to probabilistic errors. However, not all data is amenable to approximation, and errors in certain critical data can lead to invalid outputs or application crashes. Identification of critical data typically requires annotations in source code. Transparent protection mechanisms attempt to automatically protect applications from critical data errors without programmer intervention. This work proposes and compares alternatives to transparent data protection for approximate DRAM. We alleviate the impact of errors on application quality by triggering approximate re-executions when invalid outputs are detected. Furthermore, we evaluate transparent hardware and software-level resilience mechanisms for approximate memory that can avoid a large fraction of critical errors. Our results show that adding resilience mechanisms to approximate DRAM reduces crashes and invalid outputs when compared to non-resilient approximate DRAM (up to 3×), and saves energy when compared to standard DRAM (14–31%).

Keywords: Approximate computing · Approximate DRAM · Error tolerance · Interfaces for approximate data

1 Introduction

Memories represent more than 50% of the energy consumption of computational systems on memory-intensive workloads [3]. The main memory system holds the major part of this consumption, achieving 65% of the total energy in the memory hierarchy [17]. Dynamic Random Access Memory (DRAM) is the common choice for the main memory system due to its high density and low cost [8]. The nominal specification of DRAM parameters, such as voltage, delay, or refresh rate, is defined to guard-band the worst case of process variation, temperature, and other

This work was supported by the São Paulo Research Foundation (FAPESP) grant #2018/24177-0; National Council for Scientific and Technological Development - Brazil (CNPq) grant #438445/2018-0; and Coordination for the Improvement of Higher Education Personnel - Brazil (CAPES) - Finance Code 001.

C. Hochberger et al. (Eds.): ARCS 2021, LNCS 12800, pp. 35–50, 2021.
https://doi.org/10.1007/978-3-030-81682-7_3

environment variables [2]. Lowering parameters below the nominal specification can reduce energy consumption or increase performance [8]. However, below the guard-banding, memory cells are exposed to noise that may lead to bitflips. Without any control, these errors can quickly lead to broken systems.

Approximate memories are designed to achieve energy or performance benefits at the cost of controlled errors in stored data [8]. These errors may affect critical application data, leading to execution crashes and invalid results [6,13]. Executions that produce invalid results make computational efforts to be wasted, reducing the potential benefits of approximations. Transparent mechanisms protect application without requiring programmer annotations [6,15]. These mechanisms act mainly on execution resilience, improving the chances of a valid result. However, this transparent protection does not guarantee valid outputs, and re-executions may be necessary to retain the quality of the results.

Checkpointing and rollbacking mechanisms can reduce the error impact on results, improving average quality by recovering broken results, but at the cost of instrumentation or modifications in the programming language [9,16]. A transparent re-execution restarts the execution without these interventions but requires twice initialization overheads [15]. An approximate re-execution can alleviate the cost of restarting an application [9], but memory approximations are probabilistic, and re-executing into the same approximation level may lead to another invalid result. Thus, we propose to predetermine approximation levels to perform re-executions at a higher level with a lower probability of a new invalid result. Furthermore, we introduce acceptance tests with simple verification that detects invalid results produced by execution crashes or Silent Data Corruption (SDC). These functions check, without a golden accurate output, whether an approximate execution result is valid and contains the required data format.

In this work, we explore alternatives for transparent resilience of applications with approximate DRAM and recovering by approximate re-executions. Previous interfaces [6,15] model an error-prone memory as a single high-level entity that is solely responsible for storing all data, which is not compatible with the hierarchical design found in modern computing platforms. We reduce the effects of errors by pushing the approximations to DRAM, a more energy intensive point in the memory hierarchy, which is accessed through error-free caches. Our main contributions are: (1) An approximate re-execution mechanism for instances that generate invalid results; (2) Detection of invalid results through lightweight acceptance tests without having a golden accurate output; and (3) A comparison between state-of-the-art alternatives for transparent resilience in an execution scenario more compatible with systems with multi-level memory hierarchy.

Mechanisms of transparent protection have the potential to eliminate execution crashes at some operating points. Nevertheless, to transform these crashes into instances that fit a quality requirement, these executions have to generate a valid and higher quality result. We compared and mixed features from two resilience interfaces from the literature, AxRAM [6] and Crash Skipping [15], in our proposed environment. Our results show that approximate re-execution improves energy savings by up to 4 percentage points (pp) when compared to accurate re-execution, with negligible impact on quality. A combination of features from transparent resilience interfaces avoids up to 70% of crashes and achieves energy savings from 14% to 31%, depending on the application, with acceptable quality degradation.

2   Background and Related Work

DRAM approximation can be performed by adjusting operating parameters, such as refresh rate, voltage, and access latency [2,3,11]. The voltage scaling of DRAM can reduce power quadratically due to the relation between these variables. Voltage reduction influences the dynamic DRAM power on active, precharge, and refresh operations as well as the static power from the DRAM array. However, reducing voltage below guard-band values results in errors in stored data. The error rate grows exponentially as voltage decreases [3].

Errors in data stored into approximate memories impact application and may reflect in quality degradation of outputs [6,11]. The more errors are presented, the higher is the impact on the quality, which may trespass a limit of tolerable degradation for each application. Furthermore, some application data are critical and do not tolerate error, crashing the execution without generating a valid output. Therefore, errors should be controlled to avoid wasting computational resources and decreasing the approximation benefits.

Execution crashes happen when the program is prematurely terminated because of application stalling, loss of the control flow, or an attempt to access an invalid memory location [6]. Application stalling takes place when errors in control variables prevent the program from meeting a stop criteria. Other crashes are caused by reference loss when errors affect data that indicate critical information to the output, such as file headers or data pointers.

Predicting how errors can affect output quality or application executions is not trivial. The problem consists of determining automatically, for any general-purpose application and perturbation model, a guaranteed threshold in quality output and approximation benefits. The approximation level indicates the value for the variable that determines the perturbation model, the error insertion in the application, and the resulting benefits. Thus, a comprehensive solution to this problem can determine the approximation level at which a quality threshold is respected for an application without programmer intervention.

Protection of critical data is often performed by annotations in the source code to explicitly differ what data or code blocks are approximable or not [4,5,14]. In contrast, transparent interfaces perform this protection without programmer intervention [6,15]. This work aims to protect critical data transparently and improve the resilience of applications, without source code annotations, avoiding executions that would crash or lead to invalid results. AxRAM [6] works implicitly to protect regions that commonly contain critical data to avoid execution crashes and proposes a treatment of data pointers to avoid access violations. Crash Skipping (CS) [15] proposes a runtime system that detects the instructions that would cause crashes and replaces them with dummy instructions (nop), proceeding with the execution flow. Furthermore, CS has a counter of avoided crashes that prevent application stalling. In this work, we mitigate data protection and stalling prevention, combining efficient aspects of AxRAM and CS. Moreover, we include within the evaluation the memory hierarchy, a concept that has been simplified by both AxRAM and CS interfaces, that modeled the memory as a single entity exposed to errors.

3   Transparent Resilience for Approximate DRAM

Interfaces that need annotations mitigate the perturbation-outcome problem without being automatic. To be automatic, our work proposes and merges mechanisms of transparent interfaces, which execute applications developed for commodity hardware without annotations. We represent the perturbation model as bitflips originated at an approximate DRAM with an in-between precise cache to alleviate the impact of these errors and get more control over the quality degradation and approximation benefits. In this model, the memory is subjected to a discrete approximation level, which is characterized by a given value adjusted for a parameter that influences the perceived error rate, such as supply voltage or latency. Thus, the error rate grows with the approximation level, and quality degradation also follows depending on the impact of errors. Therefore, we profile applications through several executions with determined approximation levels to estimate the expected output quality for each expected energy benefit.

3.1   Impact of Errors in the Memory Hierarchy

Approximations in different levels of the hierarchy could represent different impacts on the application in terms of benefits and quality deprecation [12]. In general, caches alleviate the number of accesses into a more energy-expensive and slower main memory. In a scenario with an approximate DRAM, a precise cache also alleviates the impact of errors from this main memory because of the reduced number of accesses on the main memory. Although previous proposals mitigate approximation among more than one level in the memory hierarchy [12,17], our preliminary experiments showed that a precise cache can reduce the number of application-visible data errors from the last-level DRAM. The jpeg application, for example, can support error rates 4 orders of magnitude higher when the error source is an approximate DRAM main memory, in comparison to an approximate L1 cache, and still meet the same quality threshold. Thus, the approximation only at the DRAM main memory could maximize its energy gains with less impact on the output quality using precise caches. Moreover, an approximate DRAM maximizes energy benefits since this memory level represents the most energy-hungry point of the hierarchy, which can represent more than 60% of total memory energy breakdown [17]. Thus, this potentially represents an improvement of orders of magnitude on error resilience without programmer intervention.

3.2   Approximate Re-execution

To measure the quality of results, we need to compare the results with a reference output. The reference output is the result of an accurate execution that has no energy benefits, and, thus, is not feasible at the system-level design. Nevertheless, invalid results can be detected when caused by execution crashes or errors in critical data. To this end, we need an evaluation function for each application that distinguishes outputs that are not valid. Every invalid output is indicated with null quality and certainly needs a re-execution to generate a valid result. The re-execution is a simple mechanism that can be triggered without programmer intervention by an Operating System (OS) or a runtime system. Although an accurate re-execution generates an accurate output, it adds an energy overhead that may reduce the approximation benefits. Furthermore, in an approximate environment, an accurate output is not necessary in the first place.

To maximize the benefits of the approximation, we propose to re-execute, in approximate mode, each execution instance that produced an invalid result. Approximate re-execution has been proposed through specialized source code and programming language that re-execute parts of the application in the same approximation level [9]. However, re-executing in the same approximation level exposes the application to the same error level and the same probability of a crash or invalid outcome, and a specialized source code demands changes in applications developed to commodity hardware. To overcome these, we propose to perform the re-execution of a failed instance at a lower level of approximation than the original execution. If another invalid result is retrieved, another re-execution is scheduled in the next level, successively. A guard-banded adjustment of memory parameters defines the approximation level zero, which results in the error-free execution. As a transparent process-level mechanism, this re-execution does not demand changes in the source code nor instrumentation by checkpointing. However, each re-execution adds process initialization overheads since the application is re-executed from its beginning. On the proposed approximate re-execution method, the approximation level is decreased while there is no valid output from the last execution. In the worst case, the last execution is performed at approximation level zero without errors and thus a valid result is guaranteed. Furthermore, we can check the integrity of execution outputs based on a simple verification of the data. Thus, we propose to use acceptance tests to detect invalid results even in the case of SDC. This function returns whether an output is evaluable by a quality metric without having an accurate reference, checking labels and critical information required by the application. The simplicity of such a checking mechanism results in negligible runtime overhead to determine whether the results are valid or not.

3.3   Transparent Interface Mechanisms

Transparent protection mechanisms of critical data, in the literature, focus on resilience, trying to maintain the execution flow and converge to a valid output. Incorrect memory references are the main cause of crashes, thus protection of control flow pointers and treatment of data pointers have been proposed in AxRAM [6]. The loss of the control flow is also a concern in approximate memory environments. Mechanisms of instructions replacement by a no-operation (nop) instruction have been proposed to overcome this problem in CS [15].

We propose a combination of transparent mechanisms from AxRAM and CS into an interface that protects control flow, treats data pointers, avoids execution crashes, and prevents application stalling. The allocation of the system stack addresses into reliable memory protects control flow pointers with a minimum penalty in energy savings due to the usually small size of the stack compared to the entire application data. The treatment of data pointers into an environment with virtual addressing with MSB truncation validates non-existing addresses but is not sufficient to avoid all data crashes. Thus, we combine this addressing scheme with the replacement by nop instructions. However, these mechanisms can increase the number of instances that fall in indefinite execution, thus another mechanism counts the replaced instructions and stops the execution if a threshold of avoided crashes is reached.

4   Methodology

Transparent interfaces allow for controlling error rates at the hardware level, the OS, or a runtime system using configuration knobs. We adopt a model where non-user level instructions are protected, thus only the application is exposed to errors and the OS runs accurately.

4.1   Simulation Environment

Our environment is built upon the Spike RISC-V reference ISA simulator[1], and user-privileged memory accesses are replaced by software models that can expose data to errors [7]. These errors are bitflips persisted in memory that can occur at any bit of the row buffer with a given probability. The RISC-V Proxy Kernel controls virtual memory addresses and the execution environment. To emulate context switching on a multi-application environment, our simulator performs a cache flush every 10^5 instruction cycles, as an average estimation of an OS forcing a context switch in a time frame in the order of milliseconds for a hundreds-of-megahertz processor. In a production environment, these time and frequency values can change dynamically according to the CPU utilization. In our simulation, traces of DRAM accesses are transformed into DRAM commands and timestamp marks by Ramulator [10] to evaluate the energy consumption through DRAMPower [1]. Our simulated memory hierarchy has two independent 32 KB L1 instruction and data caches and a single 128 KB L2 cache, and the DRAM specification is DDR3 1600 MHz 64bit, 8 banks, 2 ranks, 1024 columns, 8 bytes burst length, 16384 rows, tRCD 13.75 ns, tRP 13.75 ns, and 1.35 V nominal VDD. To account for energy, we consider that each equally-sized fraction of the

---

[1] https://github.com/riscv/riscv-isa-sim.

memory contributes equally to the aggregated dynamic energy cost. Thus, if certain memory regions use a different operating point to protect or expose data to errors, their energy cost is proportional to their size in the memory.

4.2 Error and Energy Model

Our error scenario considers a controlled environment, where the approximation level refers to a calibrated static error rate. To calculate the energy impact of exposing data to a certain error rate, we derive a relation between the DRAM supply voltage of the DRAM array and the bit error probability from data collected with scaled voltage and fixed temperature and latency parameters [3], Current commercially-available DRAM does not support dynamic changes in the supply voltage of the DRAM arrays, thus, this environment requires minor changes in the power delivery of the DIMMs similar as Voltron [3]. These changes should avoid errors in the peripheral circuitry, maintaining the nominal voltage on these components while allowing dynamic adjusts in the supply voltage of the DRAM array. We assume that these modifications have insignificant energy impact. and model a median scenario of error probabilities. In steps of approximation that are not covered by the parameters from extracted data, we consider the exponential relation between voltage and error to design regressions in the form $error = A \times e^{(B \times vdd)}$, where $error$ is the bit error probability and vdd is the supply voltage of the DRAM, validating the $error$ value between 0 and 1. The values for a median error scenario are $A = 1.796 \times 10^{68}$ and $B = -155.87$ with coefficient of determination $R^2 = 98.51\%$. We did not consider other variables that could affect the error as a dynamic component of the memory, such as the temperature. However, we intend to profile the behavior and output generated by the application exposed to errors, thus a calibration over other factors is applicable to proposed techniques and also other error models.

4.3 Applications and Quality Functions

We evaluate applications from AxBench [18], cBench[2], and Polybench[3] on our experiments. The considered applications are atax, correlation, dijkstra, fft, jpeg, and sobel, which represent the behavior of general purpose applications that manipulate data that tolerate approximation in their results. For simulation purposes, we use standard input and output as the source and the destination of data. However, no other modifications were implemented within the applications, such as annotations in the source code, instructions, or data to control approximations, maintaining the transparency of the interfaces.

Our quality metrics compare an approximate output with the accurate output of the same instance (application and input) and estimate a percentage of similarity between them. The selected quality metrics are the fraction of equal

---

[2] http://ctuning.org/cbench.
[3] https://web.cse.ohio-state.edu/~pouchet.2/software/polybench/.

elements (correlations or nodes) for correlation and dijkstra; the Structural Similarity Index (SSI) for jpeg and sobel; and the mean relative error for atax and fft. The acceptance test of each application verifies if the respective output is valid without having the accurate output to trigger a re-execution. The acceptance test for jpeg and sobel checks whether the data contains a valid image header in the expected dimensions. For atax, correlation, fft, and dijkstra, the acceptance test verifies if the number of elements in the output is coherent with the size of the input data.

4.4 Approximation Levels and Metrics

We consider the approximation level zero as 1.35 V, the nominal voltage of DRAM. The predetermined approximation levels are 10 between 1.02 V and 1.11 V with 10 mV steps. To measure the energy benefits and quality degradation at the approximation levels, we perform 100 executions of each application at each approximation level. These executions intend to profile the application to determine its behavior in the approximate DRAM environment. Since the memory approximations are non-deterministic, executions in the same approximation level may produce different outputs. Thus, the expected quality and energy for each level are the average from all executions.

Each of the 100 random execution instances, at a given approximation level l, of the target application account for a relative energy cost, measured by DRAM-Power, and an output quality, given by the quality metrics. We aggregate the average energy consumption and average quality at each level as μ_{W_l} and μ_{Q_l}, respectively. We also observe the outcome of each execution instance to produce the probability of a re-execution to be triggered at the given level, δ_l. Thus, the Expected Quality (E_Q^l) and Expected Energy (E_W^l) for each level l are taken as the statistical expected value of the random variables energy cost and quality, considering the mean values μ_{Q_l} and μ_{W_l}, as shown in Eqs. 1 and 2, respectively. Considering the relative energy savings are the difference between the energy consumption from accurate (100%) and approximate executions, the Expected Energy Savings (E_S^l) are similarly given by Eq. 3.

$$E_Q^l = (1 - \delta_l) \times \mu_{Q_l} + \delta_l \times E_Q^{(l-1)} \tag{1}$$

$$E_W^l = \mu_{W_l} + \delta_l \times E_W^{(l-1)} \tag{2}$$

$$E_S^l = 1 - E_W^l \tag{3}$$

4.5 Interfaces for Transparent Resilience

The mechanisms of transparent resilience evaluated in this work are based on AxRAM [6] and CS [15]. Therefore, we implement these interfaces to show and compare the results achieved with their mechanisms in our proposed environment. We consider mechanisms of hardware and software implementation of the transparent interfaces. The hardware-level implementation of AxRAM allocates the system stack addresses into a memory region with the approximate level zero, protecting control flow pointers stored into these addresses. The other main feature of AxRAM is a treatment to out-of-bounds memory accesses that we implement with the truncation mask of 39 bits in our virtual memory environment, following the RV64 Sv39 standard page-based virtual-memory system. The CS implementation (referred to as CSi) considers the hardware mechanisms, a skipping threshold of 20 for all evaluated applications, and implements instruction granularity to skip crashes.

The base AxRAM hardware implementation to treat out-of-bounds addresses is not enough to match the expected results in a virtual memory scenario. Truncating the most significant bits covers only pointers that fall out of the allowed addressing space, but does not validate whether they are a match for an existing virtual memory page. Thus, a software-level implementation of this scheme considers the page allocation to find a likely correspondence for the virtual address. In RV64 Sv39 page-based virtual-memory system, the 39-bit addressed virtual memory space is divided into 4 KiB pages and organized into three levels, allocating a 9-bit Virtual Page Number (VPN) identifier within each level and a 12-bit intra-page offset. We consider that, when the hardware raises an access violation exception, one of these partial VPNs suffered a bitflip that corrupted the virtual address. Thus, we search the Page Table Entry (PTE) for a VPN at a hamming distance = 1 in comparison to the virtual address that caused the exception. If a correspondence is found, we create a new PTE pointing the faulty virtual address to the correspondent physical address, allowing the execution to proceed. If no correspondence is possible, the execution crashes in a segmentation fault. This alternative implementation is referred to as SW-AxRAM.

5   Results

Lowering DRAM voltage below the guard-banding of errors decreases power quadratically, improving energy gains. Nevertheless, the presence of bitflips that may affect stored data grows exponentially as voltage decreases. Without any protection, these bitflips quickly lead to invalid execution because of crashes or invalid outputs. In lower approximation levels, these errors lead to some quality degradation of outputs. The best operating point for each application is the approximation level that achieves the highest energy savings while still fitting in a quality requirement. Our experiments search for the best operating point by analyzing several executions in each approximation level. In this section, we evaluate and discuss the transparent resilience mechanisms considering acceptance tests, stack protection, re-execution models, and transparent interfaces in a voltage-scaled DRAM.

5.1   Acceptance Tests

Re-executing the entire application is a mechanism that does not require changes in the application nor checkpointing support since all initialization overhead is

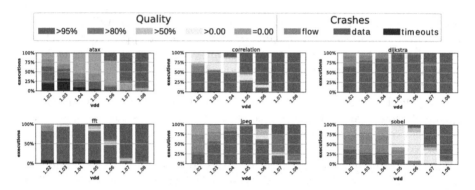

Fig. 1. Distribution of crashes and quality ranges for repeated executions with SW-AC. Crashes are predominant for lower vdds, and higher vdds produce high-quality results. Invalid and low-quality outputs are significant in the intermediate operating points.

added in the re-execution. To trigger a re-execution, we should detect which instances need to recover from invalid outputs. These outputs can result from execution crashes, which an OS can detect by hardware and software signals that indicate memory access violations, incorrect instructions, or more than expected execution time. Nonetheless, invalid outputs may also result from instances that cannot be detected by the OS because they did not trigger an execution crash. These results came from data corruption and can be detected by the acceptance tests proposed in this work.

Transparent resilience interfaces avoid behaviors that would otherwise result in a crash. However, these behaviors may result in SDC, which leads to invalid outputs. Figure 1 shows the distribution of crashes and quality ranges for all approximation levels with the combination of SW-AxRAM and CSi (SW-AC). This interface avoids execution crashes, but increases the number of instances that generate results with useless or null quality. Thus, other invalid outputs that cannot be detected by the OS may need a re-execution to generate a valid result.

Figure 2 exhibits the percentage of re-executions triggered by crashes detection, the proposed output validation with acceptance tests plus crashes detection, and an oracle that detects every execution that resulted in quality lower than 80%. Such an oracle implementation is not achievable, since it would need an accurate output as a reference to validate and measure the output quality, which nullifies the energy gains of the approximate memory. For all applications and error rates, the inclusion of acceptance tests covers more instances than crash detection only. Although the crash detection may cause false positives, such as when a crash happens after a valid result is generated, as in fft application where this trigger surpasses the oracle at some levels, it prevents false negatives from the acceptance test, such as when an image header is correctly written and the execution crashes within the pixel data region. Thus, the combination of acceptance tests and crashes detection is more efficient as a re-execution trigger than crash detection only.

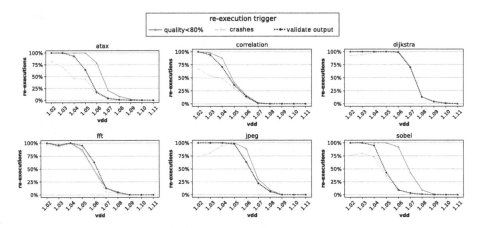

Fig. 2. Percentage of executions invalidated by crash detection only, crash detection and output validation, and an oracle with 80% target quality. Output validation improves upon crash detection performance for all operating points. Reaching oracle performance on all applications would require costly quality assessment.

5.2   Approximate Re-execution

The re-execution mechanism relies on the detection of crashes and the acceptance tests. The proposed approximate re-execution tries to generate valid outputs in the next lower approximation level instead of executing directly on an error-free nominal level, as the accurate re-execution method. The re-execution methods bring another component to the energy-quality trade-off, which adds energy overhead for each re-execution but increases the average quality by recovering invalid results. For the approximate method, this energy overhead can be softened with lower re-execution probabilities in the next approximation level, or be raised when the chances for another invalid result are high on this level. Nonetheless, higher chances for other invalid results occur at approximation levels where the low average quality of results and the nonexistent energy savings prevent these operating points to be valid levels of execution. Table 1 shows the expected savings (E_S) and quality (E_Q) for all applications without any transparent resilience mechanisms (AM model), in approximation levels from 1.07 V to 1.10 V, in which most applications present the more significant energy savings maintaining high-quality results. In all these levels and applications, the energy overhead does not make the approximate re-execution surpass the energy cost of accurate re-executions on our experiments, where the E_S of the approximate method is at most the same as the one of the accurate method.

The probability of a re-execution is a key characteristic to achieve energy savings using re-execution methods, especially for the approximate re-execution that relies on the re-execution probability of the next lower vdd. Sobel presents the highest E_S values because of fewer crashes and invalid results on lower vdds, increasing the E_S of the approximate method up to 4 pp at 1.07 V. Dijkstra, fft, and jpeg nullify the energy gains at 1.07 V through accurate re-execution,

Table 1. Expected Energy Savings (E_S) and Expected Quality (E_Q) for approximate and accurate re-execution.

vdd →		1.07		1.08		1.09		1.10	
Application	Re-execution	E_S	E_Q	E_S	E_Q	E_S	E_Q	E_S	E_Q
atax	Approximate	**10.7%**	74.8%	**18.9%**	91.1%	19.3%	98.0%	18.51%	100.00%
	Accurate	7.7%	**76.3%**	17.8%	**91.2%**	19.3%	98.0%	18.51%	100.00%
correlation	Approximate	**15.3%**	96.6%	20.0%	98.9%	19.3%	100.0%	18.52%	100.00%
	Accurate	13.3%	**96.7%**	20.0%	98.9%	19.3%	100.0%	18.52%	100.00%
dijkstra	Approximate	**1.0%**	68.5%	**12.5%**	83.5%	**18.0%**	98.7%	**17.10%**	99.67%
	Accurate	–	80.7%	8.3%	**83.8%**	17.6%	98.7%	16.92%	99.67%
fft	Approximate	–	44.9%	**15.6%**	91.6%	**17.2%**	100.0%	18.52%	100.00%
	Accurate	–	49.0%	12.9%	91.6%	16.6%	100.0%	18.52%	100.00%
jpeg	Approximate	**3.0%**	88.6%	**20.1%**	89.3%	19.3%	99.6%	18.52%	100.00%
	Accurate	–	93.2%	18.6%	**89.4%**	19.3%	99.6%	18.52%	100.00%
sobel	Approximate	**30.5%**	68.5%	**22.6%**	92.9%	19.6%	99.3%	18.52%	99.99%
	Accurate	26.5%	**69.8%**	22.3%	92.9%	19.6%	99.3%	18.52%	99.99%

because of the higher re-execution probability that adds an overhead based on the nominal energy consumption. However, this overhead is decreased by the approximate re-execution, which can present slight energy savings on jpeg and dijkstra at this approximation level. The higher number of delayed crashes and invalid results produced by SDC increases the energy overhead of fft, which postpones its energy savings to 1.08 V on both re-execution methods. Correlation presents equal E_S peaks to approximate and accurate re-executions due to the fewer invalid results and crashes in its best approximation level. Some operating points show no difference between the accurate and the approximate methods because of having small chances of triggering re-executions. For 5 out of 6 applications, the peak of E_S occurs with approximate re-execution at the cost of a decrease on the E_Q.

In general, the approximate re-execution shows higher savings at the approximation level closer to the edge of a high probability of crashes because of the minimum overhead added when compared to the accurate method. Energy savings are significantly high in comparison to the depreciation in quality. In all cases when quality and energy metrics show different results, the approximate method achieves higher efficiency in the combined efficiency. Therefore, our proposed approximate re-execution method achieves the highest energy savings for the 6 applications with a low impact on quality.

5.3 Transparent Interfaces

The number of valid results varies depending on the execution with transparent interfaces. These interfaces are orthogonal to the re-execution methods, which can recover invalid results even when no resilience mechanisms are used, as the results with AM. Resilience interfaces insist on executions that would crash or result in invalid outputs, trying to generate valid and higher quality results.

Table 2. Operating points of the best E_S for each application.

Application	Interface	vdd	E_Q	E_S	Application	Interface	vdd	E_Q	E_S
atax	AM	1.09	98.0%	19.3%	fft	AM	1.10	100%	18.5%
	SW-AC	1.07	80.3%	**20.0%**		SW-AC	1.09	100%	17.7%
	SW-ACw	1.09	**99.9%**	18.8%		SW-ACw	1.09	100%	**19.3%**
correlation	AM	1.08	**98.9%**	**20.0%**	jpeg	AM	1.08	89.3%	**20.1%**
	SW-AC	1.07	98.6%	**20.0%**		SW-AC	1.09	99.6%	18.9%
	SW-ACw	1.07	98.5%	19.3%		SW-ACw	1.09	**99.7%**	19.3%
dijkstra	AM	1.09	98.7%	**18.0%**	sobel	AM	1.07	68.5%	30.5%
	SW-AC	1.10	99.0%	10.0%		SW-AC	1.07	**74.9%**	30.5%
	SW-ACw	1.11	**100%**	17.8%		SW-ACw	1.07	71.6%	**30.6%**

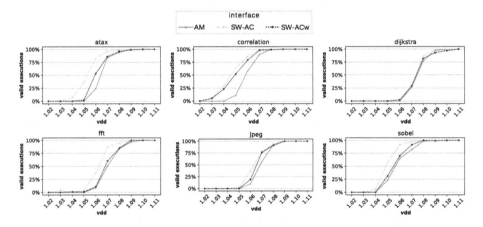

Fig. 3. Executions that produce valid outputs with the evaluated interfaces. In general, resilience mechanisms increase the percentage of these valid executions.

Valid Executions. Figure 3 shows the percentage of executions that produce valid results for two evaluated interfaces, SW-AC and SW-ACw, besides an approximate memory without implementing resilience interfaces (AM). SW-AC implements software and hardware addressing schemes from AxRAM plus CSi features and protection of the stack region from errors. SW-ACw implements all these features, except for the stack protection. SW-AC shows the higher number of valid executions, and, consequently, the lower re-execution probability.

In general, the use of interfaces decreases the need for re-executions at lower vdds, however, higher quality results are usually generated at higher vdds, where crashes and invalid outputs are not so frequent using our proposed architecture. Furthermore, in our environment, the error impact is alleviated by error-free L1 and L2 caches, which can protect small temporary variables, and the approximate re-execution decreases the impact of recovering invalid outputs, thus reducing any gains of protecting the application stack.

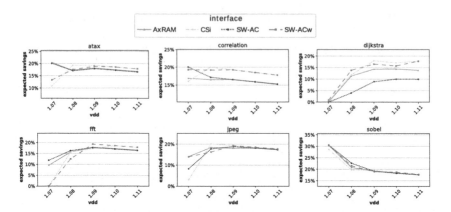

Fig. 4. Expected energy savings for evaluated interfaces. The combined interfaces benefit from the lower overhead of CSi at higher vdds, and the higher savings of AxRAM at lower vdds.

Moreover, triggering fewer re-executions does not necessarily infer more energy savings. Other factors influence these gains, such as timeouts (the more energy-wasting execution crash) and the execution phase at which a crash happens. The more delayed an execution crash is, the higher is the energy overhead of an instance.

Expected Energy Savings and Quality. In our environment, the best operating points are in the vdds where the probability for a re-execution is relatively low, and, when a re-execution is needed, the approximate re-execution is performed at a level with this probability almost equal to zero. These operating points range from 1.07 V to 1.10 V. Comparing data from this range, Table 2 shows the operating points with the highest energy savings achieved for all applications per interface, where the protection mechanisms match the highest expected quality for 5 out of 6 applications. However, the decreased cost of recovering invalid outputs or crashed instances by approximate re-executions results in higher energy savings for AM, which matches the highest savings for 3 out of 6 applications.

The software-level addressing scheme achieves the most benefits on quality and energy for 5 out of 6 applications. However, the stack protection can impact differently depending on the overhead and structures used by the application. Only for sobel this feature increases the combined benefits. The stack protection, however, is derived from correct memory allocation for the stack region and can be configured at runtime [6]. Thus, an analysis of the impact of each protection feature and its respective overhead is necessary before associating an application to an interface.

Comparison with Other Interfaces. Figures 4 shows the expected energy savings for the proposed interfaces compared with hardware-only implementations of AxRAM and CSi. From a certain point, execution crashes are rare, and thus resilience interfaces have no significant benefits and add energy overhead, especially when protecting memory regions from errors. This behavior can be noticed on the decreased benefits with sobel starting from 1.08 V.

Dijkstra is a representative application that shows the highest difference between the four interfaces. This application performs a lot of accesses on the application stack, resulting in significant overhead on its protection and favors the energy benefits of CSi, in isolation. Moreover, CSi is a low-overhead hardware-only mechanism, in comparison to the software implementation SW-AxRAM. However, if the stack protection is removed from SW-AxRAM, the energy benefits get closer to pure CSi, while still providing high-quality results and, thus, maximizing the energy-quality trade-off. This behavior pattern is perceived in most applications.

Thus, the unprotected stack is determinant for achieving high energy savings for most of the applications at higher vdds. However, interfaces that protect some critical memory region achieves higher savings at lower vdds, as seen in atax. The combined interfaces have a lower overhead at higher vdds and protect critical data at lower vdds, achieving most of the benefits of CSi and AxRAM and maintaining high quality results for a wider range of operation.

6   Conclusion

Approximate memories operate below guard-banding parameters trading energy for quality degradation of results. In the border of this guard-banding, the execution of some applications brings low or even no errors. However, as the approximation level grows, errors may lead to invalid results or crashed executions. Mechanisms for transparent resilience aim to avoid execution crashes to generate valid results and improve the chances for a high-quality result in higher approximation levels without any program annotation. This work compares and explores state-of-the-art mechanisms for transparent resilience, detecting invalid results to trigger re-execution mechanisms. Our results show that approximate re-executions achieve energy savings of 4 pp with negligible loss in quality. Furthermore, the proposed combined interfaces, that merge transparent mechanisms, have the potential to benefit from higher energy savings with lower overhead than interfaces that implement isolated mechanisms. Despite being application-specific, the use of acceptance tests as re-execution triggers can improve the detection of invalid outputs up to 30% by simple and lightweight validations. The impact on quality depends on the behavior of the application and its manipulated data, thus, to have improved quality and allow further efficiency, we intend to explore as future work the relation between application characteristics and the resulting output quality.

References

1. Chandrasekar, K., Weis, C., Li, Y., Akesson, B., Wehn, N., Goossens, K.: DRAM-Power: open-source DRAM power & energy estimation tool (2012). http://www.drampower.info
2. Chang, K.K., Kashyap, A., Hassan, H., Pekhimenko, G., Khan, S., Mutlu, O.: Understanding latency variation in modern DRAM chips: experimental characterization, analysis, and optimization. In: SIGMETRICS/IFIP, pp. 323–335 (2016)
3. Chang, K.K., et al.: Understanding reduced-voltage operation in modern DRAM chips: characterization, analysis, and mechanisms. POMACS 1(1), 1–42 (2017)
4. Cohen, M., Zhu, H.S., Senem, E.E., Liu, Y.D.: Energy types. ACM SIGPLAN 47(10), 831–850 (2012)
5. De Kruijf, M., Nomura, S., Sankaralingam, K.: Relax: an architectural framework for software recovery of hardware faults. ISCA 38, 497–508 (2010)
6. Fabrício Filho, J., Felzmann, I.B., Azevedo, R., Wanner, L.: AxRAM: a lightweight implicit interface for approximate data access. FGCS 113, 556–570 (2020)
7. Felzmann, I., Fabrício Filho, J., Wanner, L.: Risk-5: controlled approximations for RISC-V. IEEE TCAD 39(11), 4052–4063 (2020)
8. Froehlich, S., Große, D., Drechsler, R.: Approximate memory: data storage in the context of approximate computing. In: Große, C.S., Drechsler, R. (eds.) Information Storage, pp. 111–133. Springer, Cham (2020). https://doi.org/10.1007/978-3-030-19262-4_4
9. Joshi, K., Fernando, V., Misailovic, S.: Aloe: verifying reliability of approximate programs in the presence of recovery mechanisms. In: CGO, pp. 56–67 (2020)
10. Kim, Y., Yang, W., Mutlu, O.: Ramulator: a fast and extensible DRAM simulator. IEEE CAL 15(1), 45–49 (2016)
11. Koppula, S., et al.: EDEN: enabling energy-efficient, high-performance deep neural network inference using approximate DRAM. In: MICRO, pp. 166–181 (2019)
12. Maity, B., Donyanavard, B., Surhonne, A., Rahmani, A., Herkersdorf, A., Dutt, N.: AXES: approximation manager for emerging memory architectures. Technical report, UCLA Irvine (2020). http://arxiv.org/abs/2011.08353
13. Moreau, T., et al.: A taxonomy of general purpose approximate computing techniques. IEEE LES 10(1), 2–5 (2018)
14. Sampson, A., Dietl, W., Fortuna, E., Gnanapragasam, D., Ceze, L., Grossman, D.: EnerJ: approximate data types for safe and general low-power computation. In: PLDI, pp. 164–174 (2011)
15. Verdeja Herms, Y., Li, Y.: Crash skipping: a minimal-cost framework for efficient error recovery in approximate computing environments. In: GLSVLSI, pp. 129–134 (2019)
16. Wang, T., Zhang, Q., Xu, Q.: ApproxQA: a unified quality assurance framework for approximate computing. In: DATE, pp. 254–257 (2017)
17. Yarmand, R., Kamal, M., Afzali-Kusha, A., Pedram, M.: DART: a framework for determining approximation levels in an approximable memory hierarchy. IEEE TVLSI 28(1), 273–286 (2020)
18. Yazdanbakhsh, A., Mahajan, D., Esmaeilzadeh, H., Lotfi-Kamran, P.: AxBench: a multiplatform benchmark suite for approximate computing. IEEE D&T 34(2), 60–68 (2017)

Heterogeneous Computing

Automatic Mapping of Parallel Pattern-Based Algorithms on Heterogeneous Architectures

Lukas Trümper[1,2] , Julian Miller[2(✉)] , Christian Terboven[2] ,
and Matthias S. Müller[2]

[1] Huddly AS, Oslo, Norway
[2] Chair for High Performance Computing, IT Center,
RWTH Aachen University, Aachen, Germany
`lukas.truemper@rwth-aachen.de`,
{`miller,terboven,mueller`}`@itc.rwth-aachen.de`

Abstract. Nowadays, specialized hardware is often found in clusters to improve compute performance and energy efficiency. The porting and tuning of scientific codes to these heterogeneous clusters requires significant development efforts. To mitigate these efforts while maintaining high performance, modern parallel programming models introduce a second layer of abstraction, where an architecture-agnostic source code can be maintained and automatically optimized for the target architecture. However, with increasing heterogeneity, the mapping of an application to a specific architecture itself becomes a complex decision requiring a differentiated consideration of processor features and algorithmic properties. Furthermore, architecture-agnostic global transformations are necessary to maximize the simultaneous utilization of different processors. Therefore, we introduce a combinatorial optimization approach to globally transform and automatically map parallel algorithms to heterogeneous architectures. We derive a global transformation and mapping algorithm which bases on a static performance model. Moreover, we demonstrate the approach on five typical algorithmic kernels showing automatic and global transformations such as loop fusion, re-ordering, pipelining, NUMA awareness, and optimal mapping strategies to an exemplary CPU-GPU compute node. Our algorithm achieves performance on par with hand-tuned implementations of all five kernels.

Keywords: Mapping · Heterogeneous architectures · Global transformations · Parallel patterns · Performance portability

1 Introduction

Advances in science and engineering are intrinsically linked to computing power. This demand is met with large-scale clusters with many compute nodes.

Electronic supplementary material The online version of this chapter (https:// doi.org/10.1007/978-3-030-81682-7_4) contains supplementary material, which is available to authorized users.

© Springer Nature Switzerland AG 2021
C. Hochberger et al. (Eds.): ARCS 2021, LNCS 12800, pp. 53–67, 2021.
https://doi.org/10.1007/978-3-030-81682-7_4

However, these nodes are limited by their power draw, memory performance, and Instruction Level Parallelism (ILP) (cf. *three walls* [2]). Hence, current advances in hardware are driven by specialization, which leads to clusters comprising heterogeneous architectures. To effectively utilize this quickly evolving landscape of architectures, domain scientists need to continuously adapt their software, which requires a significant development effort and experience.

To reduce these efforts, current parallel programming models introduce a *second layer of abstraction* to decouple the expression of parallelism from the hardware architectures. Thus, an architecture-agnostic source code can be maintained and the optimization for a specific architecture is delegated to the transformations supported by the programming model. E.g., *Kokkos* [13] and *RAJA* [7] utilize data layout rules and *Stateful Dataflow Multigraphs (SDFG)* [8] allows to interactively transform the dataflow of a parallel algorithm for the target architecture.

With increasing heterogeneity, effective utilization of the available processors however requires fine-grained mapping decisions. This mapping needs to match algorithmic properties with processor features, e.g., assigning a compute-intensive part of the algorithm to an appropriate accelerator. Furthermore, architecture-agnostic transformations are necessary to expose global parallelism and execute large parts of the algorithm on different accelerators simultaneously.

To automatize such mappings, this work provides a combinatorial optimization approach to globally transform and automatically map parallel algorithms to heterogeneous architectures. The approach leverages a hierarchical representation of parallel algorithms [21,22] based on *parallel patterns* [19]. This representation allows for the analysis of global properties like synchronization and dataflow through *algorithmic efficiencies* [21,22]. Based on these efficiencies and the *roofline model* [25], structural transformations and a cost-based optimization is derived. Thereby, this paper focuses on the re-ordering and delinearization of routines, the separation and fusion of large subflows within the dataflow as well as data affinity on a global level. Our key contributions are as follows:

– We introduce a static performance model based on algorithmic efficiencies that allows for global transformations of parallel algorithms and their mapping to heterogeneous architectures.
– We derive a transformation and mapping algorithm based on fine-grained splits of the algorithmic structure.
– We demonstrate the approach on five typical algorithms on a modern CPU-GPU architecture. The experiments show the mapping to target architectures with respect to algorithmic properties as well as the application of several global transformations such as loop fusion, re-ordering, pipelining, NUMA awareness, and target offloading.

The remainder of this paper is structured as follows: Sect. 2 briefly summarizes related work. Section 3 introduces the used model of algorithms and architectures and Sect. 4 proposes the static performance model. Section 5 derives the mapping algorithm and Sect. 6 evaluates the approach for typical data-parallel algorithms. The results of the evaluation and extensions of the approach are discussed in

Sect. 7. At last, Sect. 8 provides a conclusion of the paper and summarizes future work.

2   Related Work

This paper focuses on the automatic transformation and mapping of parallel algorithms to heterogeneous architectures. The following sections briefly delineate this paper from related work.

Parallel Programming Models. Recent parallel programming models are designed on top of architecture-specific programming models like *OpenMP* [12], *MPI* [20], and *CUDA* [23]. The architecture-agnostic layer is typically represented by *parallel patterns* [19]. Kokkos [13] uses C++ software abstractions, where the mapping is specified by compile-time parameters. RAJA [7] follows a similar approach by expressing parallelism through loops. The SDFG framework [8] focuses on data parallelism and represents the patterns of a *python* program with graphs. Furthermore, there exists multiple skeleton-based models and interfaces [14]. These models minimize the necessary code changes for porting an application by automatically transforming the code. This paper extends these approaches by exposing additional parallelism, complex global transformations, and automatic mapping to a heterogeneous architecture. This work re-uses the pattern-based representation of algorithms found in the models above.

Transformations. Low-level transformations are applied to improve low-level and code-local performance properties for a specific architecture. Bacon et al. [3] provide an overview of loop transformations to improve the ILP. Many of these transformations are supported by the programming models discussed above and modern production compilers. *Structural transformations* are high-level manipulations of the structure of an algorithm. For instance, throughput-oriented processors typically require flat parallelism, which can be achieved by resolving nested parallelism [9] and nested loops [10]. Furthermore, skeleton-based libraries typically implement different transformation rules [17] like the fusion of skeletons. In contrast to such rule-based approaches, this work transforms and maps an algorithm based on a static performance model. This allows for structural transformations on the highest level of a parallel algorithm. By identifying substructures in the algorithm, fine-granular transformations such as the separation of a sparse dataflow and cache blocking on a routine-level are enabled.

Mapping. Various approaches for mapping a parallel algorithm on heterogeneous architectures exist. A theoretical foundation of the problem is the *MAKESPAN SCHEDULING* on unrelated machines for which different approximation algorithms were proposed [18]. Beaumont et al. [6] investigate the particular problem of matrix-partitioning on heterogeneous architectures and provide several approximation algorithms. The approaches above investigate the mapping within an isolated context, i.e., without a temporal dimension defined by subsequent routines and data dependencies. In this work, however, the mapping is part of an optimization problem over the global structure of an algorithm.

3   Parallel Algorithms

The approach proposes automatic transformations and mappings to heterogeneous architectures at compile time. The mapping algorithm thereby founds on a model of parallel algorithms consisting of a hierarchical decomposition of parallel patterns, which is introduced in [21,22]. This model is particularly applicable to the global analysis of algorithms as it combines two basic ideas making this combinatorially complex analysis feasible. First, it follows the idea of separating the structure of an algorithm from its executed function. This is mainly implemented by abstracting local routines like loops to respective parallel patterns. Second, the model introduces a two-level representation of the algorithmic structure, called the abstract pattern tree (APT). This representation contains local parallel patterns in their global context.

3.1   Parallel Patterns

A parallel pattern is an abstraction of local parallelism as often found in loops and other recurring structures. For this work, they are defined as a directed graph of operations and their data dependencies. An operation consumes and produces data and two operations o_1, o_2 are connected by a direct edge (o_1, o_2) iff o_2 consumes data produced by o_1. Data is thereby interpreted by its instant value, i.e., it does not refer to a memory location and is immutable. The only relevant data dependencies are therefore *true data dependencies* and the investigated graphs are acyclic. Local parallelism is then defined as follows:

- *Earliest-execution-time:* Let $s, o_1, \ldots, o_{n-1}, o$ be the longest directed path from some source of data s to operation o, then o is said to have *earliest-execution-time n*.
- *Parallel:* Two operations o, o' are parallel, iff there is no directed path connecting them and they have the same earliest-execution-time.

A *parallel pattern* comprises at least two parallel operations; the *serial pattern* is defined analogously. Figure 1 illustrates the concept with the example of a *map* pattern where $f_1, \ldots, f_4$ are parallel operations. In the following, local parallelism is assumed to be optimal, i.e., all true data dependencies are well-defined. For the scope of this paper, the three common parallel patterns *map*, *stencil*, and *reduction* as defined by McCool et al. [19] are considered. These patterns are data-parallel and are found in popular *Berkeley dwarfs* [2] like *dense linear algebra, spectral methods*, and *MapReduce*.

3.2   Abstract Pattern Tree

The abstract pattern tree (APT) is an internal representation of the structure of an algorithm over the execution order of parallel and serial patterns. Formally, an APT is an undirected graph of pattern nodes (parallel and serial patterns) and two types of meta nodes: The children of a *serial meta node* must be executed from left to right. The children of a *parallel meta node* can be executed

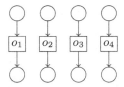

Fig. 1. The map pattern with $o_1, \ldots, o_4$ parallel operations.

in parallel. Furthermore, serial and parallel patterns may themselves be meta nodes to account for the concepts of sub-routines and nested parallelism. The term execution order corresponds to the order defined by the developer and is intentionally different from the data dependencies. As such, the developer may miss concurrency as shown by the linearization of nodes in the APT. However, it is assumed that the developer-provided code is correct, i.e., all true data dependencies are well-defined. An exemplary APT is illustrated in Fig. 2.

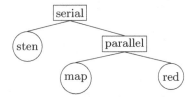

Fig. 2. An exemplary APT of a stencil (sten) and a subsequent parallel map and reduction (red).

The partitioning of operations into sets of parallel operations defines local *algorithmic steps*. Globally, algorithmic steps $STEP_1, \ldots, STEP_T$ combine the local steps according to their relation in the APT. In the following, the set of all operations is denoted $\mathcal{O}$ with $STEP_1 \,\dot{\cup}\, \ldots \,\dot{\cup}\, STEP_T = \mathcal{O}$.

4 Performance Modeling

The following section introduces the performance model, which guides the global transformations and mapping of parallel algorithms. This is based on *algorithmic efficiencies* introduced in [21,22], which are briefly summarized in the following. Algorithmic efficiencies are necessary conditions of performance defined over specific global properties of algorithms. The mapping of operations to processors must therefore be assessed within its global context defined through previous and subsequent data dependencies.

Synchronization. The *synchronization efficiency*'s purpose is to maximize the potential parallelism before mapping the operations to the processors. On the global algorithmic level, this potential is mainly limited by unidentified concurrency, e.g., due to the linearization of independent parallel patterns.

Inter-Processor Dataflow. Formally, a mapping is defined as a function $M :$ $\mathcal{O} \to \mathcal{P}$ from operations to processors, where each operation must be executed by exactly one processor. A *processor* thereby describes a homogeneous set of *cores* sharing the same processor-level cache. This corresponds to a socket of a CPU or the streaming processor of a GPU in practice. The set of processors of a cluster may be heterogeneous and can comprise different processors on the same device, node and within the same network on different nodes. Without loss of generality, the mapping can be decomposed into a sequence of step-wise mappings $M \to M_1^T$, where $M_t : STEP_t \to \mathcal{P}$ is the mapping of step t. The *inter-processor dataflow efficiency* defines the costs of a mapping through *execution costs* $E_t : \mathcal{P} \times 2^{STEP_t} \to \mathbb{R}$ and *network costs* $N_t : \mathcal{P} \times 2^{STEP_t} \to \mathbb{R}$. The criterion to be minimized by the mapping is defined as follows:

$$\sum_t \max_P \left\{ E_t(P, M_t^{-1}(P)) + N_t(P, M_t^{-1}(P); M_1^{t-1}) \right\} \to \min_{M_1^T} !,$$

where the network costs at step t may depend on previous steps and the execution costs only depend on the current step. The costs can thereby be modeled based on assumptions of existing performance models. In the following, the costs are adopted from the *roofline model* [25], where the assumption of the overlap of execution is relaxed:

– *Execution costs:* The execution of operations is captured by the number of floating point operations (Flops) divided by the peak performance π_P (clock frequency times Flops per cycle):

$$E_t(P, M_t^{-1}(P)) := \frac{\sum_o Flops(o)}{\pi_P}, o \in M_t^{-1}(P).$$

– *Network costs:* The network costs are defined as the slowest data transfer between two processors. A data transfer thereby bundles all bytes to be trans-ferred from one processor to another to satisfy the data dependencies. The bandwidth $\beta_s(P', P)$ is determined by the slowest interconnect between these two processors and a latency penalty $\Gamma_s(P', P)$ is added:

$$N_t(P, M_t^{-1}(P)) := \max_{P'} \left\{ \frac{\sum_{(o',o)} BYTES((o',o))}{\beta_s(P', P)} + \Gamma_s(P', P) \right\},$$
$$o \in M_t^{-1}(P), o' \in M_{1...t-1}^{-1}(P').$$

Intra-Processor Dataflow. Given a mapping M_1^T, the *intra-processor dataflow efficiency* seeks to optimize the execution of parallel operations assigned to the same processor. This includes the scheduling on its cores, the utilization of core-local caches, and transformations on the instruction-level to allow overlapping execution of operations of different steps via asynchronous techniques. It is a subsequent optimization after the mapping to the processors, and it is assumed to be optimized by downward compilers (cf. Sect. 2).

5   Mapping Algorithm

The mapping and transformation algorithm consists of two steps: First, the synchronization efficiency is optimized by re-ordering the APT's nodes to resolve false linearization. Second, the actual mapping is derived by sequential optimization over the algorithmic steps with respect to the inter-processor dataflow efficiency. An implementation of the presented algorithm is included in the supplemental material.

5.1   Step 1: FlatAPT

The serial meta nodes of the APT encode the algorithmic steps defined by the developer. To resolve false linearization, the children of a serial meta node need to be re-ordered according to their actual data dependencies. If two such children are parallel, the parallelism is encoded by re-inserting them as the children of a new parallel meta node into the respective sub-tree.

Due to potential parallelism across nested serial meta nodes, local optimality does not directly lead to global optimality. Instead, the APT is traversed in-order and every node is added to a new *FlatAPT*. This FlatAPT consists of only a single serial meta node, the main node, and parallel meta nodes at the second level, the algorithmic steps. A new pattern node is added as the child of a new parallel meta node to the end of the FlatAPT, which introduces a new (last) step. The node then *bubbles up* the algorithmic steps as long as there are no true data dependencies and becomes the child of an earlier parallel meta node. Since the FlatAPT consists of only a single serial meta node, the FlatAPT is constructed globally optimal. Note that the nested parallelism is not leveraged at this stage and, thus, the algorithm omits the traversal of sub-trees defined by a parallel pattern or parallel meta node (Fig. 3).

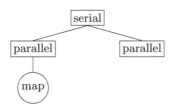

Fig. 3. Exemplary structure of a FlatAPT with a map inserted and an empty second step already created.

The worst-case computational complexity occurs if every node of the APT needs to be traversed and compared to every preceding node in the FlatAPT at insertion, i.e., every node bubbles up into the first step. Hence, the algorithm holds a quadratic worst-case complexity to the number of nodes. The feasibility and complexity of the actual data dependence analysis for each pair of nodes depend on the static information provided by the programming language as described by Hennessy et al. [15] and Banerjee et al. [5].

5.2   Step 2: Step Mappings

The inter-processor dataflow efficiency is modeled as a sequential optimization problem over the sequence of step mappings M_1^T. The optimization is thereby restricted to the following mapping space:

- *Team:* A team reserves a number of cores on a processor. The set of all possible teams is denoted $\mathcal{T}$.
- *Pattern split:* A pattern split is a subset of the parallel operations of a parallel pattern, e.g., an interval of independent iterations of the same loop.
- *Step mapping:* A step mapping is refined as a function $M_t : SPLITS_t \to \mathcal{T}$ from pattern splits to teams. There is at most one active team per processor and step.

Accordingly, the recursive formulation of the efficiency is considered instead:

$$Q(M_1^t) = \min_{M_1^{t-1}} \{d(M_t; M_1^{t-1}) + Q(M_1^{t-1})\},$$

$$d(M_t; M_1^{t-1}) = \max_P E_t(P, M_t^{-1}(P)) + N_t(P, M_t^{-1}(P); M_1^{t-1}),$$

where $d(M_t; M_1^{t-1})$ is the inter-processor dataflow efficiency of only the step mapping M_t given the history M_1^{t-1}. The optimization problem associates three decision dimensions yielding the general structure of the optimization algorithm:

- *Teams:* At each step t, select k out of K teams.
- *Assignment:* Partition the N pattern splits into k sets.
- *Time:* Assess the step mapping within the temporal context and extend the current hypotheses of partial mappings.

However, this optimization problem does not admit *optimal substructure* to the end that a globally optimal mapping can be constructed from locally optimal step mappings. Because of arbitrary temporal dependencies in the network costs, series of suboptimal step mappings might enable particularly efficient step mappings in the last algorithmic steps. By considering the full search space, the global optimum can be obtained. However, the combinatorial complexity then grows exponentially in all three dimensions K, N, T. In the following, approximation techniques are proposed to reduce this complexity.

Time. Data dependencies are assumed to be limited to a maximum length of m steps. The mapping is therefore constructed greedily over time with a lookahead of m steps:

$$Q(t) = \min_{M_t, M_{t+1}, \ldots, M_{t+m}} \{d(M_t; B(t-1)) + Q(t-1; B(t-2))$$

$$+ \sum_{\tau=1}^m d(M_{t+\tau}; B(t-1+\tau))\},$$

where $B(t)$ is a *traceback array* storing the actual step mappings of previous steps. The approximating assumption leverages the *principle of locality*. Furthermore, data dependencies refer back to the operation that initially created the data. In practice, the data may also be read by another team in the meantime and it is then transferred from this team. This effectively shortens the temporal length of dependencies.

Assignment. For a given set of teams, only the locally optimal assignments of pattern splits concerning the current step are considered. This transforms the optimization over step mappings M_1^T to one over teams U_1^T. The estimation of the locally optimal assignment is approached by the modeling as an instance of the NP-hard *MAKESPAN SCHEDULING* on unrelated machines [18]; teams are distinguishable in execution costs by hardware characteristics and network costs for accessing remote memory locations. The main difference to the original problem is that pattern splits may share data, i.e., data only needs to be loaded once from memory for two different splits. This invalidates the assumption of independent costs for the splits and the optimality bounds of existing heuristics for the original problem. The assignment is therefore based on a generic *branch-and-cut* algorithm as shown in the prototype implementation in the supplemental material.

Teams. At each step, the set of teams is determined by a variant of *local search*. The basic idea is to gradually extend an initial set of teams consisting of a single CPU team. The search compares different strategies for an extension, called moves, and follows the direction of the best move similar to *hill climbing*. Two phases of this search are distinguished that differ by the type of moves to be compared: At first, the search progresses by *local moves*. Such moves may only add new teams located on devices used by the current teams, e.g., another socket of a CPU. When a local optimum is reached, the set of teams is extended with new devices and nodes called *jump*. These two types of moves are necessary in order to avoid a collapse of hypotheses. The assignment may lead to a *subset selection* of teams by not assigning splits to some teams. This frequently occurs when extending to a new node and too few teams are added to compensate for the additional network costs. Thus, local optima of this search are always plateaus and the optimization space consists of different levels of plateaus. This variant of a local search is therefore denoted *stair climbing*.

Analysis. While the mapping based on the inter-processor dataflow efficiency is a general scheduling problem, the proposed algorithm cuts it into many local assignment problems by explicitly exposing the optimization over time and teams. Assuming the stair climbing algorithm needs to search the whole cluster, but each move doubles the number of teams on average and only two moves are compared at a time, the computational complexity of this outer optimization regarding the assignment is $T \cdot (K \cdot a(N))^{1+m}$, where $a(N)$ is the complexity of each assignment. Assuming $m = 1$, K to be constant and T to be linear in N, the complexity is $\mathcal{O}(a(N)^3)$.

6 Evaluation

In the following, the proposed optimization framework for global transformations and automatic mappings is evaluated regarding its approximation quality and achieved local optima. Since the approximation quality cannot be derived analytically for practical problems, an empirical analysis of typical data-centric algorithms such as linear equations, classifications, and neural networks is used. Each algorithm is implemented in a *baseline version* closely following its numerical definition. Furthermore, a *hand-tuned version* is derived by applying crucial transformations and mapping decisions as found in the literature and library implementations. The proposed framework transforms and maps the baseline versions, which is denoted *auto version*. The resulting optimizations are then compared to the hand-tuned version including a qualitative analysis of the optimization as well as a quantitative analysis of the estimated and actual runtimes. Once the implementation of the approach as a fully integrated tool is finished, a comparison with related approaches will be carried out.

Experimental Setup. The experiments were executed on two typical CPU-GPU nodes connected via Intel® Omni-Path with 100 Gb/s. Each node features two Intel® Skylake® Platinum 8160 processors with 24 cores each, a base frequency of 2.1 GHz, disabled HyperThreading, and 192 GB of DDR4 RAM. Two NVIDIA® Tesla® V100 GPUs with 16 GB of HBM2 memory are connected via PCI-express. The experiments were repeated 30 times and median measurements are reported.

We implement the algorithms in a *Parallel Pattern Language (PPL)*, from which the APT can be parsed directly. After optimization of the APT, the resulting mapping is manually translated into C code using the parallel programming models OpenMP 4.5, OpenMPI 3.1.3, and CUDA 10.2; the baseline versions are directly implemented in C. The OpenMP versions were compiled with gcc 9.3.0 and compiler flags *-fopenmp -std=c99 -O2*, the MPI versions with gcc 9.3.0, OpenMPI 3.1.3, and compiler flags *-fopenmp -std=c99 -O2*, and the CUDA versions with the NVIDIA compiler 10.2, gcc 8.2.0 and compiler flags *-Xcompiler -fopenmp*. If the generated pattern and data splits are large on the GPU, the block size is reduced to 512 due to the limits of the CUDA framework. The work assigned to a specific processor is statically scheduled to its cores. The implementations of the parallel algorithms, as well as the mapping reports of the optimization framework, can be found in the supplemental material.

Parallel Algorithms. The following parallel algorithms are investigated. Depending on the problem size of the evaluated parallel algorithms, different hyperparameters for the optimization algorithm are chosen. They steer the granularity of the pattern and data splits and were derived experimentally.

The *Multi Filter* algorithm represents a typical image processing task, where different filters are applied to the same image independently. In detail, the task is to compute different image derivatives: A *Sobel* filter estimates horizontal derivatives on the upper half of the image and a *Prewitt* filter on the lower half.

Furthermore, a discrete Laplacian is applied to the whole image. The size of the image is 8194×8194. The baseline version processes the three filters sequentially. The used pattern and data split sizes are 4096 and 128 respectively.

The *Batch Classification* represents a typical classification task, where the elements of a batch are processed in multiple stages separately. The first two stages extract the features by first standardizing and then integrating over the absolute inputs. The third stage classifies based on the majority vote of 4096 thresholding classifiers. To highlight potential pipelining and fusion transformations, the baseline version processes the batch in reverse during the second stage. The size of the batch is 2^{19} and each input element is a vector of size 4096. The used pattern and data split sizes are 262144.

Three linear equation systems are solved with the *Jacobi method* sharing the same coefficient matrix A. The number of unknowns is 8192 in each linear system and the number of Jacobi iterations is fixed to 50. The baseline version solves the linear systems sequentially. The used pattern and data split sizes are 4096.

The *Neural Network* algorithm defines the forward pass of an eight-layer neural network for a batch of size 2^{18}. Each layer consists of 64 neurons. The respective matrix-matrix computations admit massive data parallelism and acceleration potential. The used pattern and data split sizes are 8192.

The *Monte Carlo Pi* algorithm defines a Monte Carlo method for approximating π by accumulating the area of a unit circle. The approximation is obtained by averaging over 96 independent estimations with 10^9 random draws each. The used pattern and data split sizes are 24 and 1 respectively.

6.1 Results

The cost estimations and runtimes are reported in Table 1 for the unoptimized baseline version and the automatically transformed and mapped version.

Table 1. The estimated runtime in seconds and the measured runtime in seconds for the baseline version (base) and the automatically transformed and mapped version (auto). Moreover, the applied transformations by the proposed framework are listed.

Algorithm	Cost [s]		Runtime [s]		Transformations
	Base	Auto	Base	Auto	
Multi filter	0.013	0.010	0.038	0.030	Fusion, re-ordering, pipelining, NUMA awareness
Batch classification	0.475	0.396	1.157	0.898	Fusion, pipelining
Jacobi	0.913	0.637	1.320	0.561	Fusion, re-ordering, pipelining
Neural network	0.167	0.009	0.329	0.175	GPU offloading
Monte Carlo Pi	13.611	6.944	43.449	22.238	Distributed computing

Multi Filter: The optimization identifies the independence of the filters and the shared input data. It fuses the Sobel operator and the Laplacian splits iterating over the upper half of the image; the Prewitt and the remaining Laplacian are fused analogously. Hence, the halves of the images are pipelined and kept in the local caches across the different filters. The baseline version is estimated at 0.013 s and measured at 0.038 s. The estimated runtime costs of this automatic mapping are 0.010 s and measured 0.030 s. Due to the short runtime of the algorithm, the average of 10 repetitions with random input is used.

Batch Classification: Due to the integration over absolute values and the thresholding classifiers, the computation is dominated by branching. The framework accounts for this property by mapping to the two CPU teams of a single node with 24 cores each. Furthermore, the mapping identifies the pipelines for each input and fuses the extraction and classification stages. The estimated runtime costs for the baseline are 0.475 s while the measured runtime is 1.157 s. The estimated runtime of the automatic mapping is 0.396 s and the actual runtime is 0.898 s.

Jacobi: The framework maps the algorithm to the two CPU teams of a single node. It thereby integrates the three linear systems in a single Jacobi pass. Furthermore, the splits across the different linear systems comprising the same rows of A are assigned to the same teams. Accordingly, the same teams are used for corresponding splits over different Jacobi iterations. Hence, the respective rows of A are pipelined across the different linear systems and iterations. The baseline version is estimated at 0.913 s and measured at 1.320 s while the cost of the automatic mapping is 0.637 s and the runtime is 0.561 s.

Neural Network: The proposed framework offloads the massive data parallelism of the algorithm to a GPU. Due to the induced data transfers for a multi-GPU implementation, a single GPU is preferred by the performance model. The costs for the CPU baseline version is 0.167 s and its runtime is 0.329 s. The automatically mapped version is estimated at 0.009 s and measured at 0.175 s.

Monte Carlo Pi: The automatic mapping distributes the splits of the 96 pi estimations across four CPU teams located on two different nodes. The mapping thereby leverages the low communication costs for separating the sparse dataflow initially. The cost of the baseline version that only utilizes a single node is 13.611 s and the measured runtime is 43.449 s. The automatic version is estimated at 6.944 s and measured at 22.238 s.

7   Discussion

The paper introduces an automatic mapping algorithm utilizing a model of algorithmic efficiencies and cost-based combinatorial optimization. The evaluation investigates its approximation quality empirically on a representative set of parallel algorithms. The obtained optima consistently improve the runtime and their qualitative analysis shows that these optima comprise a rich set of global transformations as applied by an HPC expert. In the following, the results and next steps are discussed in detail.

Static Analysis. While the static analysis requires complete information about local parallelism, real-world problems often contain dynamic characteristics. To overcome this challenge, the information about the exact sizes of data structures may be relaxed to approximative estimates. Furthermore, the definition of local parallelism via a parallel pattern is general enough to be defined over concrete structures of existing programming models like directives or C++ templates, from which the APT can be parsed. This information is available for a wide set of scientific algorithms implemented in modern parallel programming models.

Evaluation. The integration of the algorithm into a parallel programming model is the next step towards a thorough evaluation of the approach. This implementation enables a performance comparison on typical benchmarks such as NAS Parallel Benchmarks [4] with existing approaches and an evaluation on proxy and real-world applications regarding the approach's practicability. The critical part of the integration is thereby the optimal use of further architecture-specific transformations as applied by Kokkos, Raja, and modern compilers. For instance, current data representations and team definitions may be refined for compatibility with other models and devices, e.g., CUDA thread blocks.

Performance Modeling. The comparison of the estimated costs for the baseline and the automatic mapping shows that the mapping decisions are well-guided by the high-level performance model. The difference between measured and estimated runtime varies by a factor of 0.9–3.2 except for the neural network, where the GPU mapping is underestimated by a factor of 19. While the model provides rich efficiency information, the implementation currently renounces architecture-specific features required for higher estimation accuracy. For instance, describing the peak performance solely via the number of cores oversimplifies the *SIMT* execution model of modern GPUs since it implies independent execution of threads on cores. The model also excludes architecture-specific acceleration features like *vector registers*, which could be included with the *LogCA model* [1]. Moreover, the overlap between execution and network costs is not investigated in detail and the modelled network costs assume that the communication of a single step occurs simultaneously in a single transfer. This latter assumption overestimates the bandwidth if many teams use the same interconnect simultaneously. This could be improved by utilizing the *LogP model* [11].

Computational Complexity. The computational complexity of the mapping algorithm is cubic with respect to the complexity of the assignment algorithm. Approaches for the assignment based on LP-relaxations and the simplex algorithm are themselves at least cubic on average [16]. Hence, efficient heuristics must be derived, which for instance group similar patterns and leverage the symmetry of modern architectures. Furthermore, the pattern and data split sizes allow to control the feasibility in practice. However, large split sizes may result in a coarse granularity of the analysis, where the degree of parallelism is reduced significantly and artificial data dependencies are introduced. To balance this, a pattern-specific split size could be applied instead of the global parameter. As this increases the number of hyperparameters, an algorithmic strategy for determining these hyperparameters is an important extension. Evolutionary algorithms based on a parallel model like the *island model* [24] may be considered.

8 Conclusion

In this paper, we investigate the problem of mapping parallel algorithms to heterogeneous architectures. To this end, we introduce a static performance model that minimizes the global execution costs. This includes global transformations to improve the dataflow and expose parallelism as well as utilizing large clusters efficiently while minimizing the required data transfers. We show that the proposed algorithm delivers complex optimizations as carried out by HPC experts and execution performance similar to such hand-tuned versions for five typical parallel algorithms. Our proposed approach is extensible in several directions: The performance model could be extended with architecture-specific features to increase its accuracy on a wide set of applications and hardware platforms. Furthermore, the computational complexity of the optimization algorithm may be lowered by heuristics and auto-tuning methods. We will integrate the approach into existing parallel programming models to conduct a larger performance evaluation on a wide set of benchmarks.

Acknowledgement. We thank Adrian Schmitz (RWTH Aachen University) for implementing the prototype language PPL and useful discussions. We also thank Huddly AS for supporting Lukas Trümper in this work.

References

1. Altaf, M.S.B., Wood, D.A.: LogCA: a performance model for hardware accelerators. IEEE Comput. Archit. Lett. **14**(2), 132–135 (2014)
2. Asanovic, K., et al.: A view of the parallel computing landscape. Commun. ACM **52**(10), 56–67 (2009)
3. Bacon, D.F., Graham, S.L., Sharp, O.J.: Compiler transformations for high-performance computing. ACM Comput. Surv. **26**(4), 345–420 (1994)
4. Bailey, D.H., et al.: The NAS parallel benchmarks summary and preliminary results. In: Supercomputing 1991: Proceedings of the 1991 ACM/IEEE conference on Supercomputing, pp. 158–165. IEEE (1991)
5. Banerjee, S.-C.C., Kuck, T.: Time and parallel processor bounds for Fortran-like loops. IEEE Trans. Comput. **C-28**(9), 660–670 (1979)
6. Beaumont, O., Becker, B.A., DeFlumere, A., Eyraud-Dubois, L., Lambert, T., Lastovetsky, A.: Recent advances in matrix partitioning for parallel computing on heterogeneous platforms. IEEE Trans. Parallel Distrib. Syst. **30**(1), 218–229 (2018)
7. Beckingsale, D.A., et al.: RAJA: portable performance for large-scale scientific applications. In: 2019 IEEE/ACM International Workshop on Performance, Portability and Productivity in HPC (P3HPC), pp. 71–81 (2019)

8. Ben-Nun, T., de Fine Licht, J., Ziogas, A.N., Schneider, T., Hoefler, T.: Stateful dataflow multigraphs: a data-centric model for performance portability on heterogeneous architectures. In: Proceedings of the International Conference for High Performance Computing, Networking, Storage and Analysis. SC 2019. Association for Computing Machinery, New York (2019)

9. Chakravarty, M.M.T., Keller, G., Lechtchinsky, R., Pfannenstiel, W.: Nepal — nested data parallelism in Haskell. In: Sakellariou, R., Gurd, J., Freeman, L., Keane, J. (eds.) Euro-Par 2001. LNCS, vol. 2150, pp. 524–534. Springer, Heidelberg (2001). https://doi.org/10.1007/3-540-44681-8_76

10. Chen, C., Chame, J., Hall, M.: Chill: a framework for composing high-level loop transformations. Technical report, Citeseer (2008)

11. Culler, D., et al.: LogP: towards a realistic model of parallel computation. In: Proceedings of the Fourth ACM SIGPLAN Symposium on Principles and Practice of Parallel Programming, PPOPP 1993, pp. 1–12. ACM (1993)

12. Dagum, L., Menon, R.: OpenMP: an industry standard API for shared-memory programming. IEEE Comput. Sci. Eng. **5**(1), 46–55 (1998)

13. Edwards, H.C., Trott, C.R., Sunderland, D.: Kokkos: enabling manycore performance portability through polymorphic memory access patterns. J. Parallel Distrib. Comput. **74**(12), 3202–3216 (2014). Domain-Specific Languages and High-Level Frameworks for High-Performance Computing

14. Gonzàlez-Vèlez, H., Leyton, M.: A survey of algorithmic skeleton frameworks: high-level structured parallel programming enablers. Softw. Pract. Exp. **40**(12), 1135–1160 (2010)

15. Hennessy, J.L., Patterson, D.A.: Computer Architecture: A Quantitative Approach, 5th edn. Morgan Kaufmann Publishers Inc., San Francisco (2011)

16. Klee, V., Minty, G.J.: How good is the simplex algorithm? Inequalities **3**(3), 159–175 (1972)

17. Kuchen, H.: Optimizing sequences of skeleton calls. In: Lengauer, C., Batory, D., Consel, C., Odersky, M. (eds.) Domain-Specific Program Generation. LNCS, vol. 3016, pp. 254–273. Springer, Heidelberg (2004). https://doi.org/10.1007/978-3-540-25935-0_15

18. Lenstra, J.K., Shmoys, D.B., Tardos, É.: Approximation algorithms for scheduling unrelated parallel machines. Math. Program. **46**(1), 259–271 (1990)

19. McCool, M., Reinders, J., Robison, A.: Structured Parallel Programming - Patterns for Efficient Computation. Elsevier, Amsterdam (2012)

20. Message-Passing Interface Forum: A Message-Passing Interface Standard. http://www.mpi-forum.org/

21. Miller, J., Trümper, L., Terboven, C., Müller, M.S.: A Theoretical Model for Global Optimization of Parallel Algorithms, Manuscript submitted for publication, RWTH Aachen University, Germany

22. Miller, J., Trümper, L., Terboven, C., Müller, M.S.: Poster: efficiency of algorithmic structures. In: IEEE/ACM International Conference on High Performance Computing, Networking, Storage and Analysis (SC 2019) (2019)

23. NVIDIA, Vingelmann, P., Fitzek, F.H.: CUDA Toolkit. https://developer.nvidia.com/cuda-toolkit

24. Sudholt, D.: Parallel evolutionary algorithms. In: Kacprzyk, J., Pedrycz, W. (eds.) Springer Handbook of Computational Intelligence, pp. 929–959. Springer, Heidelberg (2015). https://doi.org/10.1007/978-3-662-43505-2_46

25. Williams, S., Waterman, A., Patterson, D.: Roofline: an insightful visual performance model for multicore architectures. Commun. ACM **52**(4), 65–76 (2009)

Assessing and Improving the Suitability of Model-Based Design for GPU-Accelerated Railway Control Systems

Alejandro J. Calderón[1,3](✉)📵, Leonidas Kosmidis[1,2]📵, Carlos F. Nicolás[3]📵, Javier de Lasala[4]📵, and Ion Larrañaga[5]📵

[1] Universitat Politècnica de Catalunya, Barcelona, Spain
[2] Barcelona Supercomputing Center (BSC), Barcelona, Spain
leonidas.kosmidis@bsc.es
[3] Ikerlan Technology Research Centre, Arrasate-Mondragón, Spain
{ajcalderon,cfnicolas}@ikerlan.es
[4] CAF Research Department, Beasain, Spain
jlasala@caf.net
[5] CAF Power & Automation, San Sebastián, Spain
ilarranaga@cafpower.com

Abstract. Model-Based Design (MBD) is widely used for the design and simulation of electric traction control systems in the railway industry. Moreover, similar to other transportation industries, railway is moving towards the consolidation of multiple computing systems on fewer and more powerful ones, aiming for the reduction of Size, Weight and Power (SWaP). In that regard, Graphics Processing Units (GPUs) are increasingly considered by critical systems engineers, seeking to satisfy their ever increasing performance requirements. Recently, MBD tools have been enhanced with GPU code generation capabilities for machine learning acceleration, however, there is no indication whether these tools are ready for the design of time-sensitive systems. In this paper we analyse the suitability of commercial MBD toolsets by designing and deploying a model-based parallel control case study on embedded GPU platforms. While our results show promising feasibility evidence, they also reveal shortcomings which should be addressed before these toolsets become fit for developing critical systems. We propose certain improvements that have to be incorporated in these tools to achieve this goal. By implementing our proposals in the generated code, we experimentally show their effectiveness on two NVIDIA-based embedded GPUs.

Keywords: Model-based design · GPU · Control systems · Railway

1 Motivation and Introduction

The control of railway electric traction systems requires reading different types of sensors to feed the control algorithms, executing these algorithms and applying

C. Hochberger et al. (Eds.): ARCS 2021, LNCS 12800, pp. 68–83, 2021.
https://doi.org/10.1007/978-3-030-81682-7_5

their results with precision to guarantee optimal and safe operation. For this purpose, CAF group's traction control electronics use a combination of boards with microprocessors, Digital Signal Processors (DSPs) and Field Programmable Logic Arrays (FPGAs) in a modular way, to adjust costs and space to the needs of each client.

MBD tools have been used in the railway industry for many years to design electric traction control systems, allowing the suitability of the design to be verified by simulation at an early stage. It has also been possible for a long time to transfer the models into code that will be executed by the control electronics, thus facilitating validation through Hardware-in-the-Loop (HIL) simulation and also avoiding the introduction of possible errors inherent to manual intervention. CAF group employs MATLAB-Simulink capabilities to generate, from the model, C code for DSPs and Hardware Description Language (HDL) code for FPGAs. Thus, engineers can work at a higher level focusing on the control algorithms instead of their implementation in the target platforms.

Given the interest of the automotive industry in GPUs for Advanced Driver-Assistance Systems (ADAS) and autonomous driving, several GPU manufacturers are launching products that may be interesting for other functional safety sectors such as railways, especially if they facilitate reductions in costs and SWaP requirements, while allowing the code to still be generated from the models. There are already on the market boards based on System on Chips (SoCs) that integrate a microprocessor and a GPU, which in our railway traction system could replace a microprocessor board and many DSP boards, if real-time behaviour of the code generated from a model could be guaranteed. To validate this, we assess the state-of-the-art of MBD tools for the implementation of GPU-accelerated parallel control systems using a case study. We identify shortcomings which can be addressed to achieve this goal. In this direction, we propose concrete improvements, which we implement and experimentally show their effectiveness on two NVIDIA embedded GPUs.

2   Background and Related Work

2.1   Model-Based Design

A key attractor for adopting MBD to develop industrial applications is the separation of concerns, where the desired functionality can be described by a pure mathematical representation, i.e. the model. Afterwards, this will be step-wise refined until achieving a description that will be partitioned and allocated to the computing platform.

Equipment manufacturers relying on third-party embedded computing platforms expect MBD to isolate their own intellectual property, related to the functionality of the embedded software, from the particular features of a given hardware, which could jeopardise portability and make platform replacement costly. This expectation typically sacrifices optimal performance when compared to a hand-written implementation tailored to a specific platform.

MBD product development yields many additional advantages: MBD enables the validation of specifications by analysis and simulation, and allows designers to unveil potential design pitfalls at early project stages, which in turn cuts the overall development cost by lowering the time and effort required to fix undesirable behaviour. Moreover, when provided with trustworthy models of the system environment, MBD enables the systematic exploration of a multiplicity of what-if scenarios under unlikely conditions, which could be hard or completely impossible to fully reproduce in real-world tests.

A typical MBD development process starts with a pure simulation model, known as Model-in-the-Loop (MIL), which is refined and analysed in relevant simulated scenarios until an acceptable behaviour is achieved. Then an initial model-to-code transformation yields a second executable implementation. Depending on whether this implementation could be (cross-)compiled and run on the same host platform or has to be executed on the final target, the configuration is named Software-in-the-Loop (SIL) or X-in-the-Loop (XIL). In addition, depending on the target used in XIL it can be specialised as Processor-in-the-Loop (PIL), FPGA-in-the-Loop (FIL) or in this paper GPU-in-the-loop (GIL).

Recently, GPUs started attracting a strong interest for developing embedded control applications, particularly for real-time controllers involving non-conventional computations – e.g., Deep Neural Networks (DNNs) or Convolutional Neural Networks (CNNs). This also motivated the introduction of MBD toolsets intending to ease the development of GPU applications using the same modelling environments already in use for the other types of computing platforms mentioned before. The novelty of these GPU toolsets, coupled with the special programming patterns required by them, pose several challenges and face many limitations. For example, ensuring the suitability of the languages to describe functionality in a way that can be unambiguously translated to a parallel programming language adequate for coding a GPU, such as CUDA.

2.2   Control Systems

Control systems regulate the behaviour of devices or equipment using feedback control loops. Most of modern control systems implementations involve digital embedded microprocessors. Such embedded microprocessors provide interfaces to sensors and actuators, and hard real-time scheduling to guarantee the timely execution of synchronous feedback algorithms. Embedded controllers for real-world applications typically execute multiple cascaded control loops. This control structure tends to require multiple sampling rates; the inner the loop in the code control structure, the higher its required sampling rate is.

An unexpectedly long execution time could delay the action of the controller on the system under control, eventually bringing the system to an inconvenient or risky situation. Therefore, determining the worst-case execution time of the control loop is of uttermost importance for controllers operating critical or protection systems.

Scenarios involving the parallel control of multiple systems can be found in industrial controllers in applications demanding high computational throughput and scalability – e.g., as required by power converters for distributed propulsion systems comprising tens of motors, as proposed for electrification of airborne vehicles [10,12], or power-related applications such as distributed power converters for charging stations or distributed power generation.

2.3   GPUs in Critical Systems

GPUs have been initially introduced as special purpose accelerators, in particular for the production of visual content. However, their massively parallel architecture and the introduction of general purpose programmability allowed their use for computationally intensive tasks, including the extremely demanding AI processing, enabled with deep learning.

Autonomy is becoming an important aspect of future critical systems for sectors such as the automotive with the introduction of autonomous driving vehicles, avionics with Unmanned Aerial Vehicles (UAVs), space and planetary exploration with autonomous navigation as well as in industrial automation in industry 4.0 applications to name a few. For this reason, GPU manufacturers started addressing these sectors with the introduction of embedded GPU designs incorporating functional safety features. However, this is still in its infancy with several open challenges currently addressed by the research community.

Several works in the literature address the real-time behaviour of GPUs. As a complex hardware design with a black box non-preemptive behaviour, GPU requires novel approaches for scheduling of real-time tasks [5,8], reduction of offloading overheads [7], characterisation of contention [6] as well as the computation of worst case execution times [3]. Other works analyse necessary properties which need to be taken into account when GPUs are used in the context of critical systems. For example, [2,14] reverse engineered non-obvious aspects of the GPU behaviour which need to be taken into account when GPUs are used in real-time systems, while [4] reverse engineered the memory allocation of GPUs in order to achieve predictable resource consumption with regard to memory and timing. Other authors address the compliance of GPUs with regard to functional safety certification [1,11,13] by proposing the use of language subsets or the adaptation of safety standards. In this work we explore another dimension in this aspect, by using MBD to facilitate certification.

In brief, so far GPUs are mainly employed for high throughput computations but not latency sensitive ones. However, embedded GPUs targeting particularly the automotive and other critical domains are constantly improving in that matter. For example, in the keynote of the GPU Technology Conference 2020 a new GPU architecture and software infrastructure was presented, which will allow to deliver low-latency conversational AI for use in the automotive sector. This is an indication that the latency capabilities of embedded GPUs will be soon competing with other architectures, which were preferred so far for the implementation of such tasks. For this reason, in this work we propose an even more ambitious latency-sensitive parallel case study from the control domain. We assess whether such an application is feasible with the existing technology (both MBD tools and hardware capabilities) or if it will be likely available in the near future according to the current technology trends. In fact, we show that even though existing

MBD tools are not yet there, with our proposals this could be achieved even with existing embedded GPUs.

3   Case Study: Design and Implementation of a GPU-Accelerated Parallel Control System

3.1   Preliminaries

The primary objective of this work is to assess the capabilities of MBD tools regarding GPU code support for the implementation of real-time parallel control systems. To carry out a comprehensive assessment we opted to implement a case study from the control domain, which is representative of such systems and in addition has not been considered so far for GPU acceleration.

More specifically, we are interested in the evaluation of parallel code generation capabilities and the integration with GPU hardware for PIL or HIL testing. After researching the state-of-the-art in these tools, we concluded that currently, there are only two MBD tools which provide that kind of support: MathWork's MATLAB-Simulink through its GPU Coder toolbox and LabView with its GPU Analysis Toolbox. However, the GPU support in the latter is very limited. It only uses the GPU for the acceleration of some computations such as matrix operations and Fast Fourier Transform (FFT) through the CUDA provided libraries, but does not support custom code generation for GPUs. For this reason, we focus our analysis exclusively on MATLAB-Simulink, which is the only industry-ready MBD tool to support this functionality. However, if in the future any additional existing or new MBD tool includes GPU code generation, our methodology and proposed case study can be applied in order to benchmark its capabilities.

GPU Coder is a MATLAB-Simulink toolbox oriented to the generation of optimised CUDA code for NVIDIA GPUs, with special focus on tasks related to deep learning, embedded vision and autonomous systems. However, to the best of our knowledge, there is no previous analysis on the application of GPU Coder – or any other industrial or academic GPU-capable MBD tool – towards the development of a real-time application, such as a control system.

3.2   The Model

To evaluate the capabilities of GPU Coder and the integration with MATLAB-Simulink, we created an initial model to simulate the control of 8 parallel Permanent Magnet Synchronous Motors (PMSMs), as shown in Fig. 1a. We see suitable to start with controlling 8 motors in order to justify the use of the GPU in the system, since a lower number of cores can already be accelerated with existing platforms, such as the TI Delfino platform which supports control of 2 motors. Note however that while our initial model which is described next uses 8 motors, in Sect. 4.5 we perform a full scalability study for the control of up to 1024 motors. This is a reasonable upper bound of the number of potential motors which can realistically be present in a cyber-physical railway system and controlled together. Moreover, this is the maximum number of threads supported

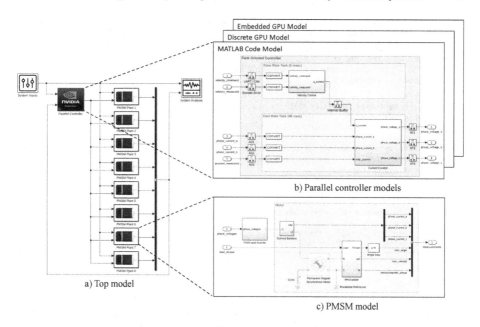

a) Top model

b) Parallel controller models

c) PMSM model

Fig. 1. Simulink model of a parallel PMSM FOC controller

Algorithm 1: Velocity control algorithm

Input	: reference_speed, measured_speed
Output	: reference_iq
InOut	: accum_error
Parameter	: kp, ki, dt

1   $speed\_error \leftarrow reference\_speed - measured\_speed$
2   $accum\_error \leftarrow accum\_error + speed\_error * dt$
3   $reference\_iq \leftarrow kp * speed\_error + ki * accum\_error$

---

by a single Streaming Multiprocessor (SM) in a GPU and it is the number of threads supported by our embedded GPU platforms, since the embedded GPU of the smaller of them contains a single SM.

In our implementation we follow the classic model-based development process with gradual refinement as introduced in Sect. 2.1. First we start with a mathematical model validating its correct behaviour through a MIL simulation. Then we refine the model by generating code executed in the discrete GPU of the host computer where MATLAB-Simulink is installed. This way we perform a HIL/GIL validation, ensuring that its behaviour is identical to the model. Finally, we create the final model which is executed on our target embedded GPU platforms, where the actual evaluation is performed. In that model in particular, we assess not only its identical functionality with the previous models, but also analyse its memory and timing properties.

Algorithm 2: Current control algorithm

Input	: reference_iq, ia, ib, angle
Output	: va, vb, vc
InOut	: accum_error_id, accum_error_iq
Parameter	: kp, ki, dt

1   $ialpha \leftarrow ia$;
2   $ibeta \leftarrow (1/sqrt(3)) * (ia + (2 * ib))$
3   $id \leftarrow cos(angle) * ialpha + sin(angle) * ibeta$
4   $iq \leftarrow cos(angle) * ibeta - sin(angle) * ialpha$
5   $id\_error \leftarrow -id$
6   $accum\_error\_id \leftarrow accum\_error\_id + id\_error * dt$
7   $vd \leftarrow kp * id\_error + ki * accum\_error\_id$
8   $iq\_error \leftarrow reference\_iq - iq$
9   $accum\_error\_iq \leftarrow accum\_error\_iq + iq\_error * dt$
10   $vq \leftarrow kp * iq\_error + ki * accum\_error\_iq$
11   $valpha \leftarrow cos(angle) * vd - sin(angle) * vq$
12   $vbeta \leftarrow sin(angle) * vd + cos(angle) * vq$
13   $va \leftarrow valpha$
14   $vb \leftarrow (-valpha + (sqrt(3) * vbeta))/2$
15   $vc \leftarrow (-valpha - (sqrt(3) * vbeta))/2$

Mathematical Description: A PMSM is a rotating electrical machine which has phase windings in the stator and permanent magnets in the rotor. To operate, it requires the interaction of the magnetic field created by the stator coils and the magnetic field created by the permanent magnets. The three stator coils are permanently energised with a sinusoidal current which is 120° apart on each phase. This creates a rotating North/South magnetic field.

In our top model shown in Fig. 1a, each one of the 8 PMSM plants has the internal structure shown in Fig. 1c. The core of this structure is a Simscape PMSM block connected to a mechanical circuit which is necessary to simulate the physical properties of the motor. The structure also includes a subsystem used for the Pulse-Width Modulation (PWM) generation and a three-phase inverter circuit to simulate the commutation needed to produce rotation in the motor.

To simplify the control of PMSMs a vector control technique known as Field Oriented Control (FOC) is used. The FOC algorithm consists of two control loops which execute at different frequencies. The first control loop is the slower one and is a simple Proportional-Integral (PI) controller, which is used to control the velocity of the motor. Algorithm 1 shows the steps executed in the velocity control loop. The output of this control loop is used as reference value for the quadrature current (*reference_iq*) in the next control loop. The second control loop is more complex and runs at a higher frequency. This control loop consists of a series of coordinate transforms of the currents to determine the time invariant values of torque and flux of the motor. These values can then be controlled using PI controllers. Algorithm 2 shows the steps executed in the current control loop.

Based on these two control loops, we defined the structure of a field oriented controller subsystem, as shown in Fig. 1b. In this configuration, the output of the speed controller is used as reference value in the current controller. However, since both control loops are executed at different frequencies, a rate transition buffer is used to hold the reference value.

In the model shown in Fig. 1a, the Parallel Controller block is a Simulink *variant* subsystem on which we implemented three different versions of the field oriented control structure, as shown in Fig. 1b.

MATLAB Code Model: In the first model, we implemented the velocity and current control algorithms using MATLAB code. The reason for using MATLAB code instead of Simulink blocks is that GPU Coder has the limitation that it can only generate CUDA code from MATLAB code. To be able to control multiple PMSMs in parallel, we created parallel versions of Algorithms 1 and 2 using vectors instead of scalar variables and replacing the scalar operators with MATLAB element-wise operators. To integrate the parallel MATLAB code into the Simulink model, we used *MATLAB Function* Simulink blocks. This first version of the field oriented controller allowed us to validate the correctness of our setup and to register the behaviour of the PMSM plants when interacting with the controller, using a MIL simulation. For this task, we applied different reference input signals for the 8 PMSM plants, as shown in Sect. 4.

Discrete GPU Model: For the second model, we used GPU Coder to generate CUDA code from the MATLAB version of the control algorithms. First, we generated a dynamic-link library with the CUDA version of the velocity and current controllers. Then, we invoked this external library from MATLAB. In the Simulink model, we included two MATLAB Function blocks to invoke the corresponding CUDA functions. This way, on each step of the Simulink simulation, the velocity and current control calculations are executed in the GPU of the host computer and their output is returned to Simulink to drive the simulated motors. In the generated code, each thread in the GPU is in charge of driving a different motor.

Embedded GPU Model: For the third model, we executed the generated CUDA code in the target embedded GPUs, to evaluate the capabilities of GPU Coder to interact with external hardware. GPU Coder includes a support package for the deployment of CUDA code in embedded NVIDIA GPUs such as the Jetson and DRIVE platforms. Moreover, the support package provides the functionality to create a PIL session between MATLAB-Simulink and a target embedded GPU platform, which allows the remote execution of code. We implemented this model using a similar approach to the previous one, but creating a PIL session as opposed to creating a dynamic-link library. In addition to the equivalence checking between the MATLAB-Simulink and the generated code for all models, we also evaluate the performance and memory consumption of this version of the application in a standalone setup instead of PIL, as described in Sect. 4.4. Then, in Sect. 4.5 we propose improvements for the generated code, which we implement and evaluate experimentally, showing their effectiveness.

4   Evaluation

4.1   Experimental Setup

We used the MathWorks MATLAB-Simulink toolset release 2021a with GPU Coder 2.1 to develop our parallel control case study, running on a computer equipped with an NVIDIA GeForce GTX 1650Ti Max-Q discrete GPU. For the final embedded GIL evaluation we used 2 different versions of the NVIDIA Jetson family of embedded GPU single board computers. The details of each embedded platform are provided in Table 1. For the performance evaluation on the embedded platforms, we installed Linux for Tegra (L4T) 32.5 with the PREEMPT RT patches. Moreover, to avoid external interference, all the experiments have been executed with a real-time priority of 98, on an isolated CPU core and with paging disabled. To guarantee the maximum performance, `jetson_clocks` has been enabled with the maximum `nvpmodel` profile for each embedded platform.

Table 1. Embedded GPU platforms

Platform	GPU architecture	Compute capability	SMs	CUDA cores	Max. threads per block	RAM
Jetson Nano	Maxwell	5.3	1	128	1024	4 GB
Jetson TX2	Pascal	6.2	2	256	1024	8 GB

4.2   Validation of the Models

For the models validation task, we designed 8 different reference input signals for the PMSM plants, which represent changes in the target speed of each motor, as shown in Fig. 2 with a continuous red line. We applied the reference signals to the controller based on MATLAB code and registered the outputs of the simulation. With this MIL simulation, we validated that the configuration was correct and that the parallel controller was in fact capable of controlling different plants with different set-points. Figure 2 shows also the response of the system with a blue dashed line, trying to adapt the speed of each motor to the requested speed. In Fig. 3 we can see the changes in the phase-voltages of each motor in response to the changes of the requested speed. As expected, identical results have been obtained also with the GIL simulations of the discrete and embedded GPUs of the target platforms, which are omitted for the sake of space, as well as because they do not offer any additional value except confirming the equivalence of the MATLAB model and the generated CUDA code.

4.3   Integration with External Hardware

In the third model, we used the GPU Coder support package for embedded NVIDIA GPUs to establish a PIL session between MATLAB-Simulink and the Jetson boards to run the simulation. In this setup, Simulink only simulates the physical motors, while their parallel control algorithm is executed in the embedded GPU. As stated in Sect. 4.2 this is functionally equivalent to the other models. However, we identified two important limitations:

First, in the PIL simulation mode the system establishes a single communication channel at a time to execute a single CUDA kernel on the target. This means that in cases such as our application where multiple CUDA kernels are used, their execution is serialised. Second, for this same reason, the execution frequency of the target GPU is limited by the communication latency between the host and the target which initiates each kernel execution, increasing the physical execution time required for the simulation.

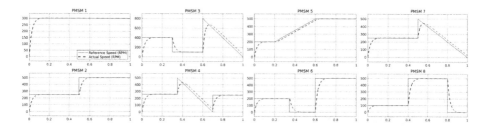

Fig. 2. Reference and actual speeds of parallel PMSMs (Color figure online)

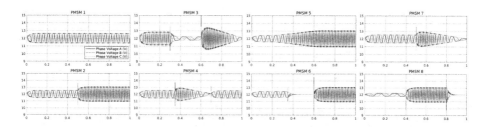

Fig. 3. Phase voltages of parallel PMSMs (Color figure online)

4.4   Evaluation of Generated CUDA Code

Performance of Generated CUDA Code: In order to evaluate the actual performance of the generated code, we ran our case study directly on the target platforms, without a Simulink PIL setup but as a standalone application. From a control systems perspective, we are interested in measuring the execution time of the instructions that will be executed on each iteration of the control loops: copying values from CPU to GPU, launching the kernel, executing the kernel, and copying the results back from GPU to CPU. On each experiment we execute one million control iterations and we register the average execution time, the maximum execution time and the standard deviation

Table 2. Execution time of generated CUDA code (µs)

Platform	Memory mode	Velocity			Current		
		Avg	Max	S.D.	Avg	Max	S.D.
Jetson Nano	Discrete	265.2	350.9	9.7	489.1	606.0	30.4
	Unified	663.8	1086.7	13.5	1335.1	2045.5	37.3
	Unified fixed	80.7	152.7	2.8	90.6	167.2	3.1
Jetson TX2	Discrete	154.2	273.4	5.7	296.6	383.6	9.5
	Unified	395.1	574.3	14.3	816.5	1013.5	17.9
	Unified fixed	49.7	92.1	2.0	65.6	111.9	8.0

(appearing as Avg, Max and S.D. respectively in the following Tables). To measure the execution time of each iteration, we used the `clock_gettime` function with the `CLOCK_MONOTONIC` clock, which has nanosecond resolution.

GPU Coder can generate CUDA code which uses either the discrete or the unified memory modes. Unified memory allows the CPU and the GPU to share the same address space, which matches the physical memory configuration of the embedded Jetson boards. However, some researchers consider this feature not suitable for critical systems [4] due to its black-box behaviour. Regardless, we perform our evaluation with both memory modes. In the evaluation, we identified that GPU Coder generates `cudaMemcpy` calls to transfer data between CPU and GPU when using the unified mode, which are unnecessary in this mode and costly as we show, given that the CUDA system automatically migrates data between CPU and GPU. This is the first shortcoming we identified. For comparison purposes, we created a fixed version of the code generated for the unified memory mode, removing these unnecessary `cudaMemcpy` calls.

Table 2 shows the execution times of the code generated for the discrete and unified memory modes on the two target platforms. We also include the execution times of the fixed version of the unified memory code. Note that the execution times of the original unified memory code are significantly higher than the execution times of the fixed version, due to the overhead caused by the extra `cudaMemcpy` calls. Therefore, there is room for improvement in the GPU Coder code generation in order to achieve the requirements of a control system.

In control systems, the maximum execution times of the control algorithms will define the maximum sampling rates the controller will be able to achieve. Unexpectedly long execution times could delay the action of the controller on the system under control, which can cause a risky situation in the system. In the case of FOC, the needed sampling rates depend on the physical characteristics of the inverters and the motors. In general, the period of the velocity control loop usually can be around a few milliseconds, while the current control loop typically has a period inferior to 100 µs.

Table 3. Profiling results for discrete memory mode (μs)

Platform	Call name	Velocity			Current		
		Avg	Min	Max	Avg	Min	Max
Jetson Nano	Kernel execution	2.0	2.0	2.0	2.6	2.5	2.6
	`cudaLaunchKernel`	50.3	45.5	60.0	56.0	47.2	69.8
	`cudaMemcpy`	46.0	30.9	74.9	50.3	32.0	89.0
Jetson TX2	Kernel execution	1.5	1.4	1.6	2.0	1.9	2.1
	`cudaLaunchKernel`	30.8	27.4	43.3	40.0	31.7	51.9
	`cudaMemcpy`	29.1	20.6	52.9	31.0	19.7	84.7

Table 4. Profiling results for unified memory mode (μs)

Platform	Call name	Velocity			Current		
		Avg	Min	Max	Avg	Min	Max
Jetson Nano	Kernel execution	2.8	2.7	3.1	3.9	3.7	4.1
	`cudaLaunchKernel`	76.9	66.6	96.7	86.6	77.0	98.9
	`cudaMemcpy`	101.4	83.3	142.6	116.1	93.5	173.7
	`cudaDeviceSynchronize`	46.7	44.9	50.6	53.7	50.5	57.3
Jetson TX2	Kernel execution	2.4	2.4	2.5	3.5	3.4	3.7
	`cudaLaunchKernel`	56.6	50.5	71.9	64.6	48.4	86.9
	`cudaMemcpy`	64.6	50.0	114.0	73.2	57.0	120.4
	`cudaDeviceSynchronize`	29.9	26.9	40.3	33.7	28.4	44.7

As shown in Table 2, while the maximum execution times of the velocity controller are in an acceptable range, the maximum execution times of the current controller are very high, limiting the maximum control frequency of the system.

To better understand the maximum execution times, we executed some iterations of the control loops using the NVIDIA `nvprof` profiler. Tables 3 and 4 show the results reported by `nvprof` for the discrete and unified memory modes.

In both versions, the maximum execution time for the actual kernel execution is in the target range for both the velocity and current controllers. The rest of the time is spent on `cudaMemcpy` and kernel launch/synchronisation calls. Therefore, if the time spent on these calls is reduced or eliminated, it is feasible to achieve the timings required for the control system. Based on this analysis, on Sect. 4.5 we propose some further improvements for the generated code.

Memory Overhead of Generated CUDA Code: In addition to the performance of the generated code, we also evaluated its memory consumption. For this task we employ the open source GPU memory allocation inspector GMAI, proposed by [4]. GMAI reports that the generated CUDA code performs 20 individual allocations and memory copies for each of the GPU variables, which is inefficient. Although the allocations occur at the application startup and thus do not affect timing, the individual memory copies significantly impact the timing, since they are quite costly as shown in Table 3. On the other hand, in terms of absolute memory consumption, this allocation strategy is beneficial, since all individual memory allocations are quite small and of the same size, so they are allocated from the same size class of the memory allocator, occupying a single memory pool which has a size of 1 MB in the Nano and 2 MB size in the TX2. Note that each of the generated GPU variables corresponds to an array with size as many elements as the number of the motors which are controlled. In total, for the 8 motor configuration, the total requested size for GPU memory from the application is less than 1 KB.

4.5   Improvement of Generated CUDA Code and Its Evaluation

In embedded platforms where CPU and GPU share the same physical memory, the memory copy overhead can be eliminated using an alternative memory configuration known as *zero-copy*. This feature allows the allocation of memory regions shared between CPU and GPU, eliminating redundant allocations as well as the copying task itself.

Regarding the kernel launch overhead, it can be reduced using the persistent threads model [9]. In this model, a persistent kernel is launched only once, which iterates waiting for work. Then, the CPU can assign new work to the persistent kernel by just changing values in memory, avoiding the kernel launch process.

Based on these two approaches we modified the generated code in two steps, creating two versions in order to evaluate the benefit obtained from each one. In the first step we replaced the traditional memory allocations with zero-copy allocations to avoid using `cudaMemcpy` calls. In the second step, besides using zero-copy memory, we replaced also the kernel launch/synchronisation with a persistent kernel launch. Table 5 shows the resulting execution times of the control algorithms with these improvements. Figure 4 shows a comparison of the maximum execution times for the different versions of velocity and current controllers on the target platforms.

Table 5. Execution time of improved CUDA code versions (µs)

Platform	Improvement	Velocity			Current		
		Avg	Max	S.D.	Avg	Max	S.D.
Jetson Nano	Zero-copy memory	32.7	74.1	3.0	34.4	81.2	2.9
	Persistent kernel	2.9	8.8	0.2	4.0	9.8	0.3
Jetson TX2	Zero-copy memory	20.3	55.5	1.3	31.5	61.9	7.3
	Persistent kernel	3.0	8.8	0.2	4.1	9.8	0.2

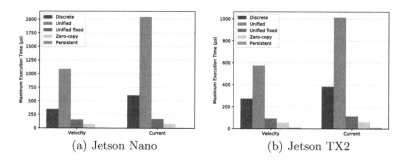

Fig. 4. Maximum execution times of generated code and proposed improvements.

Note that using zero-copy memory is enough to get maximum execution times in the target range for both control algorithms. Furthermore, when this solution is combined with a persistent kernel, the control loops can be executed significantly faster on both platforms. This improvement by an order of magnitude can be beneficial for even tighter control scenarios. In terms of memory, since we replace a host allocation and a GPU allocation with a single zero-copy allocation, the memory consumption is reduced up to 50%.

Finally, to evaluate the scalability of the improved code, we executed the control algorithms with different threads configurations, to control up to 1024 motors in parallel. Figure 5 shows the execution times on the target platforms. Note that the most stable execution times are obtained with up to 128 threads, which is the amount of CUDA cores per SM in both platforms. Even so, in all the cases, the maximum execution times do not exceed 30 μs.

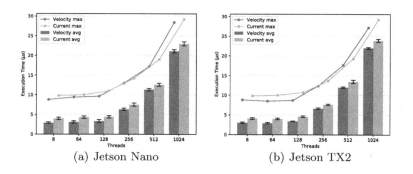

Fig. 5. Performance scalability of improved CUDA code

5   Conclusion and Outlook

In this paper we assessed for the first time the GPU code generation capabilities of MATLAB-Simulink for the design of real-time parallel control systems. We performed this evaluation by designing a novel GPU-accelerated parallel control case study, as a representative application of future railway parallel control systems, which we evaluate in 2 embedded GPU platforms.

Our results show that existing embedded GPU hardware can already support the timing requirements of such a case study, scaling up to 1024 motors, provided that the generated code is optimised according to our proposals. However, due to code generation inefficiencies, the original MBD generated code cannot meet the performance required by the control application. In particular, while the actual GPU generated code is functional, we noticed inefficiencies in the API calls which control the interaction of the GPU with the CPU part of the application. In terms of memory consumption the generated code is reasonable, however the implementation of the memory allocations and transfers is the limiting factor of the control loop frequency, together with the kernel launch overhead.

For these reasons, we conclude that to enable the use of the MathWorks toolset for model-based designing GPU-accelerated real-time control applications, it yet requires to enhance its GPU code generation capabilities at least in the following aspects: a) add support for zero-copy memory configuration which can eliminate the overhead of memory copies, and b) add support for a method to reduce or eliminate the kernel launch overhead, such as persistent threads.

Acknowledgments. This work was partially supported by the European Commission's Horizon 2020 programme under the UP2DATE project (grant agreement 871465), by the Spanish Ministry of Economy and Competitiveness under grants PID2019-107255GB and FJCI-2017-34095 and the HiPEAC Network of Excellence.

References

1. Alcaide, S., Kosmidis, L., Tabani, H., Hernandez, C., Abella, J., Cazorla, F.J.: Safety-related challenges and opportunities for GPUs in the automotive domain. IEEE Micro **38**(6), 46–54 (2018)
2. Amert, T., Otterness, N., Yang, M., Anderson, J.H., Donelson Smith, F.: GPU scheduling on the NVIDIA TX2: hidden details revealed. In: Real-Time Systems Symposium, RTSS, pp. 104–115 (2017)
3. Berezovskyi, K., et al.: Makespan computation for GPU threads running on a single streaming multiprocessor. In: Euromicro Conference on Real-Time Systems (2012)
4. Calderón, A.J., Kosmidis, L., Nicolás, C.F., Cazorla, F.J., Onaindia, P.: GMAI: understanding and exploiting the internals of GPU resource allocation in critical systems. ACM Trans. Embed. Comput. Syst. **19**(5), 1–23 (2020)
5. Capodieci, N., Cavicchioli, R., Bertogna, M., Paramakuru, A.: Deadline-based scheduling for GPU with preemption support. In: Proceedings of the Real-Time Systems Symposium, RTSS, pp. 119–130 (2019)
6. Cavicchioli, R., et al.: Memory interference characterization between CPU cores and integrated GPUs in mixed-criticality platforms. In: IEEE International Conference on Emerging Technologies and Factory Automation, ETFA, pp. 1–10 (2017)

7. Cavicchioli, R., et al.: Novel methodologies for predictable CPU-to-GPU command offloading. In: Euromicro Conference on Real-Time Systems, ECRTS 2019 (2019)
8. Elliott, G.A., Ward, B.C., Anderson, J.H.: GPUSync: a framework for real-time GPU management. In: Proceedings of the Real-Time Systems Symposium, pp. 33–44 (2013)
9. Gupta, K., et al.: A study of persistent threads style GPU programming for GPGPU workloads. In: 2012 Innovative Parallel Computing, InPar (2012)
10. Kim, H.D., Perry, A.T., Ansell, P.J.: A review of distributed electric propulsion concepts for air vehicle technology. In: 2018 AIAA/IEEE Electric Aircraft Technologies Symposium, EATS 2018 (2018)
11. Saidi, S., Steinhorst, S., Hamann, A., Ziegenbein, D., Wolf, M.: Future automotive systems design: research challenges and opportunities. In: International Conference on Hardware/Software Codesign and System Synthesis, CODES+ISSS (2018)
12. Schmollgruber, P., et al.: Multidisciplinary exploration of DRAGON: an ONERA hybrid electric distributed propulsion concept. In: AIAA Scitech 2019 Forum (2019)
13. Trompouki, M.M., Kosmidis, L.: BRASIL: a high-integrity GPGPU toolchain for automotive systems. In: Proceedings of the 2019 IEEE International Conference on Computer Design, ICCD 2019, pp. 660–663 (2019)
14. Yang, M., Otterness, N., Amert, T., Bakita, J., Anderson, J.H., Smith, F.D.: Avoiding pitfalls when using NVIDIA GPUs for real-time tasks in autonomous systems. In: Euromicro Conference on Real-Time Systems, ECRTS (2018)

DRT: A Lightweight Runtime for Developing Benchmarks for a Dataflow Execution Model

Roberto Giorgi[1]([🖂]) [iD], Marco Procaccini[1] [iD], and Amin Sahebi[1,2]([🖂]) [iD]

[1] University of Siena, Siena, Italy
giorgi@dii.unisi.it, procaccini@diism.unisi.it
[2] University of Florence, Florence, Italy
amin.sahebi@unifi.it

Abstract. Future computers may take advantage of a dataflow program execution model (PXM) for both performance and energy advantages. One key element to provide a compilation tool-chain for such machines is a framework for developing initial benchmarks. DRT (Dataflow Run-Time) is a tool that enables the fast prototyping of those benchmarks for the Dataflow Threads (DF-Threads) PXM. In this work, we show how to use DRT to develop dataflow based examples to be targeted by a future compiler for the dataflow PXM.

DRT has been written in portable C code (tested with the GNU C compiler), and it is open-source, therefore, it can be used on real machines based on architectures like x86, AArch, RISC-V ISA.

Here, we discuss some didactic examples, and we show how to study and debug the data exchange, which is flowing through frames that are detached from the data stack. We compare DRT against similar dataflow runtime libraries such as DARTS and OCR. Even though our environment is not yet optimized, we found that DRT outperforms the above runtime frameworks in terms of execution time. We also give an evaluation of the time and complexity to develop DF-Threads examples in DRT compared to the approach of using a full system simulator and FPGAs for more accurate modeling.

Keywords: Dataflow threads · Low-level API · Execution model

1 Introduction and Motivation

Dataflow architectures and their program execution models (PXMs) have been studied since the '70s [3,4,7,8,34,38]. One of the most well-known features of dataflow execution models is that they can achieve a high level of parallelism, which leads to better power consumption and better hardware efficiency [30,44]. Dataflow architectures can significantly exploit the implicit parallelism of the applications and overcome synchronization and consistency overheads generated by von Neumann machines [20,21]. Since then, some researchers have shown the

© Springer Nature Switzerland AG 2021
C. Hochberger et al. (Eds.): ARCS 2021, LNCS 12800, pp. 84–100, 2021.
https://doi.org/10.1007/978-3-030-81682-7_6

possibility of supporting a dataflow execution model for parallel threads on conventional machines [19,23,37,45]. In this work, we consider the DF-Threads execution model [19]. Other works have shown the potential of dataflow models in terms of power efficiency [6,22] and also as accelerators for High-Performance Computing and machine learning applications [9,28,29]. As can be seen in Fig. 1, the DF-Threads execution model can exhibit an important speedup compared to OpenMPI when running the Matrix Multiplication benchmark over a cluster. More details about the scalability and efficiency of DF-Threads are described in [18].

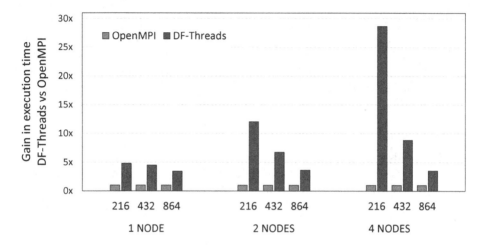

Fig. 1. Gain in execution time of DF-Threads compared to OpenMPI. The benchmark is Matrix Multiplication for different sizes of the matrices (216, 432, 864 - the block size is 8 elements) and 1, 2, 4 nodes. Data is derived from [14]

Even though dataflow models have shown many great features, conventional programming languages do not support them very well [43]. This limitation, together with the possible high performance gains, motivated us to introduce a tool, which could reduce the gap between conventional languages and dataflow execution models.

In this paper, we present the Dataflow Run-Time tool (DRT) to quickly develop and test the execution of dataflow codes based on DF-Threads API. Our contributions in this paper are:

- Introducing a dataflow runtime (DRT), which is presented first in this paper.
- Illustrating how the DRT tool can be used for debugging and studying the movement of data frames (a feature that is not available in standard debuggers).
- Comparing the execution time speedup of DRT against similar dataflow runtime.

The rest of this paper is structured as follows: in Sect. 2, we describe the background. Then in Sect. 3, we introduce the DRT tool, illustrate how to carry out an experiment, write and debug dataflow codes with DRT. Then in Sect. 4, we show the DRT runtime evaluation, and in Sect. 5, we present related works. Finally, in Sect. 6, we conclude and briefly introduce future works.

2 Background

2.1 DF-Threads

In order to demonstrate the dataflow execution model, we use DF-Threads as described in [12]. In Fig. 2, we show a simplified high-level overview of DF-Threads execution (right) and a classical (von Neumann style) execution (left). In the classical execution, the parallel threads can read/write from/to any location of the memory. Therefore, a high synchronization and coherency overhead may be generated. As mentioned in detail in [12], each of these DF-Threads has a different behavior according to the memory access pattern. Consequently, it may need different execution and hardware support. It is worth recalling that using standard libraries like *Pthreads* is not required. Here, we briefly recall the specification of the DF-Threads API:

- DF-Threads follow the dataflow semantics: a thread is ready when its input is fully available; it starts executing when the scheduler decides to assign it to a physical resource (e.g., a core).
- The management of a DF-Thread lifetime happens through the following functions, which are described in Table 1: **df_schedule**, **df_ldframe**, **df_write**, **df_destroy**.
- DF-Threads are isolated in terms of memory accesses, and their execution can be repeated in the case of faults since their inputs are retained [40].

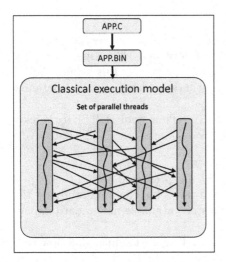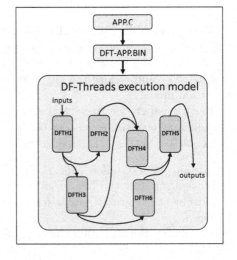

Fig. 2. Simplified representation of the DF-Threads execution model. On the left, we represent the irregular read and write of generic threads. On the right, the exchange of data among threads happens in a more regular fashion [22]

Table 1. DF-Threads function definitions [16]

DF-Threads API function	Description
uint64_t df_schedule(void* ip, uint64_t sc)	Create the DF-Thread and its associated frame; *sc* is the synchronization count, which represents the number of inputs that the DF-Thread will receive
uint64_t df_ldframe()	Retrieve the frame pointer associated with the current DF-Thread
uint64_t df_write(void* fp, uint64_t val)	The value *val* will be stored in a location pointed by *fp*, and for each write, the *sc* (which is specified by scheduler before) will be decremented
uint64_t df_destroy()	Terminate the current DF-Thread and deallocate its input frame

2.2 Writing Dataflow Codes with the DF-Threads API

This Section shows the workflow to map the desired application into a dataflow code (here DF-Threads). While this translation could be done by a compiler, we do not have such a compiler at the moment (the compiler could be future work).

We use fine-grain algorithms to show the potentiality of our tool in mapping several DF-Threads on real architectures. We choose the Recursive Fibonacci (RFIB) as a "simple yet complex enough" example to illustrate the development methodology for DF-Threads programs. The RFIB algorithm is a well-known example used to create many threads and stress the runtime and the scheduling management.

In Fig. 3, we describe the original C code and its mapping into DF-Threads, together with the dynamic behavior of the dataflow code. In this case, two DF-Threads are created: RFIB and "adder".

The key operation is the **df_schedule**, which creates a DF-Thread, whose code is specified by the parameter *ip* (the instruction pointer or the name of the corresponding function). With the same operation, a portion of memory (*frame*) is allocated and associated with the same DF-Thread. The size of the frame is determined by the number of inputs of the DF-Thread that is specified by the *sc* value of the **df_schedule**. The **df_schedule** returns the address (frame pointer) to the allocated memory space (the *frame*). The next step is to write the DF-Thread input and the output locations. This can be done by using the **df_write**. Once the frame pointer (*fp*) has been retrieved by the **df_ldframe**, the **df_write** will store the data (here n-1, n-2) in the location of $fp[1]$ and $fp[2]$, respectively. Please note that $fp[0]$ has been reserved as the output location, into which the DF-Thread will write the result. For each write into the frame, the *sc* value will be decremented by 1 (this is implied by **df_write** and it is part of the

implementation of the **df_write** itself). In the end, **df_destroy** will terminate
the current DF-Thread [17].

3 Introducing DRT

Developing a novel architecture may require considerable time when using an
architectural simulator [2,14]. To reduce this development-cycle time, in the
case of the dataflow execution model, we designed a tool that we call "Dataflow
Run-Time" (DRT). The aim of the DRT is to make it easier for the software
community to use a dataflow program execution model (here DF-Threads): by
studying the simple examples that we propose, or building new examples, the
compiler experts could derive an appropriate compilation path, which could

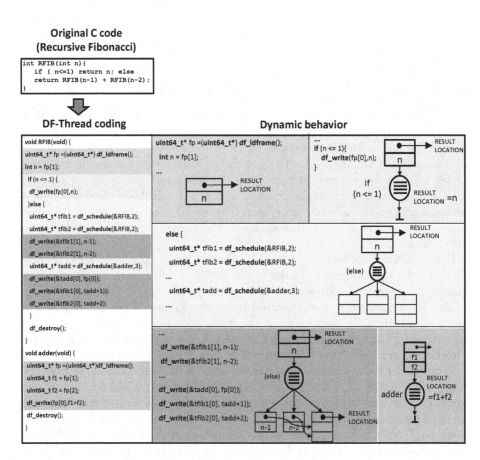

Fig. 3. Illustrating the operations of the basic DRT API functions with a simple Recursive Fibonacci (RFIB) example. On the left, there is the representation of the RFIB
function and its coding in DF-Thread style. On the right, we detail the specific dynamic
behavior. Example rearranged from [27].

target the DF-Threads PXM. This tool is compatible with real machines like x86, AArch, RISC-V. DRT only requires the installation of the GCC compiler for compiling and running DF-Threads programs.

DRT enables the fast development and debugging of the DF-Threads' API and its data exchange mechanism, which is based on *frames* (see Fig. 3).

According to an initial test done in DRT, we can reduce the development-cycle time from minutes/hours to seconds (see Table 3). As shown in Fig. 4, we currently need to map manually ('manual coding into DFT syntax') high level programs ('.c code') to the DF-Threads API. Then, the DRT enables a standard compiler (GCC in our case) to generate a binary that can run on standard architectures. The availability of DRT provides a basis for direct writing dataflow codes but also enables compiler experts to further build on this workflow and integrate it in a compiler (lower part of Fig. 4, which is not in the scope of this paper).

Similar efforts exist like the Delaware Adaptive Runtime System (DARTS) [25] and the Open Community Runtime (OCR) [27], so we compare them with DRT in Table 3. DRT is available as open-source at http://drt.sf.net[1].

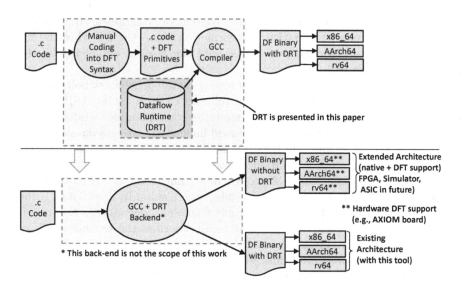

Fig. 4. The role of DRT in developing applications based on the DataFlow Threads (DFT) execution model. In the top part, we show the current setup of DRT. In the bottom part, we show the production framework that we envision. The idea is that DRT could help develop a future DRT backend of a standard compiler.

---

[1] Checkout the DRT repository by this command: svn co https://svn.code.sf.net/p/drt/code/.

3.1 Debugging with DRT

In order to check the correctness of the dataflow execution, it is crucial to monitor the movement of the data and the status of the DF-Threads. In fact, whenever new DF-Threads are created, the DRT is responsible for providing a memory block called *frame* to store data, meta-information settings, and keeping track of the DF-Thread status. When a producer DF-Thread wants to write its outputs into the consumer DF-Thread, the DRT performs the write operations and decreases the synchronization count (*sc*) of the consumer DF-Thread. When the *sc* reaches zero, the DF-Thread becomes ready to be executed, and it is moved into a ready queue by the DRT. Once a DF-Thread terminates its execution, the DRT deallocates the associated *frame* from memory, dequeues the next DF-Thread from the ready queue, and assigns it to an available core. Finally, DRT will report if the program's output is successfully calculated, e.g., making a checksum with the reference program's result. In the following, we illustrate a debugging session in detail for the RFIB benchmark (Fig. 5, Fig. 6).

DRT offers the possibility to customize the development environment through the command-line for exploring up to four levels of debugging. The debug level one displays the used frame pointers only, while the second and third level print the executed dataflow instructions and the content of the frames, respectively. The fourth level gives us the statistical information about the DF-Threads, the memory, and the queues. The user can specify the level of debugging by the environment variable DRT_DEBUG.

In Fig. 5, as an illustrative example for analyzing the benchmark behavior, we show the output of DRT when the debug level is set to three for the RFIB benchmark and its input is n = 4. We also illustrate the corresponding dataflow graph in Fig. 6. The first line describes the command line for executing a dataflow code with DRT. In the third line, the DRT initializes the environment and allocates the memory space for storing the frames based on the application requirements. Lines 4 and 5 show the creation of the scheduled function (the RFIB function, see Table 2) and the **report** function to collect the results. In lines 6 and 7, the *df_write* writes the value (*val*) in the output frame and decrements the associated synchronization count (*sc*). Lines 10 to 19 describes the recursive calls of the RFIB functions. Finally, the current DF-Thread will be terminated, and its input frame will be deallocated (line 20).

The list of *ip* and *fp* addresses that are shown in Fig. 5 correspond to the same addresses that can be retrieved through standard disassembler tools (e.g., objdump). However, the usage of such tools gives us only a static view, while DRT enables a dynamic analysis showing the entire sequence of executed instructions with additional information about the DF-Threads, memory, and queue status. For example, the $ip = 0x401795$ corresponds to the address of the code of the RFIB function (see Table 2). All the corresponding functions and their *fp* addresses generated in the function RFIB are shown in Table 2.

```
 1   ~/drt-code $ DRT_DEBUG=3 ./RFIB 4
 2   computing Recursive Fibonacci(4)
 3   -DRT: FRAME-MEM allocation+initialization done.
 4   TS: fi=0   ip=0x403a46  fp=0x609f60   sc=1/1
 5   TS: fi=1   ip=0x401795  fp=0x609fc0   sc=2/2
 6   TW: fi=1   ip=0x401795  fp=0x609fc0  val=0x609f6000   sc=1/2
 7   TW: fi=1   ip=0x401795  fp=0x609fc0  val=0x4   sc=0/2
 8   ++main
 9   -DRT: Starting Dataflow launcher.
10   TE: fi=1 ipnew=0x401795  fpnew=0x609fc0
11   TS: fi=2   ip=0x401795  fp=0x60a020   sc=2/2
12   TS: fi=3   ip=0x401795  fp=0x60a080   sc=2/2
13   TW: fi=2   ip=0x401795  fp=0x60a020  val=0x3   sc=1/2
14   TW: fi=3   ip=0x401795  fp=0x60a080  val=0x2   sc=1/2
15   TS: fi=4   ip=0x400d81  fp=0x60a0e0   sc=3/3
16   TW: fi=4   ip=0x400d81  fp=0x60a0e0  val=0x609f6000   sc=2/3
17   TW: fi=2   ip=0x401795  fp=0x60a020  val=0x60a0e001   sc=0/2
18   TW: fi=3   ip=0x401795  fp=0x60a080  val=0x60a0e002   sc=0/2
19   TD: fi=1   ip=0x401795  fp=0x609fc0   sc=2
20   TE: fi=2 ipnew=0x401795  fpnew=0x60a020
21   ++report
22   DF-Thread RFIB = 3
23   *** SUCCESS ***
```

Fig. 5. DRT sample output. DRT_DEBUG is an environment variable for specifying the debug level. The DF-Threads functions are mapped to internal operations where TS stands for thread scheduling, TE stands for thread-end, TD stands for thread drop, TW stands for thread write, ip stands for instruction pointer, and fp stands for frame pointer. Other debugging information is fi for frame index, sc stands for synchronization count, $ipnew/fpnew$ are the ip/fp just freed.

Table 2. The function name and its corresponding frame pointer address that are shown in Fig. 5 (same as in objdump tool).

Frame pointer address	Corresponding function
0x401795	RFIB
0x400d81	adder
0x403a46	report

In order to show the effectiveness of the internal modeling of the DRT function, we consider the implementation of the *df_write* function (see Fig. 7). The *df_write* needs two arguments, the pointer to the output *frame* (*fp*) and the value to write in such *frame*. Internally, the *df_write* extracts the metadata pointer from the given *frame* and, based on the *sc* information, *df_write* decides whether the DF-Thread is in ready or waiting status. Other useful debugging information, not shown in this simple example for the sake of simplicity, are the status of

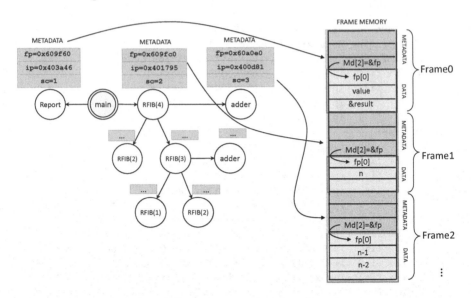

Fig. 6. An example of the RFIB(4) function of the Recursive Fibonacci (RFIB) example for illustrating the organization of data frames and their metadata. The metadata includes *fp* (frame pointer), *ip* (instruction pointer) and *sc* (synchronization count). The data illustrated here is extracted from the output of the DRT tool.

```
void df_write(uint64_t *fp, uint64_t val)
{
    *fp=val;                 //write the value
    uint64_t *md=METADATA(fp); //retrieve metadata
    md[MDSC]--;              //decrement synchronization count
    if (md[MDSC] == 0) //move the frame to READY QUEUE
        TSETREADY(md[MDQSTATUS]);
}
```

Fig. 7. An example of a modeled function in the DRT implementation, where META-DATA extracts the metadata pointer from the frame, MDSC is the offset of the synchronization count, and MDQSTATUS is the offset of the status bits that indicate whether the frame is in ready or waiting status.

queues, the total number of allocated frames, the total number of writes, total number of frames that are in ready or waiting status.

4   Evaluation

In this Section, we compare the performance of DRT against other similar environments, namely OCR [27] and DARTS [25]. OCR and DARTS use a dataflow model to manage threads, similarly to DRT: the common main idea is to decouple the higher layers of the software stack from the underlying hardware by using a possibly universal interface. For details about OCR, DARTS, and other related environments, see Sect. 5. As explained in Sect. 3, we wrote some initial benchmarks manually due to the lack of a compiler. Therefore, at this stage, we cannot afford to make more extensive tests with large benchmarks.

To demonstrate the capabilities of the DRT, we selected two simple benchmarks:

- Recursive Fibonacci (RFIB) in order to generate a high number of threads easily.
- Blocked Matrix Multiplication (BMM) as it is a very commonly used kernel in many applications (especially in Artificial Intelligence, Deep Neural Networks, etc.), and it moves much data around.

The two benchmarks are using the same exact algorithm for all three frameworks. The output of the benchmarks is validated against the output produced with other independent tools executing the same benchmarks.

For the sake of simplicity, we analyze the sensitivity with the input set by using $n = 10$, 15, 20, 25 for RFIB and $s = 128$, 256, 512, 1024 for BMM, where n is the index of the corresponding Fibonacci number and s is the size of the square matrices that are multiplied. For the block size of the matrices, we used $b = 8$, where b is the number of the elements inside a block. The purpose of DRT is to explore the correctness of the dataflow execution, not to scale the performance across cores. Nevertheless, to make a fair comparison against other environments, we restricted our evaluation to a single core execution.

For each of the three runtime frameworks (DRT, DARTS, and OCR), we measure the time spent in the Region Of Interest (ROI) of each benchmark, and we repeat at least ten times the experiments to obtain statistically valid measurements. We report the execution time speedup by using DARTS as the baseline. As we can observe from Fig. 8 and Fig. 9, DRT can outperform by one order of magnitude DARTS for smaller inputs. DRT outperforms OCR by a factor of about 13x for $n = 25$. While the OCR and DARTS are well optimized, DRT can still be improved. However, as stated before the main goal of DRT is just to provide a tool for developing DF-Thread benchmarks and a future compiler; more performance could be achieved by using DF-Thread native support as shown in Fig. 4.

4.1 DRT Versus Other Architectural Exploration Tools

DRT is also serving to explore new architectures based on dataflow concepts. While designing such a non-yet existing architecture, different approaches can be used:

- An architectural simulator (e.g., the COTSon [2]).
- A hardware prototype. In our work, we use the AXIOM board (provided by SECO [35]), which includes four 64-bit ARM cores, an FPGA, and a GPU [10,13].
- A runtime tool like DRT; in the following, we discuss how this tool can be used to understand the data exchange among the dataflow threads.

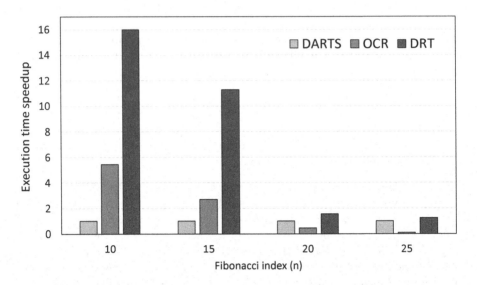

Fig. 8. RFIB execution time speedup comparison between DRT, DARTS and OCR runtime. Here OCR is the baseline. DRT reaches better performance due to a simplified management of the dataflow execution.

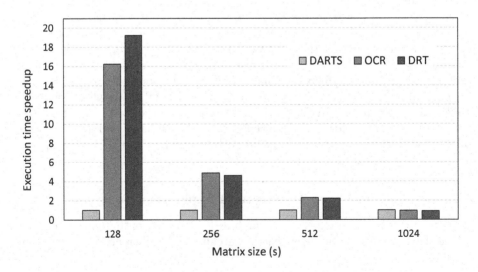

Fig. 9. Blocked Matrix Multiplication execution time speedup comparison between DRT and DARTS and OCR, with the DARTS as baseline. While for larger Matrix sizes the execution time tends to be the same for three tools, it is important to note that during the development-cycle, we typically use smaller inputs. So, the shorter execution time of DRT during tests helps focus on the development.

While it is possible to develop DF-Threads codes on a simulator or on an FPGA prototype, we found that it is more productive to use a tool such as the DRT, a minimalistic API written in around 300 lines of C code, through which it is possible to test and debug the implementation of a specific feature in seconds, while doing that on an FPGA may require days [15] (see Table 3). In Fig. 10, we show the simulation time of the COTSon simulator compared to the DRT. As we can see, we can obtain up to four orders of magnitude speedup while executing a benchmark RFIB. The speedup in simulation time of a simulator is lower compared to an FPGA, but the development-cycle time can be much higher; this is discussed below.

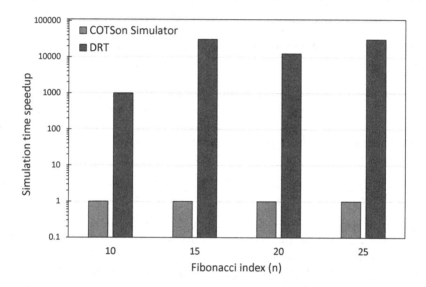

Fig. 10. Simulation time speedup comparison between DRT and the COTSon simulator by using the RFIB example. DRT significantly decreases the development-cycle time to develop a dataflow program.

Table 3. Comparing lightweight DRT with other different tools for developing dataflow codes and the related architectures. As we can see DRT, is using only 300 lines of C code.

	DRT	Simulator [24]	FPGA [33]
SLOC of the framework	∼300	∼112,000	∼1,000,000
Openness the development framework	High (open-source)	Medium (partly open-source)	Limited (proprietary tools)
Complexity of the development-cycle	Low (seconds)	High (minutes)	Very high (hours)

In terms of evaluating the DRT in relation to other approaches for developing the initial codes that use the dataflow execution model, we compare other tools for modeling new architectures like the simulator and the FPGA prototype in Table 3. The usage of these tools is necessary when exploring hardware support for the dataflow execution [14,15]. We considered the following metrics:

- SLOC[2]: these are the source lines of code of the corresponding framework; these numbers are all publicly available; for the simulator, we referred to the COTSon simulator [24], and for the FPGA, we referred to the software stack of the AXIOM board [33].
- Openness of the development framework: while DRT can be downloaded and installed in seconds, COTSon requires at least some hours to complete the setup and some days to become familiar with the modeling of the components; moreover, some parts of the code (AMD SimNow) are not open-source; regarding the FPGA-board, the software stack is open-source, but the tools are typically proprietary and may require licensing and complex setup procedures.
- The complexity of the development-cycle: while it is rather simple to make modifications, test, and debug a program through the DRT tool, it may require minutes to complete a full simulation in the COTSon simulator, and it may require hours to modify and re-generate a full design in the FPGA framework [14,15].

5   Related Work

In recent years, there have been some works regarding dataflow architectures and their execution models that we summarized below. In the following, we highlight some works that are related to ours, and we point out the differences.

BMDFM [32] is a hybrid dataflow runtime environment that provides a dataflow execution model with its extended instruction set. BMDFM has been implemented on conventional multi-core platforms to show a complete parallelization environment.

FREDDO [26] uses the distribution of Data-Driven Threads (DDT) over conventional multi-core processors. FREDDO is written in C++ and focuses mainly on Object-Oriented programs.

Sucuri [36] is a Python dataflow library to execute Dataflow Graphs (DFGs) over a multi-core distributed system. Sucuri is based on a centralized and local scheduler in each node that can execute the ready tasks in their local queues. The compiler partitions the DFG, then, during the runtime, each related DFG part will be distributed among the associated node.

Swift/T [42] is a new implementation of swift language [41] that provides high-level programmability for implicit dataflow programming. It addresses some optimization for the Swift parallel scripting language, along with Turbine compiler, which C/C++/Fortran programmers can develop their software based on this platform.

---

[2] Source lines of code.

Trebuchet [1] presents the implementation of dynamic dataflow architecture. Trebuchet presents the execution of code blocks based on a multi-thread dataflow model.

In XKaapi [11], the authors show a dataflow task acceleration on multi-core CPUs, and GPUs. XKaapi has been written in C++ language, and a work-stealing method has been presented for scheduling ready tasks via a runtime system.

These six works - BMDFM, Freddo, Sucuri, Swift/T, Trebuchet, and Xkaapi - use dataflow approaches to improve the execution time. In contrast, DRT ambition is to provide a tool for testing and debugging dataflow benchmarks, while the performance is obtained by deploying one DF-Thread implementation [12,17,39]. In particular, DRT represents a key element to develop a toolchain to support a dataflow execution model, which could be targeted by a compiler. While there are many similarities between DRT and the above works, we choose a more detailed comparison with the Codelet program execution model [5,46] and Open Community Runtime (OCR) [27,31].

In the Codelet execution model concept [46], Codelet is a fine grain event-driven unit of computation, smaller than a thread, aims to exploit the parallelism of Exascale platforms. The runtime environment DARTS [25] has been presented in such a way that a high-level program will turn into Codelet Graph with the API interface, and the runtime executes the Codelets based programs to exploit the maximum parallelism and power efficiency of the underlying hardware. DARTS uses a double level hierarchy to structure programs: threaded procedures (TP) and Codelets; TP includes several Codelets. In contrast, DF-Threads leaves more freedom to the programmer by using a flat hierarchy of threads.

The Open Community Runtime [27] is based on event driven tasks. OCR is a runtime that is influenced by the Codelet execution model and is inspired by the Asynchronous Many Task (AMT) models. A high level program written in OCR runtime is organized with Directed Acyclic Graph, which is structured with relocatable data-blocks, events, or tasks. These elements are called nodes connected to each other by edges, which represent the dependencies between nodes. DARTS and OCR trigger threads by using both data and events. In DF-Threads, we do not need this distinction: events can be treated as data.

DF-Threads [12] introduces a low-level API, which enables a high-level code into a hybrid dataflow model that can benefit from the high parallelism while parallel computations are the potential to distribute over nodes and cores.

6   Conclusion and Future Work

In this paper, we present Dataflow Run-Time (DRT), a tool for fast prototyping of benchmarks written for a dataflow program execution model (PXM). While running such benchmarks on an architecture that provides dataflow support could provide a large speedup (e.g., up to 28×) compared to OpenMPI counterparts, the compiler technology is not yet developed enough. Therefore, the contribution of this paper helps bridge the gap between future compilers and a dataflow

PXM. In fact, DRT is a step-forward to have a general compiler for executing in a dataflow style. Through DRT, we can develop dataflow codes/benchmarks, test and debug them with a better development-cycle time than other modeling tools like architectural simulators or FPGAs. We also describe how to perform the debugging of the data flow among DF-Threads' frames, and we compare the efficiency of DRT against other similar environments such as DARTS and OCR.

We illustrate and evaluate more in detail two simple benchmarks (RFIB, BMM); however, we have provided other programs in our repository (http://drt.sf.net).

DF-threads is a general approach to execute parallel programs in a more efficient way than with the von Neumann paradigm. We hope that in the future, with the help of the fully fledged compiler, we could extend our work to more general applications.

Acknowledgements. We would like to thank the anonymous reviewers for their insightful comments and suggestions. The work of this paper is partly funded by the European Commission on AXIOM H2020 (id. 645496), TERAFLUX (id. 249013), HiPEAC (id. 871174).

References

1. Alves, T.A.O., Marzulo, L.A.J., Franca, F.M.G., Costa, V.S.: Trebuchet: exploring TLP with dataflow virtualisation. Int. J. High Perform. Syst. Archit. **3**(2/3), 137–148 (2011)
2. Argollo, E., Falcón, A., Faraboschi, P., Monchiero, M., Ortega, D.: COTSon: infrastructure for full system simulation. SIGOPS Oper. Syst. Rev. **43**(1), 52–61 (2009)
3. Arvind, Culler, D.E.: Dataflow architectures. Ann. Rev. Comput. Sci. **1**, 225–253 (1986)
4. Arvind, K., Nikhil, R.S.: Executing a program on the MIT tagged-token dataflow architecture. IEEE Trans. Comput. **39**(3), 300–318 (1990). https://doi.org/10.1109/12.48862
5. CAPSL: The codelet execution model. https://www.capsl.udel.edu/codelets.shtml
6. Chen, Y., Emer, J., Sze, V.: Using dataflow to optimize energy efficiency of deep neural network accelerators. IEEE Micro **37**(3), 12–21 (2017)
7. Dennis, J.B.: Data flow computation. In: Broy, M. (ed.) Control Flow and Data Flow: Concepts of Distributed Programming. Springer Study Edition, vol. 14, pp. 345–398. Springer, Heidelberg (1986). https://doi.org/10.1007/978-3-642-82921-5_8
8. Dennis, J.B., Misunas, D.P.: A preliminary architecture for a basic data-flow processor (1974)
9. Farabet, C., Martini, B., Corda, B., Akselrod, P., Culurciello, E., LeCun, Y.: NeuFlow: a runtime reconfigurable dataflow processor for vision. In: CVPR 2011 Workshops, pp. 109–116 (2011)
10. Filgueras, A., et al.: The AXIOM project: IoT on heterogeneous embedded platforms. IEEE Des. Test., 1–6 (2019). http://www.dii.unisi.it/~giorgi/papers/Filgueras19-ieee_dnt.pdf. ISSN 2168-2356

11. Gautier, T., Lima, J.V.F., Maillard, N., Raffin, B.: XKaapi: a runtime system for data-flow task programming on heterogeneous architectures. In: 2013 IEEE 27th International Symposium on Parallel and Distributed Processing, pp. 1299–1308 (2013)
12. Giorgi, R., Faraboschi, P.: An introduction to DF-Threads and their execution model. In: IEEE MPP, Paris, France, pp. 60–65, October 2014
13. Giorgi, R., Khalili, F., Procaccini, M.: AXIOM: a scalable, efficient and reconfigurable embedded platform. In: IEEE Proceedings of DATEi, pp. 1–6, March 2019
14. Giorgi, R., Khalili, F., Procaccini, M.: A design space exploration tool set for future 1k-core high-performance computers. In: ACM RAPIDO Workshop, pp. 1–6 (2019)
15. Giorgi, R., Khalili, F., Procaccini, M.: Translating timing into an architecture: the synergy of COTSon and HLS (domain expertise - designing a computer architecture via HLS). Hindawi - Int. J. Reconfigurable Comput. **2019**, 1–18 (2019). https://doi.org/10.1155/2019/2624938
16. Giorgi, R., Procaccini, M.: Bridging a data-flow execution model to a lightweight programming model. In: 2019 International Conference on HPCS (2019)
17. Giorgi, R., Scionti, A.: A scalable thread scheduling co-processor based on data-flow principles. Future Gener. Comput. Syst. **53**, 100–108 (2015)
18. Giorgi, R.: Scalable embedded computing through reconfigurable hardware: comparing DF-Threads, cilk, OpenMPI and jump. Microprocess. Microsyst. **63**, 66–74 (2018)
19. Giorgi, R., et al.: TERAFLUX: Harnessing dataflow in next generation teradevices. Microprocess. Microsyst. **38**(8, Part B), 976–990 (2014)
20. Hum, H.H.J., Maquelin, O., Theobald, K.B., Tian, X., Gao, G.R., Hendren, L.J.: A study of the EARTH-MANNA multithreaded system. Int. J. Parallel Program. **24**(4), 319–348 (1996). https://doi.org/10.1007/BF03356753
21. Kabrick, R., Perdomo, D.A.R., Raskar, S., Diaz, J.M.M., Fox, D., Gao, G.R.: CODIR: towards an MLIR codelet model dialect. In: 2020 IEEE/ACM Fourth Annual Workshop on Emerging Parallel and Distributed Runtime Systems and Middleware (IPDRM), pp. 33–40. IEEE (2020)
22. Kavi, K., Arul, J., Giorgi, R.: Performance evaluation of a non-blocking multithreaded architecture for embedded, real-time and DSP applications. In: 14th International Conference on Parallel and Distributed Computing Systems (ISCA-PDCS-2001), Richardson, TX, USA, pp. 365–371, August 2001
23. Kavi, K.M., Giorgi, R., Arul, J.: Scheduled dataflow: execution paradigm, architecture, and performance evaluation. IEEE Trans. Comput. **50**(8), 834–846 (2001)
24. HP Labs: COTSon: Infrastructure for full system simulation. https://sourceforge.net/projects/cotson/files/
25. Stéphane., Z.: DARTS: An asynchonous fine-grained runtime based on the codelet model. https://github.com/szuckerm/DARTS. Accessed Jan 2021
26. Matheou, G., Evripidou, P.: FREDDO: an efficient framework for runtime execution of data-driven objects. In: International Conference on Parallel and Distributed Processing Techniques and Applications (PDPTA), January 2016
27. Mattson, T.G., et al.: The open community runtime: a runtime system for extreme scale computing. In: 2016 IEEE High Performance Extreme Computing Conference (HPEC), pp. 1–7 (2016)
28. Najjar, W.A., Lee, E.A., Gao, G.R.: Advances in the dataflow computational model. Parallel Comput. **25**(13–14), 1907–1929 (1999)
29. Nowatzki, T., Gangadhar, V., Ardalani, N., Sankaralingam, K.: Stream-dataflow acceleration. In: Proceedings of the 44th Annual International Symposium on Com-

puter Architecture, ISCA 2017, pp. 416–429. Association for Computing Machinery, New York (2017)

30. Nowatzki, T., Gangadhar, V., Sankaralingam, K.: Heterogeneous Von Neumann/dataflow microprocessors. Commun. ACM **62**(6), 83–91 (2019)

31. OCR: Open community runtime v1.0. https://xstack.exascale-tech.com/git/public/ocr.git. Accessed Jan 2021

32. Pochayevets, O.: BMDFM: a hybrid dataflow runtime parallelization environment for shared memory multiprocessors. MS thesis in Computer Engineering (2006)

33. AXIOM Project: Agile, extensible, fast I/O module for the cyber-physical era. https://git.axiom-project.eu/. Accessed Jan 2021

34. Sarkar, V., Hennessy, J.: Partitioning parallel programs for macro-dataflow. In: Proceedings of the 1986 ACM Conference on LISP and Functional Programming, LFP 1986, pp. 202–211. Association for Computing Machinery, New York (1986)

35. SECO s.r.l. http://www.seco.com

36. Silva, R.J.N., et al.: Task scheduling in sucuri dataflow library. In: 2016 International Symposium on Computer Architecture and High Performance Computing Workshops (SBAC-PADW), pp. 37–42 (2016)

37. Stavrou, K., et al.: Programming abstractions and toolchain for dataflow multithreading architectures. In: Proceedings of the 8th International Symposium on Parallel and Distributed Computing (ISPDC 2009), pp. 107–114. IEEE, July 2009

38. Swanson, S., Michelson, K., Schwerin, A., Oskin, M.: Wavescalar. In: Proceedings of the 36th Annual IEEE/ACM International Symposium on Microarchitecture, MICRO-36, p. 291. IEEE Computer Society (2003)

39. Verdoscia, L., Giorgi, R.: A data-flow soft-core processor for accelerating scientific calculation on FPGAs. Math. Probl. Eng. **2016**(1), 1–21 (2016). Article ID: 3190234

40. Weis, S., Garbade, A., Fechner, B., Mendelson, A., Giorgi, R., Ungerer, T.: Architectural support for fault tolerance in a teradevice dataflow system. Int. J. Parallel Program. **44**(2), 208–232 (2014). https://doi.org/10.1007/s10766-014-0312-y

41. Wilde, M., Hategan, M., Wozniak, J.M., Clifford, B., Katz, D.S., Foster, I.: Swift: a language for distributed parallel scripting. Parallel Comput. **37**(9), 633–652 (2011). Emerging Programming Paradigms for Large-Scale Scientific Computing

42. Wozniak, J.M., Armstrong, T.G., Wilde, M., Katz, D.S., Lusk, E., Foster, I.T.: Swift/T: large-scale application composition via distributed-memory dataflow processing. In: 2013 13th IEEE/ACM International Symposium on Cluster, Cloud, and Grid Computing, pp. 95–102 (2013)

43. Yazdanpanah, F., Alvarez-Martinez, C., Jimenez-Gonzalez, D., Etsion, Y.: Hybrid dataflow/von-Neumann architectures. IEEE Trans. Parallel Distrib. Syst. **25**(6), 1489–1509 (2014)

44. Liu, Y., Furber, S.: A low power embedded dataflow coprocessor. In: IEEE Computer Society Annual Symposium on VLSI: New Frontiers in VLSI Design (ISVLSI 2005), pp. 246–247 (2005)

45. Zuckerman, S., Landwehr, A., Livingston, K., Gao, G.: Toward a self-aware codelet execution model. In: 2014 Fourth Workshop on DFM, pp. 26–29 (2014)

46. Zuckerman, S., Suetterlein, J., Knauerhase, R., Gao, G.R.: Using a "codelet" program execution model for exascale machines: position paper. In: Proceedings of the 1st International Workshop on Adaptive Self-Tuning Computing Systems for the Exaflop Era, EXADAPT 2011, pp. 64–69. Association for Computing Machinery, New York (2011)

Instruction Set Transformations

Performance Gain of a Data Flow Oriented ISA as Replacement for Java Bytecode

Alexander Schwarz[✉] and Christian Hochberger

Technische Universität Darmstadt, Merckstr. 25, 64283 Darmstadt, Germany
{schwarz,hochberger}@rs.tu-darmstadt.de

Abstract. Java Bytecode is used as binary format for a number of programming languages and programming systems. Since Java virtual machines exist for many platforms, it can be regarded as a universal execution format. Consequently, several hardware implementations of Bytecode processors exist. Unfortunately, they all suffer from the inefficiencies of the Bytecode principle. Particularly, the operand stack and the local variable storage are bottlenecks during execution. In this contribution, we evaluate the performance gain that can be achieved by replacing Bytecode with a data flow oriented instruction set architecture (ISA). We describe the changes that are necessary to adapt an existing Bytecode processor to the new ISA. Ultimately, we compare execution times and HW resources for both processors, which are based on identical ALUs and heap memory model. Execution times are evaluated using the SPEC JVM98 benchmark and a set of micro benchmarks which have a very flat call graph. SPEC JVM98 reaches a speedup of 1.76 and the micro benchmarks even gain a factor of 2.80.

Keywords: Instruction set architecture · Microarchitecture · Self-timed · Java processor · Online synthesis

1 Introduction

Java Bytecode was originally conceived as a binary representation for Java classes. The main goal was to retain a high abstraction level of the instructions and to generate a compact storage layout. Due to the wide availability of Java virtual machines (JVM), Bytecode has become popular as binary representation for many other programming languages and programming systems as well.

Naturally, a number of Bytecode processors have been invented which use the Bytecode as their native instruction set (see Sect. 2). Most of the recent developments are targeting embedded systems. The nature of the Bytecode as a stack based language implies many data transfers to and from the operand stack. This becomes a bottleneck in almost all implementations. Although sophisticated countermeasures e.g. instruction folding have been invented, they cannot fully eliminate this bottleneck with reasonable hardware effort [4].

© Springer Nature Switzerland AG 2021
C. Hochberger et al. (Eds.): ARCS 2021, LNCS 12800, pp. 103–117, 2021.
https://doi.org/10.1007/978-3-030-81682-7_7

Thus, in previous work [9] we have presented a modified ISA, which sacrifices compactness in favor of a more efficient execution. Nevertheless, the abstraction level of the instructions is retained to enable mapping of instruction sequences to accelerators. In this paper we present a real processor implementation using this optimized ISA. It achieves a speedup of 1.76 for the SPEC JVM98 benchmark and a speedup of 2.80 for micro benchmarks with a flat call graph.

The contribution is structured as follows: Sect. 2 gives information on related work. It is followed by an overview of the old Bytecode processor which we use as our comparison baseline in Sect. 3. Section 4 then recapitulates the new ISA and explains the necessary changes to execute it. A thorough evaluation is given in Sect. 5. We conclude with a short summary and an outlook.

2   Related Work

Several other Java Bytecode processors exist, one of the first being picoJava-II [11,12]. Like most other Bytecode processors, it uses a RISC pipeline in its core which is assisted by microcode for realizing multi-cycle instructions. The most complex instructions trigger software traps, e.g. for exception handling or memory allocation. Runtime services like garbage collection and thread scheduling are implemented in software. aJ-200 from aJile Systems [1] is another commercial Java processor. It can run two independent programs in parallel. JAIP [14] implements even complex tasks like garbage collection, thread scheduling, and exception handling in hardware. Jamuth [15] focuses on real-time capabilities. Thus, it provides thread scheduling in hardware and four parallel instruction fetch stages for fast thread switching. JOP [8] and SHAP [18] are other Java processors supporting hard real-time requirements. They translate all instructions into microcode before execution. In contrast to the previously mentioned designs, the Java processor discussed in this work does not use a pipeline to process instructions but spreads execution over several independent functional units to allow higher flexibility for runtime reconfiguration.

The operand stack has already been identified as performance limit in pico-Java. Therefore, instruction folding has been introduced, which combines multiple instructions before execution in order to reduce stack operations [11]. Extensive research has been done on instruction folding schemes. Although instructions can be reduced considerably with advanced instruction folding schemes [13,17], they result in complex hardware, which increases costs and lowers clock frequency [4]. Synthilation [6] is another approach for accelerating Bytecode execution. It compiles a sequence of instructions into an optimized sequence of microinstructions at run time. However, this approach is only feasible for sequences which are small enough to fit into microcode memory.

The ISA discussed here is based on control flow but borrows ideas from data flow architectures for passing operands between instructions. With pure data flow architectures [2,5], programmers do not specify a sequence in which instructions are executed. All instructions are executed as soon as their operands are available. Although this allows to exploit a maximum of instruction-level parallelism, the

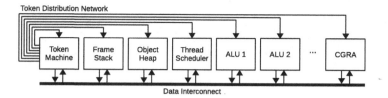

Fig. 1. Structure of the processor

overhead in terms of hardware resources and execution time per instruction is considerably larger than for control flow architectures. Also, complex data structures or arrays are difficult to implement with pure data flow paradigm [7].

3   The Bytecode Based AMIDAR Processor

3.1   The AMIDAR Principle

Processors based on the AMIDAR principle [3] are composed of separate functional units (FUs) which work highly independent from each other. This facilitates hardware design and provides opportunities for runtime reconfiguration. The structure of a Java Processor based on this principle is shown in Fig. 1. The Token Machine is a special FU. It decodes instructions into tokens which are sent to all FUs using the token distribution network. A token contains the operation to execute and the target of the operation result. Instruction-level parallelism is exploited automatically by parallel processing of tokens. FUs exchange data using a common data interconnect. When implementing an FU, assumptions about the timing of other FUs, the data interconnect, or the token distribution network are neither allowed nor necessary. Communication between FUs is self-timed.

Apart from its role as instruction decoder, the Token Machine executes operations which change control flow. Furthermore, it delivers constants to other FUs. Local variables of methods are stored in method frames, which are organized as stack. Frames are pushed on method calls and popped on returns. This is done by the Frame Stack FU. If Java Bytecode is used as ISA, this FU also contains the operand stack, which stores operands and results of instructions. The Object Heap FU stores objects, arrays and static variables. The Thread Scheduler FU is required for scheduling and synchronization of threads. Several ALUs exist for integer and floating point arithmetic. A coarse grained reconfigurable array (CGRA) is used as flexible hardware accelerator [16].

3.2   Java Bytecode as Instruction Set Architecture

Each Bytecode instruction is translated into a set of tokens. Most instructions use the operand stack as source and sink of data. This leads to typical execution sequences as illustrated in Fig. 2. The Java statement is compiled into six instructions. ILOAD_0 pushes the content of local variable 0 onto the operand

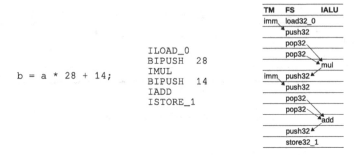

Fig. 2. Exemplary execution of a Bytecode sequence

stack. This instruction corresponds to a single token because both local variables and the operand stack reside in the Frame Stack. BIPUSH 28 creates the constant 28 in the Token Machine and pushes it onto the operand stack. IMUL pops two data words from the operand stack, executes the multiplication on the integer ALU and pushes the result back onto the operand stack. The same procedure is repeated with the addition and the final result is stored in local variable 1 by ISTORE_1. The illustrated sequence assumes an ideal instruction decoder and ignores both execution and data transmission latencies. However, it clearly shows that most operations are executed by the Frame Stack, which limits execution speed. Since most instructions both start and end with a Frame Stack operation, most operations are executed strictly sequentially. The concurrency provided by the concept of independent FUs can hardly be exploited.

3.3 Data Interconnect

The Bytecode based processor uses 64 bit wide dedicated data connections between FUs. Only the connections required by the token sets are realized. As most token sets use the operand stack as source and sink of data, this effectively results in a star topology with the Frame Stack as its center.

An important aspect of AMIDAR processors is the mechanism for synchronizing data and operations. The Bytecode based processor uses tags for this purpose. The required hardware components are depicted in Fig. 3. The token machine puts operation, tag and target into the *token queue* of an FU. A target consists of the FU where the result should be delivered to, the tag of the operation which uses the result as operand, and a port which allows to distinguish between multiple operands of one operation. When all operands of the operation at the front of the operation queue have been received in the *port registers*, the operation is executed and its target is stored in the *target queue*. When computation is finished, the result is stored in the *result register*. It is sent to the target FU using information from the target queue. Data is only accepted and stored in the port register when its tag matches the tag of the operation at the front of the operation queue. Otherwise, the source FU must retry until data is accepted.

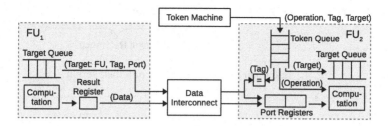

Fig. 3. Data transmission in the Bytecode based processor

Data transmission requires one clock cycle from result register to port register. Only one transmission is allowed per port register and clock cycle. If multiple FUs try to send to the same FU and port simultaneously, one of them is selected by fixed priority arbitration.

3.4 Context Switch

Switching threads is accomplished easily when using Java Bytecode as ISA. Apart from the current code position, all thread specific data resides in the Frame Stack between instructions. Consequently, this FU provides separate stacks for all live threads. When threads are switched, the Token Machine waits until the current instruction is fully decoded, instructs the Frame Stack to change its active stack, and continues executing from the code position of the next thread.

3.5 Garbage Collection

Garbage collection for deleting unreachable objects and arrays is implemented in hardware as part of the Object Heap. Handles are used as references to objects and arrays. Cooperation with the rest of the processor is required when collecting the root set of reachable objects. This root set consists of handles found in static fields and in stack frames. As static fields are stored in the Object Heap as well, they can be examined directly inside the FU. The Frame Stack provides different operations for storing primitive values or handles. This allows to mark all handles in this FU with a handle flag. The Object Heap has a dedicated connection to the Frame Stack to retrieve these handles during root set collection.

4   The AMIDAR Processor with New ISA

4.1 Concept of the ISA

The operand stack has been identified as bottleneck in Sect. 3.2. A new ISA [9] has been developed to remove this bottleneck while keeping the high level of abstraction of Java Bytecode, which is beneficial for software/hardware migration. The main idea of this ISA is to allow data to be transferred directly between

Fig. 4. Assembler representation of one instruction

computational FUs without central intermediate storage. This is accomplished by specifying data flow between instructions explicitly.

Figure 4 shows the four components of an instruction. Every instruction contains an operation code. Some operations require an additional constant. If an instruction produces a result, the *result reference* defines which instruction will receive this result. It consists of an instruction offset and a port. The offset counts the number of instructions to execute after the current instruction until the result is received. A value of 0 references the next instruction. This offset is limited by the *resolution size*, which is a parameter of the processor. The port allows to distinguish between multiple operands of the target instruction.

```
                    read  0 -> 1:0        TM    FS          IALU
                    imm  28 -> 0:1        imm   load32_0
    b = a * 28 + 14;    mul      -> 1:0   imm              mul
                    imm  14 -> 0:1                    add
                    add      -> 0:0       _____
                    write 1               store32_1
```

Fig. 5. Exemplary execution of an instruction sequence

The example from Sect. 3.2 is depicted for the new ISA in Fig. 5. The resulting instructions have almost the same semantics as the Bytecode instructions. However, data is transferred directly between instructions without the operand stack. read 0 -> 1:0 for example has 1 as its instruction offset and 0 as target port. Consequently, it reads local variable slot 0 and sends it to port 0 of the second instruction after the current instruction (mul). Looking at the idealized FU execution sequence, one can clearly see that Frame Stack operations and data transfers have been reduced, which leads to much faster execution.

This technique of specifying data flow between instructions has similarities to data flow machines but control flow determines which instructions are executed. Figure 6 shows an assembler code example together with corresponding control and data flow. This short program iterates over the elements of an array in backwards direction and computes their sum. The handle of the array can be found in local variable slot 0, the index counter is stored in local variable slot 1, and the sum is finally stored in local variable slot 2. While the loop is executed, the sum is directly passed to the next iteration without intermediate storage.

Lines 1 to 5 store the total number of array elements minus 1 to local variable slot 1 as starting value for the index counter. Line 6 generates the initial value of the sum. The fwd (forward) in line 8 receives this value and sends it to port 0 of the add in line 15 without modifications. Lines 9 to 11 load the next element

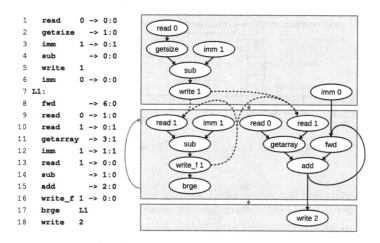

```
1    read       0 -> 0:0
2    getsize       -> 1:0
3    imm        1 -> 0:1
4    sub           -> 0:0
5    write      1
6    imm        0 -> 0:0
7  L1:
8    fwd           -> 6:0
9    read       0 -> 1:0
10   read       1 -> 0:1
11   getarray      -> 3:1
12   imm        1 -> 1:1
13   read       1 -> 0:0
14   sub           -> 1:0
15   add           -> 2:0
16   write_f    1 -> 0:0
17   brge       L1
18   write      2
```

Fig. 6. Loop example (blue: control flow, solid black: explicit data flow, dashed black: implicit data flow using local variable memory). (Color figure online)

	23	22	21	20 19 18 17 16 15 14	13 12 11 10 9	8 7	6 5 4 3 2	1 0
R-Type	0	0	res	Funct7	Param6	K	Offset	Port
I-Type	0	1	res	Imm14			Offset	Port
J-Type	1	0	res	Imm21				
B-Type	1	1	res	res	Funct3	Imm17		

Fig. 7. Binary encoding of instructions

from the array and send it to the other port of the **add**. Lines 12 to 14 decrement the index counter and send it to the **write_f** in line 16. The **add** in line 15 sends its result to the first instruction executed after the branch. This can be either the **write** in line 18 or the **fwd** in line 8 depending on the branch decision. The **write_f** (write and forward) in line 16 stores the decremented index counter to local variable slot 1 and sends a copy to the **brge** in line 17, which compares it to zero and decides whether the loop is left.

The **add** has two mutually exclusive targets for its result but has only one instruction offset. Therefore, both targets must have the same position in the flow of execution relative to the **add**. We call this the *multi-target problem*. Because one target (in line 18) immediately follows the branch, the other target must be positioned at the beginning of the loop. As the **add** cannot be positioned there, the **fwd** must be inserted. If the sum is not immediately required after the loop and other instructions can be inserted between line 17 and 18, the **fwd** can be avoided. In this case, the **add** can send its result to itself for the next iteration.

The binary encoding of instructions is illustrated in Fig. 7. It has been compacted compared to [9] by removing the separate S format and adding a field for small constant parameters, which are transferred to FUs within tokens. This field is currently used for scratchpad memory operations only. Most instructions utilize format R. Format I is for immediate values, J for unconditional jumps,

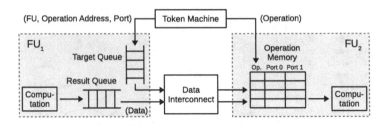

Fig. 8. Data transmission in the new processor

and B for conditional branches. The encoding is fixed for all processor variants. Sizes of the fields have been determined by analyzing the distribution of values in our benchmarks. A transpiler transforms Java class files into a binary for the new ISA. Transformation of code sequences is more complex than one-to-one mapping of instructions. This includes measures to avoid deadlocks.

4.2   Data Interconnect

The new processor also uses 64 bit wide data connections between FUs. However, data is now required to be transmitted between all FUs. Dedicated connections would result in a full crossbar topology. With 12 FUs, such an interconnect consumes a significant amount of hardware resources and causes timing problems. Therefore, a topology with parallel data buses has been implemented. Each FU can send to all buses but can only receive from one bus. Evaluation shows that already two buses provide performance close to a full crossbar (see Sect. 5.3).

The mechanism for synchronizing data and operations has been changed as proposed in [9] and is explained in the following. The new components for data transmission can be seen in Fig. 8. Tokens are split into two parts which are delivered separately to the FUs. Token queues have been replaced by operation memories and target queues. Tags have been replaced by operation memory addresses. When the Token Machine decodes an instruction, it only delivers the operation at first. This operation is stored in the *operation memory*. Each line of this memory stores an operation together with its operands. When all operands for an operation have been received, they are sent to execution. The result is stored in the *result queue*. As soon as the Token Machine has decoded the target instruction, it sends corresponding target information consisting of FU, operation address, and port to the *target queue*. As targets are sent in the same order as operations and operations are executed in exactly this order, the contents at the front of result queue and target queue belong to each other. They are removed and sent to the correct position in the operation memory.

This mechanism avoids tag comparison and acknowledgment to the sending FU because for each target delivered by the Token Machine guaranteed storage exists in the target FU. Furthermore, this mechanism allows more concurrency since data can be accepted for more than one operation waiting at the FU. On the other side, additional operand storage increases hardware costs. Operation memories and queues are implemented using distributed lookup table RAM.

Data transmission requires one clock cycle from result queue to operation memory like in the Bytecode processor. While the Bytecode processor allows one transmission per port and clock cycle, the new processor only allows one transmission per bus and clock cycle. If multiple FUs try to use the same bus simultaneously, one of them is selected by fixed priority arbitration.

4.3   Context Switch

In contrast to the Bytecode processor, not all thread specific data is stored in the Frame Stack after each instruction. When decoding is stopped, result references may exist whose target instructions have not been decoded yet. Data belonging to these unresolved references is located in result queues. Usual concepts for flushing internal state of out-of-order processors cannot be applied because unresolved references are part of the visible program state. The ISA has no concept of a central register file which comprises all state information. Consequently, a process is required for saving and restoring this data on context switches.

This process is illustrated in Fig. 9. Execution is stopped after the first three instructions, which leaves data in the result queues of integer ALU, integer multiplier, and Object Heap. The Token Machine starts the collection process (1) by generating a `collect` operation for each remaining data word. For each of these operations a corresponding target is sent to all FUs which hold data in their result queues. This causes the data to be transmitted to the Token Machine where it is stored in an internal memory. Afterwards, the Token Machine sends a `threadswitch` operation to the Frame Stack together with the ID of the next thread (2). This causes the Frame Stack to switch its internal thread context. Finally, the distribution process begins (3). The Token Machine puts the stored data of the next thread into its result queue. A separate result queue for context switches is available to prevent deadlocks. The corresponding unresolved references are restored internally. When decoding is started again, these references will be resolved automatically. The restored data will be sent to the original target, the floating point ALU in this example. However, data must be distributed in the same order as the corresponding result references will be resolved to avoid deadlocks. As this order can be different from the order of collection, the Token Machine must reorder data before it is distributed (indicated by colors in Fig. 9).

4.4   Garbage Collection

When the root set of reachable objects and arrays is generated for garbage collection, a similar problem arises like during context switches. Not all handles are stored in the Frame Stack. They can be located in operation memories, in result queues, or on the data interconnect.

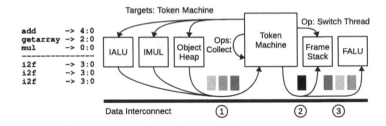

Fig. 9. Example for context switch

The first step to solve this problem is to mark handles not when they enter the Frame Stack but when they leave the Object Heap. Handle flags are assigned to all results of this FU which represent handles. They are transmitted over the interconnect together with data and are stored in all locations where handles can appear. The internals of the Object Heap are the only exception as the garbage collector has its own mechanism for identifying handles stored in heap memory.

The second step makes use of the collection and distribution processes for context switches. In contrast to the Bytecode processor, the garbage collector requests root set handles not only from the Frame Stack but also from the Token Machine. When the Token Machine receives such a request, it stops execution, collects all remaining data, examines this data for handles, re-distributes it, and continues execution. A real thread switch is not required.

4.5   Functional Units

Most FUs can be used for the new processor only with interface modifications required. An FU for data forwarding has been added, which directly passes its operands to the result queue without modifications. It is used to solve the multi-target problem as described in Sect. 4.1 and to avoid deadlocks. A new Token Machine had to be implemented because it is responsible for decoding the new ISA. The hardware for the exception handling mechanism has been replaced by a software routine. The Frame Stack has also been re-implemented because operand stack functionality has been removed. It still contains the stack of method frames for storing local variables. Pushing data is now only used for passing parameters to methods. The garbage collection mechanism in the Object Heap has been modified slightly as explained in Sect. 4.4 and the hardware implementation for multi-dimensional array allocation has been replaced by a software version. A Scratch Pad Memory FU [9] is not part of the current implementation as it does not provide significant speedup (see Sect. 5.2). Read and write operations access the local variable slots of the Frame Stack instead. The Debugger FU has been adopted to the new synchronization mechanism described in Sect. 4.2.

5 Evaluation

5.1 Test Setup

All systems have been synthesized to a Xilinx Artix 7 FPGA (xc7a200tsbg484-1) using Vivado 2019.1 with a target frequency of 100 MHz. Two sets of benchmarks are used for evaluation. Micro benchmarks comprise 9 encryption algorithms, 10 hash algorithms, 4 image filters, ADPCM encoding/decoding, JPEG encoding, and regular expression matching. These benchmarks have flat call graphs and run for a few milliseconds only. SPEC JVM98 benchmark suite [10] with problem size 100 is used for evaluation of practical and complex applications which run for minutes. The following benchmarks are contained in SPEC JVM98:

compress (using modified Lempel-Ziv method), jess (based on NASA's CLIPS expert shell system), raytrace (raytracing algorithm rendering one scene), db (loads a data base file and executes operations on it), javac (Java compiler from JDK 1.0.2), mpegaudio (decoder for MP3 files), mtrt (multi-threaded variant of the raytracer with two worker threads), and jack (early version of JavaCC parser generator).

First, implementation variants of the new processor are evaluated in Sects. 5.2 and 5.3. This is done using the micro benchmarks in behavioral HDL simulations. They differ from hardware only in the external DRAM and its controller. This controller has been replaced by a simplified model whose parameters have been measured on hardware. The error in terms of execution time has been confirmed to be 0.068% on average and 0.224% at worst across all benchmarks.

Second, the Bytecode based and the new processor are compared on hardware using all benchmarks in Sect. 5.4. An SDHC card connected via SPI provides input files and reference data for SPEC benchmarks. Both processor cores have been configured for 16 threads and 64 monitors with 4096 words stack size per thread. Resolution size is 16. Operation memories have 8 lines and result queues can store 4 words (division FUs, Thread Scheduler, Debugger half of these values). The values have been determined by reducing them incrementally as long as performance has not been impacted considerably.

5.2 Scratch Pad Memory

The Scratch Pad Memory FU contains a small but fast memory for duplicating data. However, the local variable slots of the Frame Stack can be used for the same purpose. The Frame Stack is not much slower than the Scratch Pad Memory (2 vs. 1 clock cycles for a read access). Figure 10 shows average speedup and hardware resources consumed by the whole system for both variants from 4 to 64 storage slots. All values are shown relative to the variant with dedicated FU and 4 slots. The variant without dedicated FU exhibits a significantly higher performance and consumes less resources. The increased performance can be explained by the fact that Scratch Pad Memory contents must be saved on method invocations. Because hardware resource consumption is almost constant for this variant, the maximum number of slots is chosen for further evaluation.

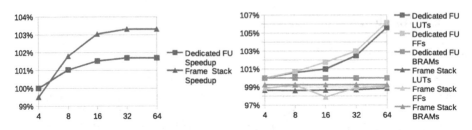

Fig. 10. Speedup (left) and hardware resources (right) for scratch pad memory variants

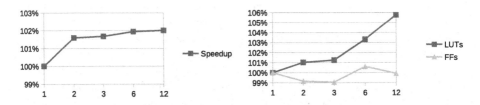

Fig. 11. Speedup (left) and hardware resources (right) for number of buses

5.3 Data Interconnect Topology

The amount of parallel data transfers allowed by the data interconnect can be varied by the number of buses. Figure 11 shows average speedup and hardware resources consumed by the whole system for interconnect configurations with different number of buses. All values are shown relative to the variant with a single bus. The variant with 12 buses is equivalent to a fully connected crossbar. Because speedup hardly increases with more than 2 buses, this interconnect topology is chosen for further evaluation. 2 buses are sufficient because traffic is heavily asymmetric (see distribution of FU operations in Fig. 14).

5.4 Comparison of ISAs

A speedup of 1.76 is achieved on average (geometric mean) for SPEC JVM98 benchmarks and 2.80 for the micro benchmarks as shown in Fig. 12. Hence, the new ISA provides significant gain compared to Java Bytecode. The reason for the notable difference between the two benchmark sets is the much more complex control flow with many method invocations in SPEC benchmarks. Consequently, the new ISA is especially beneficial for data dominated applications. The slightly lower speedup of *mtrt* (multi-threaded raytrace) compared to *raytrace* reveals that the more sophisticated context switch mechanism hardly impacts performance.

Speedup is achieved mainly by elimination of unnecessary FU operations. Figure 13 illustrates this elimination. This presumably leads to reduction of energy consumption as well. However, we have not measured it yet. Again, the micro benchmarks show higher reduction than SPEC JVM98 benchmarks. Some benchmarks exhibit significantly lower reduction than others. This is mainly

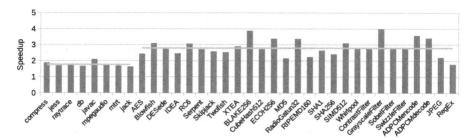

Fig. 12. Speedup in comparison to Java Bytecode (geometric mean in red). (Color figure online)

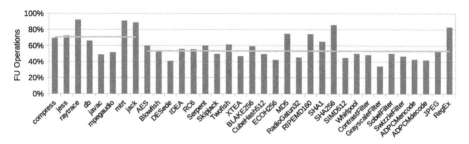

Fig. 13. Number of executed FU operations in comparison to Java Bytecode (geometric mean in red) (Color figure online)

caused by method invocations which require more instructions than with Bytecode. The Bytecode processor stores constants required for management of stack frames in tables inside the Token Machine. The new processor puts them into the code using normal instructions instead. Furthermore, preparing method parameters is more expensive. The Bytecode instruction `iload_1` can be used to push local variable 1 as method parameter. It is executed by a single operation on the Frame Stack. The new ISA instead uses a combination of `read 1` and `push32`. A similar situation occurs when pushing the constant 1 as method parameter with `iconst_1`, which is replaced by `imm 1` and `push32`. These characteristics especially have an effect if very small methods are called frequently.

Figure 14 shows for each FU the sum of executed operations in all benchmarks. Most operations are eliminated for the Frame Stack (by 56%, which has been the primary goal of the new ISA. Token Machine operations are reduced mainly because less constants are required for addressing local variable slots. Operations for the integer ALU are reduced primarily because comparisons with 0 for branches are executed directly by the Token Machine instead of the integer ALU. The Forward FU, which exists only in the new processor, is used rarely. Further speedup is achieved by allowing more operations to be processed in parallel since not all intermediate data must be stored in the Frame Stack.

Figure 15 illustrates the amount of hardware resources consumed by both systems. In total, the number of LUTs has been increased by 4.7%, the number of flip flops is lowered by 7.6%, and the number of RAM blocks is lowered by

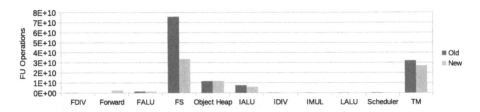

Fig. 14. Number of executed FU operations summarized over all benchmarks

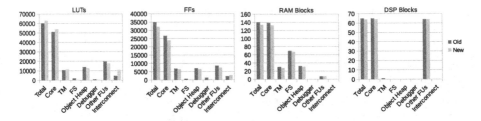

Fig. 15. FPGA resources consumed by both systems

4.3%. One DSP block has been removed from the Token Machine. Consequently, hardware resource requirements are reduced slightly.

Each system is composed of the processing core, one AXI interconnect, one DRAM controller and peripherals. Only the processing core has been modified. The core can be partitioned in its functional units and the data interconnect. Hardware resources for these components are depicted in Fig. 15. FUs which have not been modified have been summarized by "Other FUs". However, the given values are not exact because optimization across module boundaries has been enabled during synthesis. Furthermore, some components being part of the FUs in the old processor are now part of the interconnect. This explains why LUTs and flip flops have been reduced for the "Other FUs". The most significant change is the increase of LUTs for the data interconnect. It is caused by operation memories and queues which are implemented using distributed RAM.

6   Conclusion and Future Work

In this contribution, we have shown the benefit of a data flow oriented ISA over the Java Bytecode ISA. The new ISA sacrifices compactness to eliminate many data transports that were required in Java Bytecode. Yet, the new ISA retains the abstraction level and the self synchronization features of the AMIDAR principle. In total, the new ISA has a speedup of 1.76 for the SPEC JVM98 benchmark and an even higher speedup of 2.80 for micro benchmarks with a shallow call graph.

In the near future, we want to explore the gain that can be achieved by mapping compute intense parts of the application to the CGRA. Also, some optimizations of the instruction set are conceivable. E.g. method invocations could be improved by a combined "read x push32" instruction. Similarly, often occurring additions with one constant operand could be encoded in one instruction.

References

1. aJile Systems: Real-time, Low Power Network, Multimedia Direct Execution Microprocessor For The JME Platform aJ-200. Technical Reference Manual (2010)
2. Dennis, T.: Data flow supercomputers. Computer **13**(11), 48–56 (1980)
3. Gatzka, S., Hochberger, C.: The AMIDAR class of reconfigurable processors. J. Supercomput. **32**(2), 163–181 (2005)
4. Gruian, F., Westmijze, M.: Investigating hardware micro-instruction folding in a Java embedded processor. In: JTRES 2010, pp. 102–108. ACM, New York, August 2010
5. Gurd, J.R., Kirkham, C.C., Watson, I.: The Manchester prototype dataflow computer. Commun. ACM **28**(1), 34–52 (1985)
6. Hochberger, C., Jung, L.J., Engel, A., Koch, A.: Synthilation: JIT-compilation of microinstruction sequences in AMIDAR processors. In: DASIP 2021, pp. 1–6, October 2014 (2014)
7. Lee, B., Hurson, A.R.: Issues in dataflow computing. In: Advances in Computers, vol. 37, pp. 285–333. Elsevier, January 1993
8. Schoeberl, M.: A Java processor architecture for embedded real-time systems. J. Syst. Archit. **54**(1), 265–286 (2008)
9. Schwarz, A., Hochberger, C.: Engineering an optimized instruction set architecture for AMIDAR processors. In: Brinkmann, A., et al. (eds.) ARCS 2020. LNCS, vol. 12155, pp. 124–137. Springer, Cham (2020). https://doi.org/10.1007/978-3-030-52794-5_10
10. Standard Performance Evaluation Corporation: SPEC JVM98 Benchmarks. https://www.spec.org/jvm98/, Accessed 24 Mar 2021
11. Sun Microsystems: picoJava-II Microarchitecture Guide. Technical Report (1999)
12. Sun Microsystems: picoJava-II Programmer's Reference Manual. Technical Report (1999)
13. Ton, L.R., Chang, L.C., Shann, J.J., Chung, C.P.: Design of an optimal folding mechanism for Java processors. Microprocess. Microsyst. **26**(8), 341–352 (2002)
14. Tsai, C., Lin, C., Chen, C., Lin, Y., Ji, W., Hong, S.: Hardwiring the OS kernel into a Java application processor. In: ASAP, pp. 53–60 (2017)
15. Uhrig, S., Wiese, J.: jamuth: an IP processor core for embedded Java real-time systems. In: JTRES 2007, pp. 230–237. ACM, New York, September 2007
16. Wolf, D.L., Jung, L.J., Ruschke, T., Li, C., Hochberger, C.: AMIDAR Project: lessons learned in 15 years of researching adaptive processors. In: ReCoSoC 2018, pp. 1–8, July 2018
17. Yiyu, T., Fong, A.S., Xiaojian, Y.: An instruction folding solution to a java processor. In: Li, K., Jesshope, C., Jin, H., Gaudiot, J.-L. (eds.) NPC 2007. LNCS, vol. 4672, pp. 415–424. Springer, Heidelberg (2007). https://doi.org/10.1007/978-3-540-74784-0_42
18. Zabel, M., Spallek, R.G.: Application requirements and efficiency of embedded Java bytecode multi-cores. In: JTRES 2010, pp. 46–52. ACM, New York, August 2010

Towards Transparent Dynamic Binary Translation from RISC-V to a CGRA

Ramon Wirsch[(✉)] and Christian Hochberger

Computer Systems Group, Technische Universität Darmstadt,
Merckstr. 25, 64283 Darmstadt, Germany
{wirsch,hochberger}@rs.tu-darmstadt.de

Abstract. Dynamic binary translation (DBT) transforms machine code
at runtime into an optimzed form. DBT can have cross platform compatibility, better energy efficiency or improved performance as its goals. The
goal of this work is to improve performance by executing perfomance critical parts of the binary code on a Coarse Grained Reconfigurable Array
(CGRA). We show how the CGRA is integrated into the system and
explain how performance critical parts of the binary code can be identified. We demonstrate the feasibility of a dynamic binary translation
from RISC-V ISA to a CGRA, give details about the employed optimizations and show that the performance of a whole benchmark set can
be improved by a factor of 1.7 without the need for any user intervention.

Keywords: Dynamic binary translation · CGRA · RISC-V

1 Introduction

Computer users always demand more processing power. Starting in the 2000s, the
usual methods to increase the performance did no longer work (higher clock frequencies, improved microarchitecture like superpipelining or larger cache sizes).

Since clock frequencies, pipeline depths and cache sizes are saturated and
further progress with these parameters is hard to achieve, computer architects
started to exploit instruction level parallelism. Two concepts are popular in this
area: 1) Super scalar processing, where the processor core dynamically decides
which instructions can be executed in parallel. The benefit here is that the
instruction stream does not need to be tailored for the specific instance of the
processor (# of issues) 2) Very Large Instruction Word (VLIW) processors,
where the compiler already groups individual instructions into instruction words
that can be executed in parallel. This is only possible if the source code of the
application is available and the compilation must be executed for each different
degree of parallelism in the processor.

Increase of performance can also be achieved by adding hardware accelerators
like Coarse Grained Reconfigurable Arrays (CGRA) which are one type general
purpose hardware accelerators. In such a CGRA many Processing Elements (PE)
work in parallel (and typically in lockstep). Each can have PE its own register file

© Springer Nature Switzerland AG 2021
C. Hochberger et al. (Eds.): ARCS 2021, LNCS 12800, pp. 118–132, 2021.
https://doi.org/10.1007/978-3-030-81682-7_8

and a limited connectivity to its neighbours. Thus, CGRAs are highly scalable without severe clock penalty. In turn, programming CGRAs requires a concurrent solution of the problems scheduling of operations, placement (of operations and data) and routing of data.

In order to support a transparent accelleration of arbitrary applications without the need to adapt them to the acceleration features, dynamic binary translation (DBT) can be employed. DBT transforms a sequence of machine instructions of the host processor into a more suitable form. In the past, DBT has been used to emulate different instruction set architectures or to optimize the energy consumption. In our case, DBT computes configurations for the CGRA that replace compute intensive parts of the application.

In this contribution, we show that a DBT from a RISC-V processor to a CGRA is feasible and that it provides meaningful speedup. We explain, how the CGRA is integrated into the overall system and how a kernel invocation on the CGRA is realized. Also, we describe the transformation process from RISC-V instructions to CGRA configurations in detail. Particularly, we give details about the many optimizations that are required to get meaningful speedup. In the evaluation, we show that a speedup of 1.7 on average can be achieved for the PolyBench set of benchmarks.

The paper is structured as follows: The next section presents related work. It is followed in Sect. 3 by an explanation of our system setup. Section 4 explains the translation process and the optimizations. A detailed evaluation of our CGRA accelerated system is given in Sect. 5. We conclude with a short summary and an outlook onto planned extensions and further related research.

2   Related Work

In a simplification of [19], related work falls mostly into four categories. The first three use DBT for varying target architectures: VLIW, CGRA and FPGA. Lastly, there is work, that statically compiles for CGRAs.

DBT for VLIW. Previous work like Transmeta Crusoe [9], Daisy [10,16] uses DBT to execute code for one ISA on another VLIW ISA. This requires significant investment into supporting the entire ISA. Our work, in contrast, is an opportunistic accelerator. It can pick and choose parts of the executing program it can accelerate well and does not have to support all features, as long as unsupported situations are recognized and left to the processor. Nvidia Denver [5], as well as [8,13,23,24] propose supporting multiple ISAs. The original ISA for which the binary was compiled, is executed on a subset of the VLIW-Processor. DBT is used to fully utilize the VLIW architecture. VLIW processors do not scale well (other than CGRAs) since they have a common register-file, which becomes a bottleneck. Placement of operations on the other hand is trivial. Work like [3,18], in addition handle the translation in hardware, which limits the scope of the optimizations that can be applied during translation, but reduces the time until the target accelerator can be utilized.

Some concepts have specific HW optimizations for the targeted accelerator [9,18] like transactional-memory to recover from miss-speculations. These simplify the translation-process but make the accelerator more complicated.

DBT for CGRA. [6] combines a feed-forward CGRA with ARM processors and only applies some speculative techniques to optimize the instructions executed on the CGRA. Since they operate on basic-blocks instead of loops, they require tighter integration with the host-processor. Otherwise, the overhead of transferring the execution to the CGRA would exceed the gained acceleration. [7] has equally close integration with the processor. [25] maps loops to a CGRA and applies optimizations like Loop Unrolling similar to us. Of multiple possible target architectures, DySER is identified as most profitable. DySER also requires tight integration into an out-of-order core to execute loops efficiently. DySER also has wide memory-ports and thus benefits from using already vectorized x86 code as basis. This means they do not have to specially handle memory disambiguation, as that is implied for vectorized workloads. Our CGRA takes a more generic approach with multiple separate and independently addressable memory-ports. It only requires the host-processor to translate and transfer the execution. Our CGRA can be ported to arbitrary host processors and platforms, since no modification of the processor is required (besides loop-profiling). [11] proposes a CGRA that is less tightly integrated and uses modulo-scheduling. Because modulo-scheduling is time-consuming, Ferreira et al. make concessions in using crossbar interconnects to reduce placement constraints. Our work aims to approximate the performance gains of modulo scheduling by applying optimizations like unrolling combined with a simpler scheduling method. This is combined with a less hardware-intensive interconnect.

DBT for FPGA. FPGAs are more configurable than CGRAs and can achieve higher-speedups, especially for algorithms that operate on a bit-level. However, the increased configuration-space makes it much more expensive to synthesize accelerators. Warp Processors [14] thus target a specialized and simplified FPGA.

Static Translation for CGRA. DySER [12], Libra [17] and ADRES [15] statically compile for CGRAs which is also related to this work as the main principles of identifying candidates for acceleration and translation to the CGRA remain. The integration into the regular compilation-flow however, affords much more metadata, such as type-information. Also, it allows more time for optimization/synthesis. On the other hand, runtime profiling information to identify the most processing-time-intensive parts is either missing, or has to be collected in an additional compute-intensive step. Ahead-of-time knowledge of the targeted accelerator is required. A toolflow that works with DBT, such as ours, can easily be applied statically, although it will most likely achieve less performance than an otherwise equivalent toolflow designed to operate on source-code. In contrast, our work does not rely on existing compilers or toolchains to minimize the amount of code that needs to be ported for dynamic translation.

3   System Setup

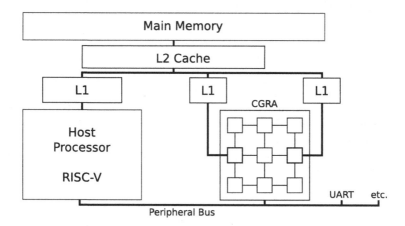

Fig. 1. Schematic of a CGRA attached to a RISC-V processor with memory coherency

The system evaluated in this work consists of a System-On-Chip (SoC) with a RISC-V processor, together with our CGRA, as shown in Fig. 1. To support acceleration of a wide range of code sequences, henceforth called kernels, the CGRA is attached to the system in a cache-coherent fashion. Some of the CGRAs Processing Elements (PEs) have access to the systems memory, each via its own L1 cache. For this work, we use 2 memory ports across all CGRA configurations and host processor and CGRA share a common L2 cache.

Furthermore, the CGRA is attached to the host processor via the peripheral bus. This is used to control the CGRA and transfer local variables to and from the CGRA at the start and end of each kernels execution. To run any kernel on the CGRA, the kernels instructions, called contexts from now on, need to be present in the CGRA. The host processor will then command the CGRA to prepare execution of a specific kernel identified by an integer ID. The host will then send all register contents required in the kernel (called live-ins) via the peripheral bus and trigger the actual execution of the prepared kernel. While the CGRA executes this kernel, the host processor could theoretically execute a different process. Although currently, it will only wait for the kernel to complete by polling the CGRA for its state. After the CGRA has finished a kernel, still needed local variables that where calculated by the kernel (called live-outs) are then transferred back to the processor, also using the peripheral bus.

Besides attaching the CGRA to the memory hierarchy and peripheral bus of the host processor, no other modifications to the hardware of the processor are required, in order to have the system run. This is much less intrusive compared to related approaches [6,7,25] that require access to the processors register-file. For identifying the most often executed code sequences as candidates for kernels, we use a loop profiler attached to the processor. The profiler only needs to monitor the addresses of executed instructions, without a need to access the instruction memory itself. The process of translating code-sequences to kernels for the CGRA is described in Sect. 4. The acquired loop-profiles are also used to compare the performance of various inner loops against the CGRAs execution to identify localized bottlenecks.

3.1 Host Processor

As host processor, we are utilizing a scalar in-order pipelined RISC-V processor that implements the RV32IMFC instruction set specified in [22]. This specifies a 32-bit processor with hardware-multiplication, single precision floating-point unit and support for the 16-bit compressed instruction set.

3.2 CGRA

The CGRA employed is based on the one used with UltraSynth [27], enhanced with better pipelining. It also has more localized state to make it more scalable and its contexts have been redesigned be more memory efficient. It consists of a configurable number of PEs, that each have their own register-file and multiple pipelines for various operations. The CGRA also has a specialized unit that computes conditions for the predication of operations and for direct branches which the entire CGRA needs to execute simultaneously. For this work, the CGRA is homogeneous with regard to the supported arithmetic operations. Every PE supports the same arithemetic operations available to the RISC-V processor, including single-precision floating-point. Each PE can only use 1 register per instruction from its own register-file, a second register can be output to its neighbors. For additional inputs PEs mostly have to rely on their available neighbors. We use a neighbor-interconnect that follows a *matrixStar*-pattern for the planar CGRA (Fig. 2a), whereby the PEs are layed out in a 2D-grid and each PE is connected to its direct neighbors on the vertical, horizontal and diagonal axes. The cube-like CGRA (Fig. 2b), on the other hand, only uses a matrix-pattern, which omits the diagonal connections. The 2 PEs with access to main-memory have an additional register-file read-port to support memory-writes with a base address and an additional offset, much like the RISC-V instruction set has.

3.3 Simulation

The proposed system is tested and evaluated using a custom simulator that encompasses the entire system shown in Fig. 1. The simulator can model multiple distinct pipelines. Every supported operation can be assigned to a pipeline and has a blocking and non-blocking latency. Thus the simulator can accurately model the behavior of a scalar, in-order, pipelined (Integer, Floatingpoint and Memory Pipeline) processor including scoreboarding for the register-file. For memory accesses, two levels of caches and their latencies, together with Dragon

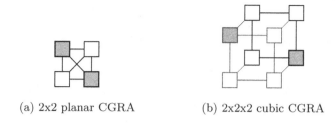

(a) 2x2 planar CGRA   (b) 2x2x2 cubic CGRA

Fig. 2. Evaluated CGRA variants

Coherency Protocol [4] are simulated. The processor-simulator can execute statically linked ELF-binaries, much like the QEMU user-space simulator can. It
supports printing to the terminal by means of recognizing calls to libc-functions,
like printf, putc etc. File-IO is not yet supported as it requires emulating many
different functions. A simulator of the CGRA is also included and models above
described interaction between CGRA and host processor. The latencies of the
CGRA's arithmetic operations are configured with the latencies of our existing
HDL implementation. The processor is configured to match the CGRA's latencies and pipelining, so that all RISC-V and CGRA operations take the same
amount of cycles on the CGRA as on the processor.

In the current stage of development, the contexts of the CGRA are not
configurable from RISC-V code, but instead are configured either ahead-of-time
or through halting the simulation in between cycles. This is also where the kernel
translation and synthesis currently happens, so realistic measurements of time
taken for translation and synthesis are not yet possible.

4   Binary Translation

The translation used for this work, shown in Fig. 3, is designed to be ported to
an embedded host-processor in the future, where it can be run dynamically as
new hot spots are discovered. It operates on the memory images of the simulator that are created from ELF binaries. During refinement of the translation it
can be executed statically, but uses only information that it would have access
to at runtime. It is currently not compiled to the RISC-V instruction set, as it
reports and tracks data for debugging and evaluation purposes that do not make
sense for dynamic execution inside the simulated RISC-V processor. Translation
starts with a custom tool that disassembles the instructions from memory, and
translates them into the a Control Flow Graph (CFG) in Static Single Assignment (SSA) form in a single pass. The CFG was designed with instructions that
map predominantly directly to operations on the CGRA. The conversion can
start at any valid instruction address and ends when all paths reached return
instructions or a predefined address limit representing the boundary of the loop
recognized by the profiler. The SSA form allows to resolve most occurrences of
indirect control flow such as jump-tables in the same pass. As the source ISA is

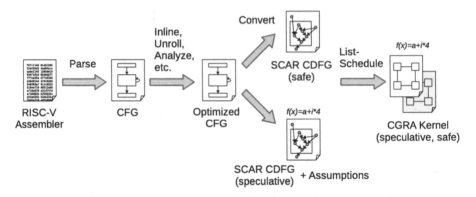

Fig. 3. DBT process from RISC-V assembler to executable CGRA kernel, including memory disambiguation

RISC, almost all instructions map to a single CFG-instruction as well as a single CGRA-operation. A custom CFG format was chosen to support unresolved calls, where the call-target, some or all of the arguments and return values have not been found or cannot be statically determined.

Since the CGRA cannot execute calls or any indirect control flow, only CFGs that contain no more call instructions can be mapped onto the CGRA. Therefore, every call must be inlined. While this would cause extensive code-size-increases if done by regular compilers, if only done for actual hotspots of the program, it is most likely preferable for performance anyway. Previously unresolved arguments are resolved during the inlining process. The translation fails, if a call can neither be inlined, proven to be dead code or mapped directly to a native operation on the CGRA. While not ideal, this is still valid, because the host processor can still execute the original code, just without any acceleration. The resulting CFG is then optimized mainly to increase the Instruction Level Parallism (ILP) for the CGRA. The CFG-optimization runs passes much like a compiler, because this affords much more flexibility in evaluating the effects of optimizations during development of a dynamic binary translation. At the moment there are 20 such passes, 13 of which are unique. They start with the already described inlining, then continue with passes designed to cleanup the CFG, to make it easier to analyze. These include Copy Propagation, Dead Code Elimination, Empty Basic Block Removal and Sparse Conditional Constant Propagation (SCCP) [26] with partial constant propagation for additions and subtractions that commonly occur in pointer-arithmetic.

4.1   Unrolling

The following passes center around preparing for loop-transformations by simplifying the loop-structures to a canonical Loop-Closed-SSA Form [1]. This decouples instructions following a loop from the effects of loop-transformations. Loop-Invariant Code is also hoisted to before the loop. Just before the main

ILP-generating pass of Loop Unrolling is executed, the CFG is analyzed with regard to the addresses of memory accesses and their relation to each other, especially inside loops. The gathered symbolic descriptions of memory-addresses form the basis for the memory disambiguation that will be applied later. The Partial Loop Unrolling itself is simplified, but based on LLVMs implementation [2]. It can currently partially unroll any reducible loop, by replicating its exit-condition for each unrolled iteration. For loops that are forward-predicated with known, constant stride and without side-effects in the loop-header, Loop-Splitting can also be performed. In this case, the entire loop is used twice, once supporting only iteration counts that are multiples of the unrolling-factor and a second version for the rest. This is shown in Fig. 4. The yellow and blue highlighted instructions indicate, how the simple unrolling with Partial Constant Folding can decouple the second memory access from the first ones' address calculation, but cannot elide the need to predicate the second load. At this time, the unrolling-factor is statically configured on a per loop-nesting-level basis and only applies to leaf-loops, i.e. loops that contain no further loops. This is due to the fact that the CGRA can only execute controlflow such as branches globally, which means that no 2 loops can be executed in parallel, unless they could be fused into a single loop in the CFG.

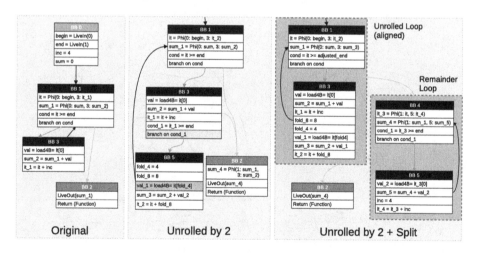

Fig. 4. Simple partial loop-unrolling & with splitting. Both with partial constant folding applied

Another collection of cleanup-passes is run, again including the Constant Propagation, Dead Code Elimination and Empty Basic Block Removal. These serve to remove artifacts of the loop-transformation and, in most circumstances, can decouple the unrolled iterations from one another. For example, instead of calculating the induction-variable for a second unrolled iteration only after the first one completed, using Partial Constant Propagation will fold multiple increments of the induction-variable into separate calculations consisting only of one addition if the stride was constant. This is also shown in Fig. 4.

4.2 SCAR-Conversion

The resulting optimized CFG is then converted into the Scheduler Application Representation (SCAR) Control and Dataflow Graph Format consumed by our CGRA-Scheduler. The SCAR-Format exposes the scheduling constraints in a convenient way for the scheduler. Reducible loops are primitives in this format, because it allows the scheduler to directly identify loop boundaries. It operates on single instructions instead of Basic Blocks as the CFG does, to allow the scheduler to only respect explicit data-, control- or order-dependencies. It currently represents traditional control-flow (branches) as speculative execution with predication. Thus, if-else constructs in the CFG will result in both branches being executed in parallel, with operations that have side-effects, such as memory accesses being predicated with the branch-condition. Phi-Instructions in the CFG are converted to conditional register-writes and reads, Phi-Instructions of loop-carried dependencies can be mapped to unconditional writes before the loop and at the end of each iteration. Figure 5 shows the loops used as example in Fig. 4 in SCAR-Format. It shows, that the predication caused by the yellow highlighted instruction in the CFG could be removed due to loop-splitting.

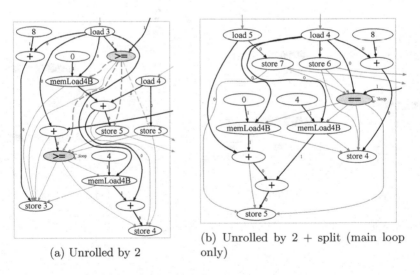

(a) Unrolled by 2

(b) Unrolled by 2 + split (main loop only)

Fig. 5. Shows SCAR-Representation of unrolled loops from Fig. 4. Black: Data-Dependency, Grey: Order-Dependency: Dotted: Predication. Yellow Conditions and their predications could be reduced/eliminated by loop-splitting.

4.3   Memory Disambiguation

Two variants of this conversion exist. One outputs a safe kernel by applying Total Store Order constraints to all memory operations in the kernel. In effect, constraining all memory accesses to the exact order they appeared in the CFG, relaxed only if it can be statically proven that two neighboring accesses cannot overlap or alias (Static Memory Disambiguation). Thereby, it drastically limits the ILP otherwise achievable with Partial Loop Unrolling, as most loops contain memory-writes that have to be serialized. The other variant applies static and dynamic conditional memory disambiguation by making the assumption that memory accesses that use different live-ins as base addresses do not overlap. This means that the second variant is only correct, if the assumptions are proven correct, which needs to be checked before the CGRA changes any memory contents. Currently all these checks are global, meaning that they solely rely on the knowledge of the live-in variables. The checks are executed on the CGRA, but since the SCAR-Format has yet to support expressing branches, the host-processor chooses between the two variants based on the checks' result. If the checks fail, the safe kernel is transparently swapped in instead of the speculative kernel. Because execution-transfer to the CGRA is patched into the original binary-code by overwriting the instructions in memory at some point during the execution, executing the checks on the host-processor and falling back to its original implementation was deemed too impractical. The patched instructions would need to be replaced by the original instructions and immediately executed. Although RISC-V is position-independent, moving only a fragment of a program will break all relative control-flow from that fragment to the rest of the program and thereby prevents executing code from a different location than originally linked for.

4.4   Scheduling

The last step in translating a kernel from RISC-V for the CGRA is scheduling. Utilizing a highly customized resource-constrained list-scheduler still under development, a statically timed schedule is created. Memory loads and stores are given a static latency in the schedule that allows them to complete if the requested address resides in the local cache. Otherwise, the CGRA is stalled until the data becomes available.

A huge benefit of such a static schedule is, that the runtime of each linear instruction-sequence is known. This way, as a final pass before replacing the RISC-V code with the patch to use the CGRA, we can validate the execution-speed of any inner-most loop in the schedule against the loop-profiles recorded by the processor with the original code. By way of this check we can avoid most of the cases, where our CGRA-Kernel would still be slower than the original code. Cases, where the "accelerated" kernel still underperforms are exceptions, where the execution time is not dominated by the inner-most loops or the actual kernel is slower than the schedule due to cache misses, that are not factored into the performance estimation of the schedule.

5   Evaluation

Since processor and CGRA are configured with matching latencies for all operations, the results are clock-frequency independent. Speedups for the CGRA are only possible through exploitation of parallelism beyond what the pipelined processor is capable of. We evaluate the proposed system with the PolyBench Benchmark suite [20], because the benchmarks are self-contained and do not use File-IO. Every benchmark consists only of setup of input data, a kernel and dumping the results. To select kernels for synthesis, we currently choose the last call-target-address before the profiled loop with the most execution time. While we can also synthesize loops with strict boundaries, this heavily increases the live-ins and live-outs needed. It may also hide certain constants or the relation between pointers derived from function arguments from our optimizations. We compiled all benchmarks for 'rv32imfc-ipl32f' with version 10.2 of GCC, built from the RISC-V GNU Compiler Toolchain [21] using newlib as libc implementation. Every Benchmark is executed once to gather reference performance and loop-profiles and again with translation applied during startup of the simulation. Because Memory Disambiguation is a vital part of achieving speedup for the PolyBench suite of benchmarks and our translation makes speculations, the made assumptions about the live-in variables need to be checked before executing a kernel that relies on these assumptions. These checks are still unoptimized, but in our experience take at most 50 cycles on the CGRA. Optimization level -O3 is used and PolyBench's Dataset size is configured to *medium* for all benchmarks. At this size, the whole-program-speedup and kernel-only-speedup factors start to converge and the time taken for checks that only execute once becomes irrelevant.

Speedups are calculated by executing a PolyBench benchmark in the RISC-V simulator without any use of the CGRA and taking the total number of clock-cycles taken for the execution as reference. Then a separate simulation is started, where the kernel-function of that benchmark is replaced by a kernel for the CGRA. To have the second simulation use the CGRA, the kernel-function is patched in-memory to transfer execution to the CGRA for the entirety of the kernel, then finish the rest of the benchmark back on the host processor. Again, the total number of clock-cycles simulated is used as the passed time.

Correct functionality is validated by comparing the output of the PolyBench benchmarks and by comparing the contents of all writes to memory that occurred during the execution of the kernel.

The configured optimzations unroll each innermost loop of each kernel by a factor of 8, with applied loop-splitting where supported.

As can be seen in Table 1, some kernels are unsupported because either the SCAR-Graph cannot express them or they include instructions that cannot be mapped to the CGRA. Examples are *jacobi-1d*, which includes hardcoded double-constants that result in unsupported float-operations with a mix of hard- and soft-float, *deriche*, which uses the *FCLASS.S* instruction that calculates 10 different flags classifying a floating-point value, and is currently not available as single operation on the CGRA. The kernels *trmm* and *gramschmidt* contain unsupported irreducible loop structures due to compiler optimization.

Table 1. Speedup-Results for PolyBench Medium -O3. "Kernel %" shows amount of cycles part of the kernel. Column **S** indicates whether the kernel was executed on the CGRA (✓). **L** and **I** indicate whether the kernel was unsupported due to loop-structure or instructions

CGRA name	Tot. cycles 10^6	Kernel %	2 × 2 (f2a)		2 ×2 × 2 (f2b)		Too slow	UNS
			Speedup	S	Speedup	S		
2 mm	421	98	1.830	✓	1.765	✓		
3 mm	599	99	1.706	✓	1.662	✓		
adi	1142	100	1.958	✓	1.956	✓		
atax	13	60	1.442	✓	1.474	✓		
bicg	13	59	1.473	✓	1.497	✓		
cholesky	2122	12	1.020	✓	1.017	✓		
correlation	238	98	1.736	✓	1.601	✓		
covariance	236	98	1.701	✓	1.601	✓		
deriche			1.000		1.000			I
doitgen	175	93	1.627	✓	1.593	✓		
durbin	3	99	1.795	✓	1.901	✓		
fdtd-2d	583	98	2.487	✓	2.551	✓		
floyd-warshall	1882	99	0.933	✓	0.850	✓		
gemm	334	98	2.706	✓	3.112	✓		
gemver	22	77	1.781	✓	1.772	✓		
gesummv	7	43	1.320	✓	1.311	✓		
gramschmidt	347	97	1.000		1.000			L
heat-3d	1406	100	3.594	✓	4.534	✓		
jacobi-1d			1.000		1.000			I
jacobi-2d	637	99	2.692	✓	3.027	✓		
lu	2417	22	1.018	✓	1.003	✓		
ludcmp	2237	17	1.059	✓	1.061	✓		
mvt	13	61	1.363	✓	1.327	✓		
nussinov	305	99	0.930	✓	0.963	✓		
seidel-2d	1342	99	1.158	✓	1.158	✓		
symm	246	97	2.156	✓	2.193	✓		
syr2k	352	97	2.613	✓	2.989	✓		
syrk	196	96	2.701	✓	2.755	✓		
trisolv	4	45	0.987	✓	0.974	✓		
trmm	137	96	1.000		1.000			L
avg			1.660		1.722			

For benchmarks like *floyd-warshall*, *nussinov* and *trisolv* there are multiple accesses to different entries of the same array inside a single iteration. Since we currently only support global checks for aliasing, we cannot verify whether the memory accesses overlap if they not only depend on the kernels arguments. In the case of Floyd-Warshall, only single iterations out of the many executed would actually contain overlapping accesses. This would require localized aliasing checks instead of global ones. Since our memory disambiguation does not yet support localized assumptions, it makes reduced assumptions that hold actually true, but do not achieve any relevant speedup.

A few kernels, like *cholesky*, *durbin* and *seidel-2d* would be slower than the host-processor executes them, but are caught by our static speedup-checks and thus never executed. This is mostly caused by our current memory disambiguation not being able to remove memory dependencies. With Total-Store-Order the CGRA cannot beat the processor.

PolyBench benchmarks, for which the memory disambiguation works, achieve speedups. How much a specific kernel benefits from increased unrolling, depends, among other things, on the composition of instructions. The current CGRA configurations support memory-operations only on 2 PEs whereas all PEs can execute floating-point and integer arithmetic. Thus, memory-bound loops will benefit much less from unrolling than arithmetically-bound loops. Furthermore, the memory-operations are currently not restricted to a specific memory-port/cache. Meaning that increasing the amount of memory-ports also increases the amount of stalls, due to transfers from one cache to another, when the same memory-locations are accessed or even written to from different memory-ports. This can cause above average differences in the statically computed cycles per iteration of a schedule and the actual runtime.

As shown by the fact that some benchmarks like *heat-3d* and *syr2k* scale with more PEs, while others do not, or are even adversely affected, we are running into bottlenecks. These are mostly caused by artifacts of the scheduler, that is still under development and center around variable placement. The largest bottleneck however is caused by a limitation to only supply one predicate for conditional execution per cycle, which will be lifted by a redesign of the condition logic in the future. Especially when loop-splitting is impossible and thus every unrolled iteration has its distinct predication, which also depends on the previous iterations condition, this is quite limiting and causes under-utilization. When first enabling the loop-splitting optimization for forward-predicated loops we saw a noticeable jump in performance for these loops. Modern compilers however, prefer backward-predicated loops to reduce the number of mispredicted branches, and will convert forward-predicated loops into backward-predicated ones for their higher optimization levels. This causes the majority of loops to not be eligible for our loop-splitting optimization and thus limits how many instructions can actually execute in parallel. The condition facilities of the CGRA were also designed for kernels created from strictly structured, forward predicated loops. The above mentioned redesign would also further improve the efficiency of our condition logic for RISC-V code.

Additionally, the naive method by which Phi-Instructions are converted for the CGRA is less efficient compared to what modern compilers do and causes a static overhead of one additional register-write beyond what the host-processor is executing, even without any loop-transformations applied. This overhead per iteration becomes less relevant the more instructions the original loop-body contained, but weighs heavy on smaller loops with multiple loop-carried-dependencies.

Kernel-Synthesis takes about 1.2 s on average on a desktop PC, most of which is consumed by the scheduling. Parsing and optimizing the CFG takes about 0.1 s on average.

6 Conclusion

In this contribution, we have shown the feasibility of a dynamic binary translation from RISC-V ISA to a CGRA. We can achieve meaningfull speedups for the PolyBench set of benchmarks. Some applications achieve high speedups of upto 4.4, while others cannot gain performance through the mapping to the CGRA.

There is still substantial room to improve. The microarchitecture of our CGRA was optimized for the mapping of a different ISA. As we now see, it can be further optimized for the needs of RISC-V binaries (condition computation). The current version of the scheduler has some limitations that we hope to lift in the near future (better register placement, utilization of more than one predication/condition signal per clock, improved routing of data). Nevertheless, we will also improve the translation process itself. E.g. memory accesses should be classified such that accesses with the same base address are mapped to the same memory port. Additionally, the aliasing checks should also be possible on inner loop levels such that each outer iteration can either use the non-aliasing or the safe inner kernel. Ultimately, we plan to enable loop splitting also for backward predicated loops (which are the majority in compiled code).

References

1. LLVM loop terminology. https://llvm.org/docs/LoopTerminology.html
2. LLVM loop unrolling. https://llvm.org/doxygen/LoopUnroll_8cpp_source.html
3. Almog, Y., Rosner, R., Schwartz, N., Schmorak, A.: Specialized dynamic optimizations for high-performance energy-efficient microarchitecture. In: CGO, pp. 137–148 (2004)
4. Atkinson, R.R., McCreight, E.M.: The dragon processor. In: ASPLOS, pp. 65–69 (1987)
5. Boggs, D., Brown, G., Tuck, N., Venkatraman, K.S.: Denver: Nvidia's first 64-bit ARM processor. IEEE Micro
6. Brandalero, M., Shafique, M., Carro, L., Beck, A.C.S.: TransRec: improving adaptability in single-ISA heterogeneous systems with transparent and reconfigurable acceleration. In: DATE, pp. 582–585 (2019)
7. Clark, N., Kudlur, M., Hyunchul Park, Mahlke, S., Flautner, K.: Application-specific processing on a general-purpose core via transparent instruction set customization. In: MICRO, pp. 30–40 (2004)

8. Deb, A., Codina, J.M., González, A.: SoftHV: A HW/SW co-designed processor with horizontal and vertical fusion. In: CF (2011)
9. Dehnert, J., et al.: The transmeta code morphing software: using speculation, recovery, and adaptive retranslation to address real-life challenges. In: CGO (2003)
10. Ebcioğlu, K., Altman, E.R.: DAISY: dynamic compilation for 100% architectural compatibility. In: ISCA, pp. 26–37 (1997)
11. Ferreira, R., Denver, W., Pereira, M., Quadros, J., Carro, L., Wong, S.: A runtime modulo scheduling by using a binary translation mechanism. In: SAMOS, pp. 75–82 (2014)
12. Govindaraju, V., Nowatzki, T., Sankaralingam, K.: Breaking SIMD shackles with an exposed flexible microarchitecture and the access execute PDG. In: PACT, pp. 341–352 (2013)
13. Liu, F., Ahn, H., Beard, S.R., Oh, T., August, D.I.: DynaSpAM: dynamic spatial architecture mapping using out of order instruction schedules. In: ISCA (2015)
14. Lysecky, R., Stitt, G., Vahid, F.: Warp processors. In: DAC, pp. 659–681 (2004)
15. Mei, B., Vernalde, S., Verkest, D., De Man, H., Lauwereins, R.: Exploiting loop-level parallelism on coarse-grained reconfigurable architectures using modulo scheduling. In: DATE, p. 10296 (2003)
16. Nair, R., Hopkins, M.E.: Exploiting instruction level parallelism in processors by caching scheduled groups. In: ISCA, pp. 13–25 (1997)
17. Park, Y., Park, J.J.K., Park, H., Mahlke, S.: Libra: tailoring SIMD execution using heterogeneous hardware and dynamic configurability. In: MICRO, pp. 84–95 (2012)
18. Patel, S.J., Lumetta, S.S.: rePLay: a hardware framework for dynamic optimization. IEEE Trans. Comput. $50(6)$, 590–608 (2001)
19. Paulino, N., Ferreira, J.a.C., Cardoso, J.a.M.P.: Improving performance and energy consumption in embedded systems via binary acceleration: a survey. ACM Comput. Surv. 53 (2020)
20. Pouchet, L.N.: Polybenchc-4.2.1 beta. https://github.com/MatthiasJReisinger/PolyBenchC-4.2.1
21. RISC-V Foundation: RISC-V GNU compiler toolchain. https://github.com/riscv/riscv-gnu-toolchain
22. RISC-V Foundation: The RISC-V Instruction Set Manual, Volume I: User-level ISA, 20190608-Base-Ratified. https://github.com/riscv/riscv-isa-manual/releases/download/Ratified-IMAFDQC/riscv-spec-20191213.pdf
23. Rokicki, S., Rohou, E., Derrien, S.: Hybrid-DBT: hardware/software dynamic binary translation targeting VLIW. IEEE Trans. Comput Aid. Des. Integr. Circuits Syst. 38(10), 1872–1885 (2019)
24. Uhrig, S., Shehan, B., Jahr, R., Ungerer, T.: A two-dimensional superscalar processor architecture. In: 2009 Computation World: Future Computing, Service Computation, Cognitive, Adaptive, Content, Patterns, pp. 608–611 (2009)
25. Watkins, M.A., Nowatzki, T., Carno, A.: Software transparent dynamic binary translation for coarse-grain reconfigurable architectures. In: HPCA, pp. 138–150 (2016)
26. Wegman, M.N., Zadeck, F.K.: Constant propagation with conditional branches. In: ACM Transactions on Programming Languages and Systems, pp. 291–299 (1985)
27. Wolf, D., Engel, A., Ruschke, T., Koch, A., Hochberger, C.: UltraSynth: insights of a CGRA integration into a control engineering environment. J. Sig. Process. Syst. 93, 463–479 (2021)

Organic Computing

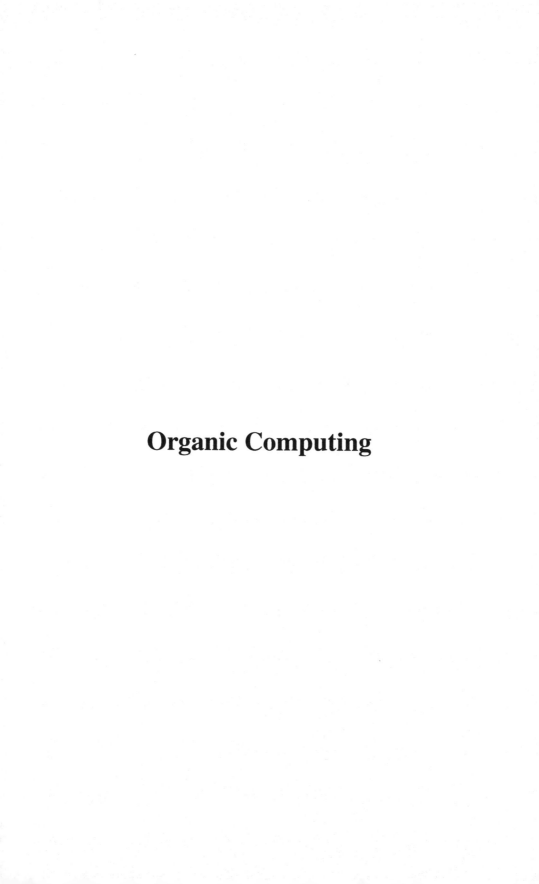

An Organic Computing System for Automated Testing

Lukas Rosenbauer[1]([⊠]), David Pätzel[2], Anthony Stein[3], and Jörg Hähner[2]

[1] BSH Hausgeräte GmbH, Im Gewerbepark B10, 93059 Regensburg, Germany
`lukas.rosenbauer@bshg.com`
[2] University of Augsburg, Eichleitner Str. 30, 86159 Augsburg, Germany
`{david.paetzel,joerg.haehner}@informatik.uni-augsburg.de`
[3] University of Hohenheim, Garbenstr. 9, 70599 Stuttgart, Germany
`anthony.stein@uni-hohenheim.de`

Abstract. Testing is a vital part of the development of a new software product. With the rise of test automation, companies more and more rely on large sets of test cases. This leads to situations in which it is unfeasible to run all tests due to a limited time budget which eventually results in the need for selecting an optimal subset of tests to execute. Recently, this test selection problem has been approached using machine learning methods. In this work, we design an *Organic Computing* (OC) system which makes use of these methods. While OC design techniques have originally been targeted at creating embedded systems, we show that these methodologies can be employed to software verification as well. We are able to demonstrate that the implemented system is a robust and highly autonomous solution which fits modern development practices such as continuous integration well.

Keywords: System architecture · Testing · Continuous integration · Organic computing

1 Introduction

Software verification has become a crucial part of the development of most products. With techniques such as test-driven development being employed more and more consistently, the number of tests for a single piece of software has increased significantly. The fact that running large test suites may take a lot of time makes it necessary to carefully decide when to run which tests [23]. On the one hand, investing too little time into running tests may lead to undetected errors and as a result unsatisfied customers. On the other hand, spending too much time may result in, often expensive, delays in the development cycle. It has been shown that, economically, testing has a major impact on total development cost [5]. Hence, innovation in software verification is a lucrative endeavor.

In this work we are considering a use case from *continuous integration* (CI). CI is the practice of frequently integrating the source code of the individual

© Springer Nature Switzerland AG 2021
C. Hochberger et al. (Eds.): ARCS 2021, LNCS 12800, pp. 135–149, 2021.
https://doi.org/10.1007/978-3-030-81682-7_9

software engineers with the goal of avoiding big software forks which can be hard to merge–this reduces costs and helps to ensure quality. Usually, CI is enabled by automatization tools such as *Jenkins* [4]: Jenkins checks out source code, builds it, tests it and, if the test results indicate that it is OK to do so, deploys it. These steps form a pipeline each run of which is coined a CI cycle.

Our work exclusively focuses on the testing stage. During this phase, any kind of test may run, ranging from unit tests to system tests. There are situations where it is not feasible to run all available tests due to time constraints. For example, the practice of smoke testing aims at getting first insights into a new software version. It tries to decide whether further testing is sensible or whether the version under test should be rejected outright [3]. For such use cases, critical test suites that fulfill certain goals have to be assembled.

Throughout a project's lifetime, the corpus of available tests may change due to practices such as early testing which emphasizes the implementation of tests as soon as possible and parallel to software development [7]. Furthermore the way software is developed has also changed since there has been a move to agile methods which propagate extending the source code iteratively leading to frequent changes of individual modules [2]. This may lead to both errors being fixed as well as new bugs being introduced into the software. Thus the testing environment is underlying constant changes.

Organic Computing (OC) is a research area which aims at designing systems that can cope with an ever changing environment [9]. OC systems are usually adaptive, autonomous and possibly distributed structures. They further have certain self-x properties such as self-learning or self-optimizing. Typical use cases may be found in embedded systems such as traffic control [20] or camera systems [14]. However several of the aforementioned properties are also desirable for our testing use case. Hence OC methodologies are of interest for software verification.

The focus of this work is to show how OC design patterns can be used to create a testing system for usage in CI. Our main contributions are:

- An adaption of the existing *multi-layer observer controller* (MLOC) architecture [9] to serve as a test system architecture.
- Sensors and actors are typically seen as hardware constructs in OC; we underline that instead they can be seen as an abstract concept which is not necessarily linked to hardware. For our system we define virtual sensors and actors that sense and execute test cases.
- We evaluate our MLOC-based architecture quantitatively regarding its degree of autonomy, self-organizing capabilities and robustness. We take special focus on the latter and use actual data sets from industry in order to have a realistic insight on the system's performance.

In Sect. 2, related work is discussed. This is followed by an introduction of an OC architecture template (Sect. 3). We evaluate the system in Sect. 5. We close this work with a conclusion and brief discussion of future work (Sect. 6).

2   Related Work

Our use case is of interest from several points of view. The task of choosing an appropriate test suite is coined *test selection problem* in software engineering. Various methods exist that try to solve different test objectives as described in a survey by Yoo and Harman [23]. A recent trend is to employ *reinforcement learning* (RL) to the task; for example, Spieker et al. [16] designed a neural network-based agent which determines critical test cases solely using data collected by CI systems. Their agent turned out to be superior to several other more traditional methods such as random or greedy selections in finding faults.

From a systems engineering perspective, our work is deeply linked to OC which relies heavily on so-called *observer-controller* architectures [9]. These split the monitoring process from the adjustment part which was shown to be a useful abstraction.

OC makes use of results of other fields of computer science, most prominently artificial intelligence [9]. Thereby OC systems often rely on *learning classifier systems* (LCSs) which are a family of rule-based machine learning methods that can be used for RL or *supervised learning* tasks. We already successfully developed an LCS for the task [13].

Continuous integration is a major part of modern software development. There is a lack of appropriate CI architectures due to the novelty of the field [18]. A survey could only find two CI architectures with one of them focusing on visualization of a CI process and the other one deals with the CI process as a whole [19]. We found another paper that proposes an architecture for CI which tries to cover the entire CI process [1]. However, the authors mention testing only briefly, stating that crucial tests should be selected and executed; it is left open how this should be done (both from an architectural as from an algorithmic point of view).

In summary, there is, to our knowledge, no well-defined system for the testing stage available. There is a need for such a system as testing can take up to fifty percent of development cost [8] and is of importance for the quality of the product. Due to the success of LCSs and the machine learning method's links to OC we deem its architectural concepts as desirable.

3   MLOC in a Nutshell

A commonly used MLOC architecture consists of four different layers which are shown in Fig. 1. Each layer serves as an abstraction of layers lower in the architecture. The lowest layer, termed *productive layer*, or, layer 0, wraps the *system under observation and control* (SuOC) whose state it measures and manipulates, e.g., using a set of sensors and actors.

Layer 1 (*reactive adaptation layer*) is structured by an observer-controller architecture. The observer reads sensor data and preprocesses it. It may also store and retrieve historical data linked to the data just received and make simple predictions based on that. The acquired data is summarized in a state

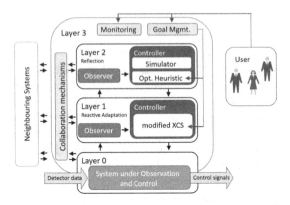

Fig. 1. MLOC architecture as defined in [9].

description and provided to the controller. The controller decides based on the given state description how the SuOC should be manipulated; here, RL techniques come usually into play [9]. In the past, LCSs have been used especially often for this control task [10] with the *XCS classifier system* [21] being an especially prominent choice, mainly due to it being easily adapted to a certain use case.

An LCS maintains a set of rules which map the given state to an action. The rules are created via internal mechanisms and their experience may be tracked. Thus the system's decisions and experience are traceable. Hence the OC system can detect whether it deals with a situation where it is unskilled. Under such circumstances layer 1 requests from the *reflection layer* (layer 2) rules which fit the novel observation. New rules in an LCS are usually either discovered at random or generated using a *genetic algorithm* (GA) [22]. The latter creates new rules based on existing ones. These new, untested rules might be detrimental for the system's performance. Hence layer 2 evaluates new rules in a simulation and only the ones that perform reasonably well are sent to layer 1 in order to be applied in the real case. It usually makes sense conceptually to move the overall process of rule generation to this layer (and thus out of layer 1).

The aforementioned layers result in an autonomous but isolated system. A third layer (*collaboration layer*) serves as an interface to neighboring systems (e.g., systems with a similar architecture) as well as the users. Communicating with neighboring systems enables adding collaboration mechanisms such as sharing of parameters or state information. The interface for users usually contains functionality for monitoring the system's performance as well as adjusting the system's goals.

4   An Organic Test System

Within this section we go over the four layers of the presented MLOC architecture and discuss which adaptions of the template were necessary for our use case. We also give a broad overview of how the system was implemented for one of our industrial partners.

Before we describe the system itself, we want to underline its goals once more. The system should prioritize and select test cases in order to quickly find errors. A widespread metric to measure the effectiveness of test case selection and prioritization methods is the *normalized average percentage of faults detected* (NAPFD) [11]. The metric ranges from zero (worst) to one (best). A prioritization technique achieves large values if it marks a high number of tests that are going to fail as important whilst being able to identify test cases that will just pass. Due to spatial restrictions we refer the reader to the works of Qu et al. [11] for a formal definition of the NAPFD metric.

4.1 Productive Layer

The SuOC is the *device under test* (DUT) which may be anything between a software component and a full product (e.g. a car or a web application). It is interfaced via a test framework. Engineers write or generate tests that are available as source code. These automated tests are maintained in a repository and can be executed using the corresponding testing framework. It usually makes sense conceptually to move the overall process of rule generation to this layer (and thus out of layer 1). In context of the original MLOC template values can often be observed in a sample rate of some clock time. However, here we differ since our time unit is not motivated by physics or embedded systems. Our time axis is the CI cycle mentioned from Sect. 1. It is worth mentioning that the original SuOC metaphor was actually inspired by electronic component tests [9].

4.2 Reactive Layer

In layer 1, the observer senses the available test cases and at the end of the CI cycles the results of the ones executed. Further, it collects CI metadata to give the controller a more detailed knowledge of the available test cases (thus no detailed knowledge about the tests or the software is required). For each test, it stores its

- **test history:** A vector of previous test outcomes, for example [failed, failed, passed, failed].
- **last execution:** A test might not be executed every CI cycle. The observer thus stores the time step (i.e. the CI cycle) the test has been performed last.
- **execution times:** Encountered durations of the test case which can be used to approximate the test cases duration.

The observer can estimate the test case's duration based on the execution time. Together with the test history, this signal can be used to estimate whether it is a short test that often fails or whether it is a rather long test that usually passes. The last execution can be used to guide exploration: For example, it allows to check whether a previously passing test that has not been run for quite a while still passes or has begun to fail more frequently.

Our reactive layer contains another abstraction mechanism: it generalizes from the given testing framework. We deem this as necessary since there are different testing frameworks for specific test levels. The abstraction from the test engine enables the reusability of the system across several test levels and makes its components independent of the test level.

The acquired information about the tests is given to the controller which uses it to compute an appropriate test suite that takes the available execution time into account. We perform our selection using a modified *XCSF classifier system* which was first used that way by Rosenbauer et al. [12]. They used it to model continuous priorities (which serve as actions) for test cases (states) and selected the test cases greedily until the time budget is exhausted. The prioritization is done with the goal of maximizing a reward function aiming at detecting as many errors as possible.

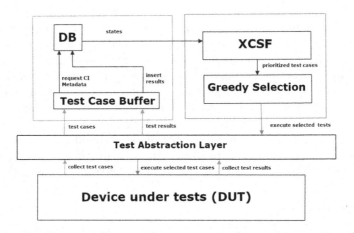

Fig. 2. Interaction of layer 1 with the DUT using the test abstraction layer. The green box represents the observer and the red box the controller. Together they form layer 1.

After executing the test cases, their results as well as additional CI metadata (durations, CI cycle) are retrieved and the observer combines the information and uploads them to a *database* (DB). This makes the data reusable for the succeeding CI cycle. We visualized the entire flow of data and separation of the building blocks of our layer 1 in Fig. 2. For the sake of simplicity, we regard the DUT and the test engine as one block.

4.3   Reflection Layer

As mentioned in Sect. 3, layer 2 usually creates rules for situations where the system lacks experience. We slightly deviate from the template in that our system does not create new rules solely using a metaheuristic and that it does not evaluate them in a simulation. Instead, we rely on two other mechanisms to develop strong rules:

- **Transfer Learning (TL):** A previous study has shown that the usage of rules created for other software projects may also be applied to another project. These reused rules can improve the system's performance [12]. Hence, if the rule base is too poor for a given situation, then layer 2 can use the collaboration mechanisms to ask neighbouring systems for fitting rules.
- **Experience Replay (ER):** Stein et al. [17] discovered that LCSs such as XCS benefit from reusing previous experiences (state-action-reward tuples) as this improves data efficiency as well as the LCS's performance. This is also the case for our test case prioritization use case [13]. ER is executed periodically after a fixed number of CI cycles.

In our system, learning is solely performed using ER and TL, both of which are part of layer 2. TL is additionally used when the system is the first time created as we transfer knowledge from a pretrained XCSF instead of creating a new population entirely at random.

The system might further benefit from other testing activities. For example, before shipping software to customers, *all* tests are run. The data created in the process can be used for additional training and evaluation of the quality of the proposed rules. This data has the advantage that the complete knowledge of the outcome of all tests is available (other than during our system's runtime, where only a subset of tests is executed at any time).

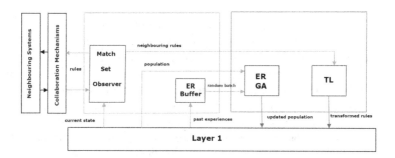

Fig. 3. Interaction of layer 2 with layer 1 and neighbouring systems. The green box represents the observer and the red box the controller. Together they form layer 2. (Color figure online)

We summarized the behaviour of the reflection layer schematically in Fig. 3. The match set observer checks if the size of the match set (set of rules that fit to the given state) is too small. If this is the case, it requests matching rules from neighbouring systems (using the collaboration layer) and injects them to the TL component of the controller which inserts the transformed rules into the match set (hence giving them to layer 1). The ER buffer saves past experiences and periodically sends a random batch to the controller in order to refine the rule basis.

4.4   Collaboration Layer

The collaboration layer enables the tester's to set two goals. 1) the time budget
for the test suite 2) A reward function for the XCSF-based agent (in our case it
is currently just one that rewards failure revealing capabilities).

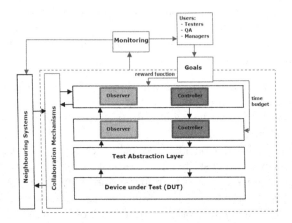

Fig. 4. Interaction of the collaboration layer with the remaining parts of the system.

Test engineers are not the only users of an autonomous testing system as
described by this work. Software developers, *quality assurance* (QA), and project
managers often need knowledge of the status quo of testing as well. Hence the
monitoring of systems such as ours is a part of some kind of overall project
reporting. In order to meet this requirement, our system's logging is integrated
into a global monitoring system which is realized as a dashboard app. However,
due to this work's space restrictions we can not provide any more details.

Collaboration with other systems can be enabled using some form of message-
based communication or shared memory. We decided to use the latter since
neighbouring systems solely exchange rules. We maintain the populations of
individual XCSFs in a software artifact management system called *Jfrog Artifactory* [6].

We summarized the interaction of the collaboration layer in Fig. 4. One can
see there that collaboration is limited to the reflection layer. Additionally the
reflection layer is the only section whose goals can be set. Further, it displays
the stakeholders and our change to a global monitoring system[1]. The content
outlined by the dashed lines represent an individual agent which may work
autonomously.

It is also worth discussing what a *neighbouring* system in our context is.
From a mathematical point of view, neighbouring means closeness in terms of
some distance or similarity measure. We instead use closeness from a testing and

---

[1] In the original MLOC variant the monitoring focuses on one isolated agent.

development perspective. We search the populations of other XCSFs of different variants of the same product[2] and different test levels of it. This simple heuristic limits the search time whilst enabling the reuse of rules. If the reflection layer requests matching rules, an exhaustive search through the neighbourhood is performed after which the rules found are transformed as described by [12] and then provided to the reactive layer.

5   Evaluation

The XCSF approach employed by our system has already been heavily benchmarked using *key performance indicators* (KPI) which are frequently used in software verification [12,13]. However, OC has its own KPIs to evaluate a system. Within this work we examine some of them.

5.1   Autonomy

In OC, a certain degree of *autonomy* is desired in order to deal with the encountered complexity of the task. A system is regarded as autonomous if its decisions are solely based on an internal control mechanism. Neither full autonomy is desired as the system would become uncontrollable nor full external control is wished. This goal is also desirable from a CI perspective since this DevOps practice requires a high amount of automatisation which can be seen as a side-effect of a system with a high degree of autonomy.

OC measures of autonomy relate the number of parameters which are set by the internal control mechanism to the number of parameters set by external influences (e.g. testers that change some goals). In our current implementation the configuration space consists out of the test cases that can be run, the time budget and the reward function to be used.

The test suite to be run is computed by the greedy-selection XCSF. If n tests are available then the chosen test suite can be encoded as a bit vector of length n (the i-th entry indicating the i-th test shall be executed or not). Note that this is encoding is common in the testing context [23]. The time budget can be encoded as a floating point variable of constant length c_b and the reward function using an ID which also has a constant size c_r (e.g., if the reward functions are maintained in some enum datatype). Both these constants are also measured in bits (note the rewards/time budgets are not constants but the size of their respective datatype).

In OC, the *static degree of autonomy* α is defined as follows:

$$\alpha = \frac{V_{int} - V_{ext}}{V_{int}} \tag{1}$$

---

[2] For example Bosch and Siemens home appliances are from the same producer and a Bosch home appliance often shares many things with a Siemens one.

where:

- V_{int} corresponds to the internal variability of the system which in our case corresponds to the number of tests n.
- V_{ext} is the external variability which corresponds to the number of external control variables (here, c_r and c_b) and internal parameters that are changed externally (e.g., by corrective measures).

α has a maximum value of one and a high value indicates a high degree of autonomy.

The externally changed internal parameters are in our use case the test cases manually set or excluded by the test engineers. We could observe that this has, up to now, never been done by our testers. Thus we can compute α as follows:

$$\alpha = \frac{n - c_r - c_b}{n} \tag{2}$$

Within the projects of our industrial partners we often observed several hundreds of test cases, sometimes even several thousands. Hence n is by far the dominating factor which leads to a value of α close to one. Therefore, we employed a system with a high degree of autonomy which enables user control, allowing to disable the autonomy in extreme situations. It is worth mentioning that, next to the static degree of autonomy, there exists the *dynamic degree of autonomy* measure β [15]. It differs from the static one by only taking the bits into account that are applied at a fixed time t. Within our current projects we could not observe yet that the testers often changed the time budget and the reward function was yet only set at the start. Thus we can make similar observations for the dynamic degree of autonomy.

5.2 Self-organization

There exist several ways to define *self-organization* (SO) within OC [9]. One focuses on the number of control mechanisms k, their distribution among the m agents and the agents' degree of autonomy. As seen in the prior subsection, our system is highly autonomous. SO in an OC context requires at least a partially distributed system (which is true for ours). Each of our agents has two control mechanisms by design (one for the reactive layer and one for the reflection layer), hence $k = 2 m$. Systems with these properties are said to be *strongly self-organizing* [9].

It is worth mentioning that self-organisation itself is not a quality indicator. There are both examples of self-organisation that lead to undesired effects or help to achieve a system goal [9]. Here the different agents can only communicate by exchanging experienced rules which is known to be beneficial [12]. Hence we regard this form of self-organisation as rather positive.

5.3 Robustness

OC has partially been developed to cope with an ever-changing environment. To this end, quality measures have been designed to assess how well a system can cope with a given disturbance δ. This assessment is based on their influence on the system performance, which is quantified using some sort of utility function U (here U corresponds to NAPFD). In our use case, disturbances may range from bugs in internal or third party software, issues connected to testing itself such as deprecation or broken test environments. These KPIs are coined *robustness*.

There are mainly two definitions for robustness in the literature [9]. *Passive robustness* measures how strongly a disturbance influences the system's utility function:

$$r_{\text{passive}} = \frac{\partial U}{\partial \delta}$$

This not only requires the disturbance to be differentiable but, more essentially, assumes the magnitude of the disturbance itself to be observable (and not just its impact on the utility function). However, this latter magnitude is very difficult to measure for the kinds of disturbances that we identified. Hence we neglect this KPI in our analysis. It is worth mentioning that passive robustness is nevertheless a well-defined KPI for some applications—especially ones that are linked to physics where many disturbances are measurable and usually smooth.

Active robustness measures how fast the system recovers when a disturbance impacts the system's performance. A disturbance is detected when the utility drops below a predefined level l. Then we can measure the active robustness as follows:

$$r_{\text{active}} = \frac{\partial U}{\partial t}$$

where t denotes time. The measurement stops when the utility is again greater than l. We follow Müller-Schloer et al. [9] and approximate active robustness as follows:

$$\frac{\Delta U}{t_{\text{rec}}} \tag{3}$$

where ΔU is the maximum drop in utility (during the performance break in) and t_{rec} is the time the system needs to recover from this drop.

In order to evaluate our system we rely on a series of open source industrial data sets which were originally introduced by Spieker et al. [16]. An overview is given in Table 1. The paintcontrol and iofrol dataset are from a Scandinavian robotics company and gsdtsr is a Google dataset.

Table 1. Summary of the three examined datasets (paintcontrol, iofrol, gsdtsr). Note the number of test executions is not a multiple of the test cases as these grew over the project's lifetime.

	paintcontrol	iofrol	gsdtsr
CI cycles	312	320	336
test cases	114	2086	5555
test executions	25594	30319	1260617
failed (%)	19.36	28.43	0.25

Before we dive into the empirical robustness evaluation we want to point out that we performed several evaluations of the employed LCS with regards to NAPFD [12,13]. There we also compared against a state of the art artificial neural network which is also in use by Netflix.

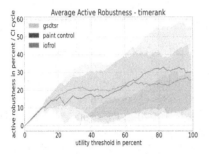
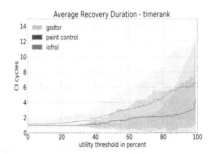

(a) Averaged active robustness times ± (b) Averaged recovery times ± standard
standard deviation σ.   deviation σ.

Fig. 5. Robustness and recovery time evaluation.

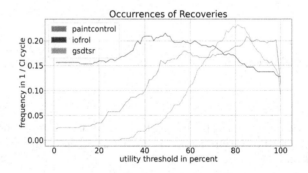

Fig. 6. Frequency of performance drops with regards to different utility thresholds.

We follow [16] who also give their system fifty percent of the total execution time as a time budget, run the system 30 times on the data sets and use averaged results. Furthermore we examine different levels l since this parameter is vital for the notion of active robustness. We display the average results including their standard deviation σ in Fig. 5a. As can be expected, both robustness and its variance generally increases with increasing utility thresholds. Notably there is a reduction in the active robustness for the paintcontrol data set if the utility threshold rises above 80%. In this range the NAPFD values are several times slightly below this value but recover in one CI cycle which in turn reduces the active robustness (the ΔUs are very small). For gsdtsr we set the active robustness to zero until a threshold of about thirty percent since for these values we could not observe any performance break downs below that level. On the first blink the measured active robustness (recovery speed) may seem low, but one may keep in mind that our utility function only has a small limited range (0 to 100%). Thereby our system is capable to recover rather quickly.

Figure 5a also indicates that our system performs differently for each considered data set. We evaluated this hypothesis using a Friedman test[3] that was significant (using a significance level of 0.05) and thus we infer that the structure of the project to test also has an impact on our test system's performance.

The previous evaluation focused on how fast the system reaches a predefined utility threshold after a performance break down. In Fig. 5b we switch the focus on how long it takes to recover in such situations. The plot shows that, for all considered data sets, the performance recuperates after 1–3 CI cycles if the threshold is below 50%. For higher thresholds the required CI cycles increase but are still on average single-digit. It is also worth mentioning that our system was always capable of recovering. Furthermore we can observe once more that the three data sets lead to different recovery times which we once more can confirm using a Friedman test and the aforementioned significance level.

After elaborating how fast the system recuperates and how long these events take, we switch our focus towards how frequently such events occur. We measured the frequencies (in $\frac{1}{CI\ Cycle}$) for different thresholds in Fig. 6. For all three considered data sets we can observe that the frequencies increase with the thresholds until reaching a threshold value in the range of 70 to 80%. After that, the frequencies start to decrease since multiple small events that were counted separately for lower thresholds tend to be merged into fewer, longer events as the threshold is increased (which is in line with our evaluation of the recovery times).

We can observe differences in the frequencies for utility thresholds lower than 50%. The highest frequencies can be observed for the iofrol data set, a lower one for the paintcontrol data set and the lowest for gsdtsr. For the latter there is often a frequency of zero (no event at all). These differences are not at random and an additional significant Friedman test underlines this (reusing a significance level of 0.05). Thus the cause is linked to the internal structure of the data sets. One difference between gsdtsr respectively paintcontrol and the iofrol data set is the frequency of the test runs. For the first two projects, tests were run on a daily basis (sometimes even several times) and for iofrol usually only once per month. Hence two succeeding iofrol software versions can be considered as more different if compared to gsdtsr or paintcontrol and it is naturally more difficult to create precise test case prioritization based on historical data. However, the frequencies are still rather small and if we also take the high active robustness values and short durations of the recovery processes into account then one can see that our system can be regarded as robust for these three data sets.

---

[3] We decided to use a Friedman test over a more widespread ANOVA test as it does not require equality of variance. The latter is not given here which renders an ANOVA analysis unfeasible.

6   Conclusion and Future Work

Continuous Integration (CI) has become a vital technique for coping with the ever increasing complexity of software and its development. This approach focuses on frequent automated building and testing of software. While testing has a major impact on development costs and duration, there still is a lack of appropriate test systems that deal with the special requirements of a CI environment. Besides, there is often not enough time to exhaustively execute all available tests; hence, a subset of critical test cases has to be compiled. The ideal composition of this subset usually changes over time as development progresses making it necessary to adapt it to an updated software. As CI processes are highly automated, selecting critical test cases should be done autonomously by the test system.

A system's engineering discipline that focuses on the design and evaluation of autonomous, adaptive systems is *Organic Computing* (OC). OC concepts have been designed to be employed for embedded systems. Within our work we showed that several OC ideas can also be applied to the aforementioned testing use case. We designed and implemented an autonomous OC test system that can be integrated easily into CI processes. In our evaluation we showed that it is self-organizing, highly autonomous, and has a robust performance in terms of selecting test cases. Thus, as it is capable of adapting to an ever-changing software, it can be directly applied to CI-based software projects.

For the future we intend to analyse for which kind of projects structure the approach suits best. Furthermore we want to analyse the impact of several other signals such as requirement artifacts which might further push the system's performance.

References

1. Angara, J., Gutta, S., Prasad, S.: DevOps with continuous testing architecture and its metrics model. In: Sa, P.K., Bakshi, S., Hatzilygeroudis, I.K., Sahoo, M.N. (eds.) Recent Findings in Intelligent Computing Techniques. AISC, vol. 709, pp. 271–281. Springer, Singapore (2018). https://doi.org/10.1007/978-981-10-8633-5_28
2. Dingsyr, T., Dyb, T., Moe, N.B.: Agile Software Development: Current Research and Future Directions, 1st edn. Springer, Heidelberg (2010). https://doi.org/10.1007/978-3-642-12575-1
3. Dustin, E., Rashka, J., Paul, J.: Automated Software Testing: Introduction, Management, and Performance. Addison-Wesley Longman Publishing Co. Inc., Boston (1999)
4. Ferguson, J.: Jenkins: The Definitive Guide. O'Reilly, Beijing (2011)
5. Herzig, K., Greiler, M., Czerwonka, J., Murphy, B.: The art of testing less without sacrificing quality. In: 2015 IEEE/ACM 37th IEEE International Conference on Software Engineering, vol. 1, pp. 483–493 (2015)
6. Jfrog: Jfrog Artifactory (2020). https://jfrog.com/artifactory/. Accessed 26 Jan 2021
7. Larman, C., Vodde, B.: Scaling Lean and Agile Development: Thinking and Organizational Tools for Large-Scale Scrum, 1st edn. Addison-Wesley Professional, Boston (2008)

8. Lazic, L., Mastorakis, N.: Cost effective software test metrics, vol. 7 (2008)
9. Müller-Schloer, C., Schmeck, H., Ungerer, T.: Organic Computing - A Paradigm Shift for Complex Systems, 1st edn. Springer, Heidelberg (2011). https://doi.org/10.1007/978-3-0348-0130-0
10. Prothmann, H., et al.: Decentralised route guidance in organic traffic control (2011)
11. Qu, X., Cohen, M.B., Woolf, K.M.: Combinatorial interaction regression testing: a study of test case generation and prioritization. In: 2007 IEEE International Conference on Software Maintenance, pp. 255–264 (2007)
12. Rosenbauer, L., Pätzel, D., Stein, A., Hähner, J.: Transfer learning for automated test case prioritization using XCSF. In: Castillo, P.A., Jiménez Laredo, J.L. (eds.) EvoApplications 2021. LNCS, vol. 12694, pp. 681–696. Springer, Cham (2021). https://doi.org/10.1007/978-3-030-72699-7_43
13. Rosenbauer, L., Stein, A., Pätzel, D., Hähner, J.: XCSF with experience replay for automatic test case prioritization. In: 2020 IEEE Symposium Series on Computational Intelligence (SSCI) (2020)
14. Rudolph, S.: Mutual Influences in Self adaptive and Autonomously Learning Systems. Ph.D. thesis (2020)
15. Schmeck, H., Müller-Schloer, C., Çakar, E., Mnif, M., Richter, U.: Adaptivity and self-organisation in organic computing systems. In: Müller-Schloer, C., Schmeck, H., Ungerer, T. (eds.) Organic Computing—A Paradigm Shift for Complex Systems. ASYS, vol. 1, pp. 5–37. Springer, Basel (2011). https://doi.org/10.1007/978-3-0348-0130-0_1
16. Spieker, H., Gotlieb, A., Marijan, D., Mossige, M.: Reinforcement Learning for Automatic Test Case Prioritization and Selection in Continuous Integration. In: Proceedings of the 26th ACM SIGSOFT International Symposium on Software Testing and Analysis. p. 12–22. ISSTA 2017, Association for Computing Machinery, New York, NY, USA (2017)
17. Stein, A., Maier, R., Rosenbauer, L., Hähner, J.: XCS classifier system with experience replay. In: Proceedings of the 2020 Genetic and Evolutionary Computation Conference. GECCO 2020, pp. 404–413. Association for Computing Machinery, New York, NY, USA (2020)
18. Ståhl, D., Bosch, J.: Modeling continuous integration practice differences in industry software development. J. Syst. Softw. **87**, 48–59 (2014)
19. Ståhl, D., Bosch, J.: Cinders: the continuous integration and delivery architecture framework. Inf. Softw. Technol. **83**, 76–93 (2017)
20. Tomforde, S., et al.: Decentralised progressive signal systems for organic traffic control. In: 2008 Second IEEE International Conference on Self-Adaptive and Self-Organizing Systems, pp. 413–422 (2008)
21. Urbanowicz, R.J., Browne, W.N.: Introduction to Learning Classifier Systems, 1st edn. Springer, Heidelberg (2017). https://doi.org/10.1007/978-3-662-55007-6
22. Wilson, S.W.: Classifier fitness based on accuracy. Evol. Comput. **3**(2), 149–175 (1995)
23. Yoo, S., Harman, M.: Regression testing minimization, selection and prioritization: a survey. Softw. Test. Verif. Reliab. **22**(2), 67–120 (2012)

Evaluating a Priority-Based Task Distribution Strategy for an Artificial Hormone System

Eric Hutter[✉] and Uwe Brinkschulte

Goethe University Frankfurt, Frankfurt am Main, Germany
{hutter,brinks}@es.cs.uni-frankfurt.de

Abstract. One approach to handle the ever-increasing complexity of embedded systems is the Artificial Hormone System (AHS). The AHS is a middleware based on Organic Computing principles capable of assigning tasks to a distributed system's processing elements (PEs). It is completely decentralized and has no single point of failure. In case a PE fails, the affected tasks are automatically re-assigned to healthy PEs, thus self-healing the system. Furthermore, the AHS is suited for real-time systems since hard time bounds can be proven for the duration of its self-configuration and self-healing capabilities.

A recently proposed extension of the AHS supports defining *assignment priorities* for tasks. These allow to enforce a specific order of task assignment, thus allowing to e.g. start the most important tasks first during the system's initial self-configuration and to make sure these tasks are re-assigned as quickly as possible in self-healing scenarios.

Although this priority-based AHS extension's time bounds have previously been studied, its behavior has not yet been thoroughly evaluated. In this paper, we thus present evaluations of this extension, confirming and refining the known time bounds.

Keywords: Artificial Hormone System · Organic computing · Self-organization · Self-healing · Task distribution

1 Introduction

New ways of handling the ever-increasing complexity of embedded systems have to be found. One possibility to achieve this goal is to adapt biological principles to computer systems, such as self-organization and self-healing. The endocrine system of mammals, for example, handles many organism functions by exchanging so-called *hormones*, forming decentralized control loops. This basic principle has been adapted to decentrally manage tasks in distributed computing systems by the *Artificial Hormone System* (AHS) middleware [14]. The AHS exchanges digital hormones (that are modeled by short messages) via a communication network, forming a flexible system exhibiting various so-called self-x properties such as self-configuration and self-healing.

© Springer Nature Switzerland AG 2021
C. Hochberger et al. (Eds.): ARCS 2021, LNCS 12800, pp. 150–164, 2021.
https://doi.org/10.1007/978-3-030-81682-7_10

We extended the AHS in [8] in order to support *task assignment priorities*. In contrast to the original AHS that assigns all tasks in a nondeterministic order, these priorities allow to define an order of task assignment. This can be used to start the most important tasks first during a system's initial self-configuration and also to re-assign these tasks first after one of the system's processing elements failed. As a result, the most critical system functionality can be started resp. restored as quickly as possible.

We have previously analyzed the priority-based AHS extension's time bounds theoretically. This paper's contribution builds upon this prior work in two ways:

1. We evaluate the priority-based extension's behavior in different self-configuration and self-healing scenarios.
2. We improve the worst-case time bound for self-healing when task assignment priorities are utilized.

The paper is structured as follows: We first present related work and the general AHS in Sects. 2 and 3. The priority-based AHS extension is summarized in Sect. 4. Section 5 presents our evaluation results and Sect. 6 improves the extension's worst-case time bound for self-healing. Finally, Sect. 7 concludes this paper.

2   Related Work

The AHS along with its extension studied in this paper allows a distributed system to recover from hardware failures by means of automatic and dynamic (re)configuration. One approach to improve a system's robustness against such failures is the duplication of its functional units. This way, each unit has an identical redundant unit in a hot stand-by mode. In order to reduce the costs induced by this duplication, approaches like [10] instead share a single backup between multiple different functional units that can replicate a single failed unit's behavior.

In contrast, the AHS allows to distribute tasks to available computing nodes with more flexibility while the studied extension additionally allows to prioritize tasks. In contrast to the approaches just mentioned, this flexible task distribution allows to reduce the number of required backup units while still achieving the same degree of tolerance against failures [1].

The AHS is inspired by and based on various general research trends, most notably *Organic Computing* [11]: Here, computer systems are constructed by incorporating concepts inspired by biological systems and their organization principles. This allows these systems to dynamically adapt to changing operational conditions, realizing self-x properties like self-configuration or self-healing. This is often accompanied by a postponement of various decisions traditionally made at design-time to the system's run-time [9].

The resulting dynamism distinguishes the AHS from approaches like [6] where a precomputed adaptation scenario is applied in case of node failures. In particular, the AHS completely postpones the calculation of adaptation strategies from design-time to run-time, allowing a more dynamic reaction that can even respect the remaining nodes' current operational conditions.

However, the AHS and systems based on Organic Computing principles in general are by no means the only approaches to assign tasks in distributed systems.

Multiprocessor scheduling is a topic that has intensively been studied with some recent research concerning fixed-priority scheduling on multiprocessors [7,13]. However, the scheduling problem is fundamentally different from the AHS approach as it concentrates on proving whether some task set can be scheduled given some constraints, respectively finding a valid schedule. In contrast, the AHS deals with dynamically assigning tasks to a distributed system's nodes. Finding a schedule for its task set is instead left to the nodes' schedulers. Furthermore, the task priorities in the AHS are not to be confused with the tasks' individual priorities as assigned by the respective scheduler. In being dynamic, the AHS approach also differs significantly from the problem of statically mapping tasks to the partitions in partitioned multiprocessor scheduling.

Contract Net Protocols (CNPs) [12] have been used to distribute tasks to agents in multi-agent systems. For example, [16] presents an improved CNP for task assignment, also employing self-healing capabilities and task priorities. However, contrarily to the AHS, it is neither completely decentralized nor can it guarantee hard time bounds, hindering its use in real-time systems.

A CNP-based task allocation algorithm for a Wireless Sensor Network (WSN) is employed in [5]. In fact, task distribution in WSNs is an active research topic and publications like [15] have even utilized self-organization to solve this problem. However, with WSNs typically having a limited energy budget per node, energy efficiency is one of the key concerns in these works rather than guaranteeing hard real-time behavior. Additionally, WSNs conceptually do not guarantee any two nodes to have a direct communication link between them as is assumed by the AHS, thus requiring different mechanisms for task distribution.

3   The Artificial Hormone System

As already explained, the *Artificial Hormone System (AHS)* is a decentralized middleware to allocate tasks in a distributed system. It works by realizing control loops based on *hormones* that are implemented by means of short digital messages. Each *processing element (PE)* in the system participates in the exchange of three basic hormone types:

Eager values indicate a PE's suitability for a specific task. In every *hormone cycle* (a run through the hormone control loop), each PE tries to make a decision upon a task to allocate. This is done by comparing its own eager value with eager values received by other PEs. If the local PE has sent the highest eager value for some task T, it has won T and may start executing it.

Suppressors are spread by PEs executing some task T. When a suppressor is received by other PEs, it will lower their eager values for this specific task. This mechanism is used to limit the number of times task T can be taken in the system.

Accelerators act antagonistic to suppressors and *increase* PEs' eager values. In contrast to suppressors that are spread globally (i.e., to all other PEs in the system), accelerators are spread locally to all PEs in the sending PE's neighborhood. This allows to send an accelerator to all tasks *related* to the executed task (i.e., tasks frequently communicated with) to further the formation of clusters of cooperating tasks on neighboring PEs, reducing the communication latency.

Figure 1 shows the AHS' hormone control loop. All tasks are automatically distributed to the available PEs: Once all tasks are assigned, the suppressors lower all eager values to 0 and no additional task instances are taken. Thus, by finding an initial task distribution by itself, the AHS is *self-configuring*.

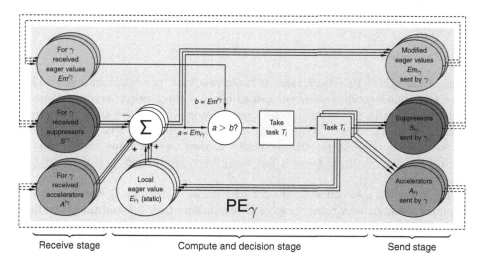

Fig. 1. The AHS' hormone control loop as executed on PE_γ. Each PE broadcasts a *modified* eager value $Em_{i\gamma}$ (calculated from its static local eager value $E_{i\gamma}$ plus received accelerators $A^{i\gamma}$ minus received suppressors $S^{i\gamma}$) for each task T_i to all other PEs. If its own modified eager value is the highest in the system, the PE may start executing T_i. As a consequence, the PE will broadcast suppressors for T_i to *all* PEs (preventing additional instances of T_i from being taken) and send accelerators for tasks *related* to T_i to *neighboring* PEs, forming clusters of cooperating tasks (called *virtual organs*).

Since the AHS is entirely decentralized, it has no single point of failure. If a PE fails, the remaining PEs will notice this failure by missing suppressor hormones. As a result, the affected tasks' eager values rise above zero again and the tasks will be re-assigned on healthy PEs. Thus, by automatically reconfiguring the system, the AHS can compensate PE failures and is therefore *self-healing*.

In addition, the AHS can guarantee hard time bounds, making it suitable for use in real-time systems: The duration of both self-configuration and self-healing can be bounded in terms of hormone cycles. Since the hormone cycles' length can be chosen arbitrarily (a lower bound is only imposed by the used communication medium's bandwidth and latency [14]), these time bounds can always be converted into absolute values. As we study a priority-based extension of the AHS in this paper, we refrain from discussing the original AHS' time bounds, the interested reader may find more information on this topic as well as further details on the AHS' operating principles in [2,4,14].

4   The Priority-Based Task Decision Strategy

As already mentioned, this paper studies an extension of the original AHS that supports *assignment priorities* and was proposed in [8]. We will thus summarize this so-called priority-based task decision strategy's key aspects in the following but refer to the aforementioned publication for further details.

4.1   Overview

Each of the AHS' PEs may take at most one task per hormone cycle. This especially allows accelerator hormones to become effective (otherwise, all tasks might be taken in the system before accelerators could have been sent, thus failing to form clusters of cooperating tasks on neighboring PEs). As a result, the so-called *task decision strategy* each PE uses to determine *which* task to take (of possibly multiple tasks it has won) has a big influence on the system's behavior.

Traditionally, a so-called *aggressive* task decision strategy [2] has been used. When employing this strategy, each PE searches its task list and takes the first task it has won.

The *priority-based* task decision strategy [8] extends this strategy: Each task in the system is given an assignment priority that is static, known to and identical on all PEs. The strategy now basically works as follows: When deciding on a task to take, each PE searches its task list in the order of *descending* priorities. If a task T is reached that the PE has won in this cycle, it may start executing it unless another PE has won a task T' of *higher* priority (and thus *might* start to execute T' in the current hormone cycle). In this case, the decision on T (as well as all tasks of *lower* priority than T') is postponed (and will automatically be re-evaluated in the next hormone cycle). This condition can easily be checked by monitoring the eager values sent in the system.

As a result, a task T cannot be assigned in the system unless all tasks of *higher* priority are already assigned. This is in contrast to the aggressive task decision strategy that assigned all tasks in a nondeterministic order.

4.2   Time Bounds

Similar to the aggressive strategy it is based on, the priority-based strategy can guarantee hard time bounds for the duration of the system's initial self-configuration and self-healing:

Theorem 1. *Let m denote the number of tasks in the system and P the set of their priorities.*

Then, the self-configuration is completed after at most $m + |P| - 1$ hormone cycles, assuming no parallel self-healing takes place.

Proof. See [8] for details. The proof idea is that each task has to be won by some PE (as one sent eager value must be the greatest among all PEs). Since each PE actively searches for tasks it has won and takes at most one task per hormone cycle, no more than m cycles are required to assign m Tasks.

However, due to the way the hormone cycle is implemented, one delay cycle occurs in which no task can be assigned in the system after the *last* task of each priority has been assigned: In a hormone cycle i, each PE has to send its modified eager values before receiving the other PEs' suppressors for cycle i. Thus, it has to rely on the suppressors from cycle $i - 1$ to calculate its eager values. Therefore, suppose some task T has been taken in cycle $i-1$ by PE_α. All other PEs will still send a positive modified eager value for T in cycle i (because they have not yet received PE_α's suppressor from cycle i that would reduce their eager values to 0). As a result, from the exchanged eager values, it *appears* that some PE_β has won T in cycle i until PE_α's suppressor is finally received. If T was the last task of its priority to be assigned, no other task can be assigned in cycle i, causing one cycle delay.

Since there are $|P|$ different priorities in the system, $|P| - 1$ delay cycles have to be considered in the worst case.   □

Theorem 2. *Let m_f denote the number of tasks that were running on a failing PE, P_f the set of their priorities and a the number of hormone cycles required to notice the PE failure.*

Then, the self-healing is completed after at most $m_f + |P_f| - 1 + a$ hormone cycles, assuming neither parallel self-healing nor self-configuration take place and the remaining PEs' combined capacities suffice to take all m_f tasks.

Proof. The PE failure is noticed after at most a hormone cycles (by missing suppressor hormones). The following re-assignment can be regarded as a self-configuration with m_f tasks and $|P_f|$ priorities, thus the bound from Theorem 1 applies.   □

Note that these bounds degenerate to $2m - 1$ resp. $2m_f - 1 + a$ hormone cycles if all m resp. m_f tasks have different priorities. This is especially important for self-healing: In general, P_f resp. $|P_f|$ is dependent on the actual distribution of tasks to the PEs and is thus hard to predict. In fact, [8] only examined the time bounds in these degenerated forms to obtain the absolute worst case possible for this reason while this paper uses the more general forms.

5   Evaluating of the Priority-Based Strategy

After having recapitulated the priority-based task decision strategy, we will now evaluate its behavior, especially with regard to its time bounds. For this reason, we implemented the strategy in an AHS simulator [3] that performs a cycle-accurate simulation of the real AHS middleware.

The self-configuration capabilities are evaluated in the following section while Sect. 5.2 presents the evaluation of self-healing.

5.1   Evaluation of Self-configuration

Figure 2 shows the number of active tasks in the system over time during a self-configuration. There exist $m = 20$ tasks with $|P| = 5$ different priorities ranging from 1 (lowest) to 5 (highest) with four tasks each per priority that were distributed to five PEs. Before we discuss the depicted behavior, we will first clarify the semantics of this diagram as well as all following ones.

Task Diagram Semantics. The time axis is given in hormone cycles since the initialization of the AHS simulator. The vertical axis shows the number of active tasks at the *end* of each hormone cycle, stacked per priority. Thus, a value of n active tasks at $t = i$ hormone cycles means that there were n tasks active at the *end* of cycle i. For example, consider the step from 0 to 1 at $t = 2$ hormone cycles in Fig. 2: At the end of hormone cycle 1, there were no active tasks, while there was one active task at the end of hormone cycle 2. This task must have been taken by some PE at some instant *during* that cycle, but the diagram does not show the precise point of time.

Self-configuration with $m = 20$ and $|P| = 5$. We can now analyze the behavior shown in Fig. 2. During hormone cycles 0 and 1, no task allocation occurs as these cycles are used by the AHS to synchronize its PEs (cf. [4]). Therefore, these cycles are not included in the time bound from Theorem 1, which is consistent with the previously published bounds (cf. [2]).

Thus, the self-configuration starts with the assignment of the first task in hormone cycle 2. After assigning one task per hormone cycle, the last task of the highest priority 5 is assigned during cycle 5 while no task is assigned in cycle 6, making it a delay cycle as predicted by Theorem 1. This pattern continues for the lower priorities 4 and 3. Afterwards, the lowest priorities 2 and 1 are assigned successively. For these two priorities, two tasks each were simultaneously assigned in the system (by different PEs) during hormone cycles 17, 18, 20 and 21. This acceleration of the task assignment in comparison to the higher priorities is due to accelerators as we defined some of the tasks to be related: Initially, there is only a *single* PE sending the highest eager value for *all* tasks of the current priority being assigned (and thus only a single task assignment happening per cycle). However, after a sufficient amount of tasks are assigned, enough accelerator hormones have accumulated so that different PEs each have the highest eager value for *different* tasks. This allows to assign more than one task in the system per hormone cycle.

Since the first of the $m = 20$ tasks was assigned during cycle 2 and the last during cycle 21, the whole self-configuration took $21 - 2 + 1 = 20$ hormone cycles while Theorem 1 estimated at most $m + |P| - 1 = 20 + 5 - 1 = 24$ hormone cycles. The difference of four cycles is due to the discussed speedup caused by accelerators.

This evaluation run thus shows that the priority-based AHS extension not only assigned all tasks in the expected order of descending priorities, but also required no more hormone cycles than predicted by Theorem 1.

Self-configuration with $m = 64$ and $|P| = 16$. Figure 3 shows a similar scenario with $m = 64$ tasks evenly partitioned into $|P| = 16$ priorities that were distributed to 16 PEs by the AHS. Again, it can be observed that all tasks are assigned in the order of descending priorities (with no defined order for tasks of the same priority imposed). The delay cycles that each occur before the first assignment of the next lowest priority level are again clearly visible. At first, there is at most one task assigned per priority, similar to the previous scenario. Later on, sometimes multiple task assignments take place simultaneously: For example, two tasks each are assigned in cycles 22 and 23 while three tasks each are assigned in cycles 25 and 67. This effect is again due to the influence of accelerators as will be seen in the next evaluation setting.

The self-configuration started in cycle 2 and was completed at the end of cycle 68 and thus took a total of 67 hormone cycles. This is again lower than the prediction of $m + |P| - 1 = 64 + 16 - 1 = 79$ hormone cycles as given by Theorem 1.

Self-configuration with $m = 64$ and $|P| = 16$, without Accelerators. To illustrate the influence of accelerators, we repeated the previous evaluation with a minor adjustment: All task relationships were removed, effectively preventing the AHS from exchanging any accelerator hormones (and thus not forming any clusters of related tasks).

The resulting self-configuration behavior is shown in Fig. 4. While being mostly similar to the previous self-configuration shown in Fig. 3, it can clearly be seen that at most one task is assigned in the system per hormone cycle. As a result, the self-configuration takes longer than the previous one, validating the claim that simultaneous task assignments are due to accelerators.

Beginning in cycle 2 and ending in cycle 80, the self-configuration took 79 hormone cycles, exactly reaching the time bound as given by Theorem 1.

Self-configuration with $m = |P| = 15$. As a final evaluation setting for the AHS' self-configuration, we decided to examine the edge case where all tasks have different priorities (thus, $m = |P|$ holds). Figure 5 shows the self-configuration for 15 tasks with 15 different priorities that were distributed to four PEs. It can clearly be seen that a delay cycle occurs after *every* task assignment as could be expected from previous considerations: Since simultaneous assignments of tasks are only possible for tasks of the same priority, at most one task can be assigned in the system per hormone cycle. Thus, it comes as no surprise that

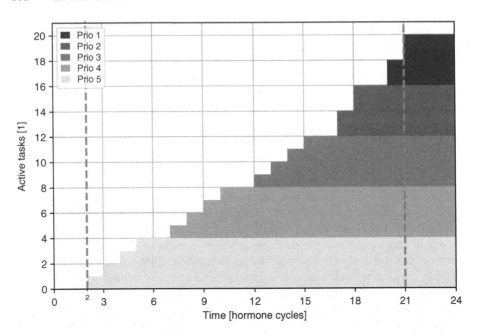

Fig. 2. Self-configuration with $m = 20$ tasks having $|P| = 5$ different priorities, on five PEs

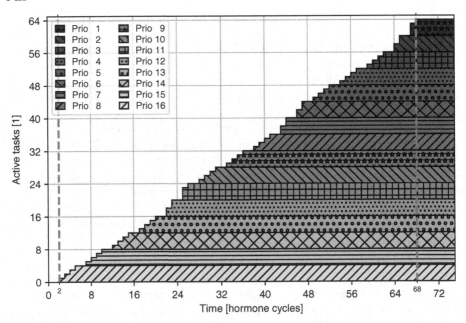

Fig. 3. Self-configuration with $m = 64$ tasks having $|P| = 16$ different priorities, on 16 PEs

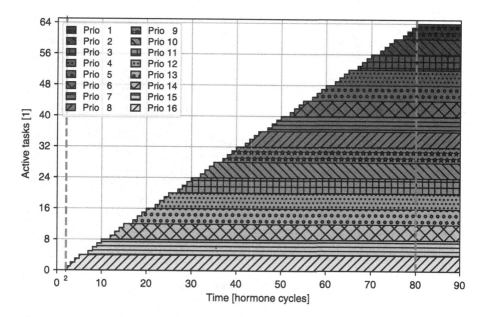

Fig. 4. Self-configuration scenario from Fig. 3 with $m = 64$ tasks having $|P| = 16$ different priorities, but with disabled accelerators, on 16 PEs

the figure applies to both the self-configuration with and without accelerators: No accelerator-induced speedup by simultaneous task assignments is possible, so the behavior is identical in both cases.

In this scenario, the self-configuration was finished at the end of cycle 30 and thus took a total of 29 hormone cycles, again exactly reaching the time bound of $m + |P| - 1 = 15 + 15 - 1 = 29$ hormone cycles as stated by Theorem 1.

Conclusion. We have evaluated the AHS' priority-based self-configuration capabilities using some example scenarios of different scales. They not only showed that all tasks are assigned in the expected order of descending priorities but also confirmed the theoretical worst-case time bound of $m + |P| - 1$ hormone cycles as given by Theorem 1. The delay cycles that occur after the last task of each priority is assigned were clearly visible in the diagrams. While for some scenarios, the self-configuration was completed faster than predicted (which is due to a speed-up caused by accelerator hormones), other scenarios exactly reached the worst-case time bound. As a result, this bound is actually a *tight* upper bound.

In the following, we will evaluate the AHS' self-healing behavior.

5.2   Evaluation of Self-healing

Since self-healing primarily consists of noticing a PE failure (through suppressor hormones no longer being sent by this PE) followed by a self-configuration of

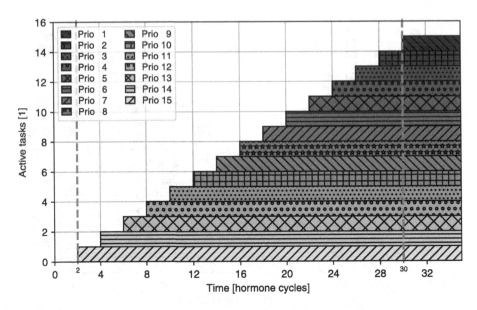

Fig. 5. Self-configuration with $m = 15$ tasks having $|P| = 15$ different priorities, on four PEs

the affected tasks, we will primarily focus on the timing of this failure detection and otherwise enforce the worst case by disabling all accelerators.

Noticing a PE Failure. The worst-case time required to notice a PE failure is said to be at most $a = 2$ hormone cycles [8]. Figure 6 shows two similar self-healing scenarios to validate this claim. These utilize a total of $m = 20$ tasks of three different priorities (eight tasks each with priorities 3 and 2 and four tasks with priority 1) running on four PEs; the initial self-configuration (that behaved exactly as predicted by Theorem 1) is not shown.

In Fig. 6a, $PE_{(1,1)}$ fails just *after* sending its hormones in cycle 40. As a result, its $m_f = 5$ tasks with $|P_f| = 3$ different priorities are no longer running on any PE at the end of cycle 40. Due to the way the AHS is currently implemented, the PE failure is recognized no earlier than in cycle 42: The suppressors $PE_{(1,1)}$ sent in cycle 40 are still used by the other PEs during cycle 41 until they have completely vanished in cycle 42. This is obviously the worst case failure detection time. In consequence, the first task re-assignment happens in this cycle and all failed tasks are re-assigned in the correct order of descending task priorities. The whole self-healing takes 9 hormone cycles as predicted by Theorem 2: $a = 2$ cycles are required to notice the PE failure, followed by $m_f + |P_f| - 1 = 7$ cycles to re-assign the affected tasks. Thus, together with the evaluations carried out for self-configuration, this result validates the worst-case time bound of self-healing.

In contrast, Fig. 6b shows the same scenario with a subtle difference: Here, $PE_{(1,1)}$ fails *before* sending its hormones in cycle 40. This is obviously the best

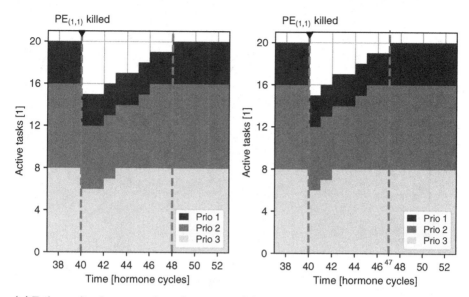

(a) Failure *after* hormones have been sent   (b) Failure *before* hormones have been sent

Fig. 6. Self-healing after failure of $PE_{(1,1)}$ in hormone cycle 40 at different instants

case for failure detection: Since no hormones have been sent in cycle 40, the other PEs will already notice the failure in the next hormone cycle. As a result, the first task re-assignment happens in cycle 41. Apart from this single saved hormone cycle, the self-healing behaves exactly as previously described since all other parameters and affected tasks are identical.

As a result, a PE failure is noticed after at least one hormone cycle and at most $a = 2$ hormone cycles.

Influence of the Number of Remaining PEs. Although the previous evaluation already confirmed the theoretical worst-case time bound, it turns out that the time required for task (re-)assignment is actually dependent on the number of (remaining) PEs participating in the process as well. Consider the situation shown in Fig. 7. Here, ten tasks exist that all have different priorities ranging from 1 to 10.

At the beginning, three PEs are executing these ten tasks. In cycle 30, $PE_{(1,1)}$ fails (at the worst-case point of time, i.e., just after sending its hormones) and two healthy PEs remain. The self-healing takes 9 hormone cycles as predicted by Theorem 2 for $m_f = |P_f| = 4$ and $a = 2$.

However, in cycle 50, $PE_{(2,1)}$ fails (also at the worst-case point of time during the cycle), resulting in a second self-healing that takes 7 hormone cycles. However, this is lower than the prediction of 11 cycles for $m_f = |P_f| = 5$ and $a = 2$: No delay cycles have occurred after the complete assignment of each priority

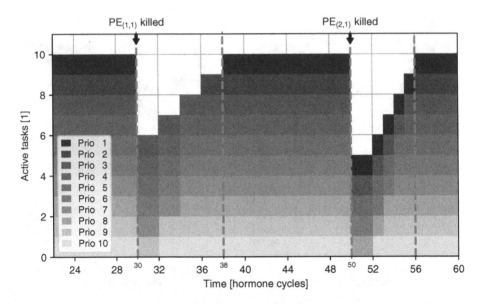

Fig. 7. System self-healing after two subsequent PE failures

level. As a result, the second self-healing is actually completed *faster* than the first one even though one additional task had to be re-assigned.

Since all other parameters were similar in both self-healing situations, the omission of the delay cycles must be caused by the fact that only a single remaining healthy PE participates in the second self-healing. This observation will be explained and exploited in the next section in order to improve the worst-case time bound in such cases.

6   Improving the Self-healing Time Bound

Although the evaluations showed that the time bounds of self-configuration and self-healing can be hit exactly in many cases, we also saw that self-healing can be finished significantly faster than predicted if only a single healthy PE remained since no delay cycles occur (cf. second self-healing in Fig. 7). This observation can be used to generalize the time bound of self-healing in this edge case:

Theorem 3. *Let m_f denote the number of tasks that were running on a failing PE, P_f the set of their priorities and a the number of hormone cycles required to notice the PE failure. Furthermore, let $v \geq 1$ denote the number of remaining healthy PEs.*

Then, the self-healing is completed after at most

$$\begin{cases} m_f & + a, & v = 1 \\ m_f + |P_f| - 1 + a, & v > 1 \end{cases} \quad hormone \ cycles,$$

assuming neither parallel self-healing nor self-configuration take place and the v remaining PEs' combined capacities suffice to take all m_f tasks.

Proof. The delay cycles occur because some PEs erroneously send a positive modified eager value since they are currently oblivious of another PE having taken some task T in the previous cycle. However, if only one healthy PE remains, there are no other PEs sending such a spurious eager value. Thus, no delay cycles occur in this case. Otherwise, the proofs of Theorem 1 and Theorem 2 apply. □

This bound enables a better estimate of a self-healing's duration if only a single healthy PE remains; otherwise, it is identical to Theorem 2.

Obviously, the time bound for the system's initial self-configuration could similarly be generalized. However, the use of a *distributed* middleware like the AHS for a system consisting of only a *single* PE is dubious, which is the reason we refrained from doing so.

7 Conclusion

In this paper, we evaluated a priority-based extension to the AHS middleware. Different self-configuration and self-healing scenarios were evaluated. The system's behavior generally confirmed the theoretical worst-case time bounds, although we derived an improved bound for self-healing if only a single healthy processing element remains in the system.

In future work, we plan to conduct research on the AHS' behavior if the communication medium is unreliable: Currently, the theoretical analyses assume all packets to be delivered correctly. Although empirical evidence suggests that a limited degree of communication failures is handled quite well by the AHS, we plan to factor in such reliability issues during the theoretical analysis, along with developing AHS improvements to improve its resilience.

References

1. Brinkschulte, U., Fastnacht, F.: Applying the concept of artificial DNA and hormone system to a low-performance automotive environment. In: Schoeberl, M., Hochberger, C., Uhrig, S., Brehm, J., Pionteck, T. (eds.) ARCS 2019. LNCS, vol. 11479, pp. 87–99. Springer, Cham (2019). https://doi.org/10.1007/978-3-030-18656-2_7
2. Brinkschulte, U., Pacher, M.: An agressive strategy for an artificial hormone system to minimize the task allocation time. In: 2012 IEEE 15th International Symposium on Object/Component/Service-Oriented Real-Time Distributed Computing Workshops. pp. 188–195. IEEE, Shenzhen, April 2012. https://doi.org/10.1109/ISORCW.2012.40
3. Brinkschulte, U., Pacher, M., von Renteln, A.: Towards an artificial hormone system for self-organizing real-time task allocation. In: Obermaisser, R., Nah, Y., Puschner, P., Rammig, F.J. (eds.) SEUS 2007. LNCS, vol. 4761, pp. 339–347. Springer, Heidelberg (2007). https://doi.org/10.1007/978-3-540-75664-4_34

4. Brinkschulte, U., Pacher, M., von Renteln, A., Betting, B.: Organic real-time middleware. In: Higuera-Toledano, M.T., Brinkschulte, U., Rettberg, A. (eds.) Self-Organization in Embedded Real-Time Systems, pp. 179–208. Springer, New York (2013). https://doi.org/10.1007/978-1-4614-1969-3_9

5. Chen, L., Xue-song, Q., Yang, Y., Gao, Z., Qu, Z.: The contract net based task allocation algorithm for wireless sensor network. In: 2012 IEEE Symposium on Computers and Communications (ISCC), pp. 600–604, July 2012. https://doi.org/10.1109/ISCC.2012.6249362

6. Fohler, G., Gala, G., Pérez, Daniel, G., Claire, Pagetti: evaluation of DREAMS resource management solutions on a mixed-critical demonstrator. In: ERTS 2018. 9th European Congress on Embedded Real Time Software and Systems (ERTS 2018), Toulouse, France, January 2018

7. Guan, N., Stigge, M., Yi, W., Yu, G.: Fixed-priority multiprocessor scheduling with Liu and Layland's utilization bound. In: 2010 16th IEEE Real-Time and Embedded Technology and Applications Symposium, pp. 165–174. IEEE, Stockholm, April 2010. https://doi.org/10.1109/RTAS.2010.39

8. Hutter, E., Brinkschulte, U.: Towards a priority-based task distribution strategy for an artificial hormone system. In: Brinkmann, A., Karl, W., Lankes, S., Tomforde, S., Pionteck, T., Trinitis, C. (eds.) ARCS 2020. LNCS, vol. 12155, pp. 69–81. Springer, Cham (2020). https://doi.org/10.1007/978-3-030-52794-5_6

9. Müller-Schloer, C., Tomforde, S.: Organic Computing – Technical Systems for Survival in the Real World. AS, Springer, Cham (2017). https://doi.org/10.1007/978-3-319-68477-2

10. Orlov, S., Korte, M., Oszwald, F., Vollmer, P.: Automatically reconfigurable actuator control for reliable autonomous driving functions (AutoKonf). In: 10th International Munich Chassis Symposium 2019. Tech Plus, Chassis (2019). https://doi.org/10.1007/978-3-658-26435-2_26

11. Schmeck, H.: Organic computing - A new vision for distributed embedded systems. In: Eighth IEEE International Symposium on Object-Oriented Real-Time Distributed Computing (ISORC 2005), pp. 201–203 (2005). https://doi.org/10.1109/ISORC.2005.42

12. Smith, R.G.: The contract net protocol: high-level communication and control in a distributed problem solver. IEEE Trans. Comput. **C-29**(12), 1104–1113 (1980). https://doi.org/10.1109/TC.1980.1675516

13. Sun, Y., Lipari, G., Guan, N., Yi, W.: Improving the response time analysis of global fixed-priority multiprocessor scheduling. In: 2014 IEEE 20th International Conference on Embedded and Real-Time Computing Systems and Applications, pp. 1–9, August 2014. https://doi.org/10.1109/RTCSA.2014.6910543

14. von Renteln, A., Brinkschulte, U., Pacher, M.: The artificial hormone system—An organic middleware for self-organising real-time task allocation. In: Müller-Schloer, C., Schmeck, H., Ungerer, T. (eds.) Organic Computing — A Paradigm Shift for Complex Systems. ASYS, vol. 1, pp. 369–384. Springer, Basel (2011). https://doi.org/10.1007/978-3-0348-0130-0_24

15. Yin, X., Dai, W., Li, B., Chang, L., Li, C.: Cooperative task allocation in heterogeneous wireless sensor networks. Int. J. Distrib. Sensor Networks **13**(10), 15501447 (2017). https://doi.org/10.1177/1550147717735747

16. Zhang, J., Wang, G., Song, Y.: Task assignment of the improved contract net protocol under a multi-agent system. Algorithms **12**(4), 70 (2019). https://doi.org/10.3390/a12040070

Low Power Design

Streamlining the OpenMP Programming Model on Ultra-Low-Power Multi-core MCUs

Fabio Montagna[1], Giuseppe Tagliavini[1(✉)], Davide Rossi[1], Angelo Garofalo[1], and Luca Benini[1,2]

[1] University of Bologna, Bologna, Italy
giuseppe.tagliavini@unibo.it
[2] ETH Zürich, Zürich, Switzerland

Abstract. High-level programming models aim at exploiting hardware parallelism and reducing software development costs. However, their adoption on ultra-low-power multi-core microcontroller (MCU) platforms requires minimizing the overheads of work-sharing constructs on fine-grained parallel regions. This work tackles this challenge by proposing OMP-SPMD, a streamlined approach for parallel computing enabling the OpenMP syntax for the Single-Program Multiple-Data (SPMD) paradigm. To assess the performance improvement, we compare our solution with two alternatives: a baseline implementation of the OpenMP runtime based on the fork-join paradigm (OMP-base) and a version leveraging hardware-specific optimizations (OPM-opt). We benchmarked these libraries on a Parallel Ultra-Low Power (PULP) MCU, highlighting that hardware-specific optimizations improve OMP-base performance up to 69%. At the same time, OMP-SPMD leads to an extra improvement up to 178%.

Keywords: Ultra-low-power multi-core MCU · Parallel programming · OpenMP · SPMD

1 Introduction

In recent years, ultra-low-power (ULP) multi-core microcontroller units (MCUs) have been introduced in low-cost, low-power IoT end-nodes and embedded systems markets [21, 22]. These platforms can provide more than one order of magnitude increase in energy efficiency with respect to high-performance single-core MCUs and carry out the computational power to support the execution of complex workloads. As a representative of this class of MCUs, the PULP platform [21] is an open-source, scalable, and energy-efficient multi-core architecture tailored for sub-mW deeply embedded applications and IoT end-nodes.

Effective programming of these architectures requires the adoption of high-level parallel programming models. However, to achieve high efficiency, we need to tune runtimes to their specific characteristics and tightly limited

© Springer Nature Switzerland AG 2021
C. Hochberger et al. (Eds.): ARCS 2021, LNCS 12800, pp. 167–182, 2021.
https://doi.org/10.1007/978-3-030-81682-7_11

resources. First, exploiting the ULP features of the hardware architecture can lead to an efficient implementation of the programming model. For instance, the PULP platform includes specialized hardware for accelerating key parallel patterns (e.g., barriers and locks). Second, parallel programming models imply unavoidable overheads to distribute the workload and orchestrate communication/synchronization among the workers. The overhead minimization in the case of fine-grained parallelism is a key challenge on these platforms. For instance, typical applications have small working sets implying relatively small parallel regions (just a few tens of cycles), making it difficult to amortize overheads.

Fork-join parallelization and Single-Program Multiple-Data (SPMD) are two common paradigms in parallel programming. In the fork/join paradigm, the program execution starts with a single thread, exploiting parallelism recruiting additional threads when a parallel region is encountered (*fork*). When the parallel region ends, only the initial thread continues the program execution sequentially after synchronization (*join*). A well-known programming model based on the fork/join paradigm is OpenMP [9,10], which allows exploiting parallelism through directives resolved at compile-time into low-level calls for a specific runtime library. With the SPMD paradigm, all the cores start the program execution simultaneously. CUDA and OpenCL programming models adopt this approach on Single-Instruction Multiple-Thread (SIMT) hardware platforms such as GPUs. However, the CUDA support is specific to NVidia platforms, while OpenCL is more portable but requires a total code refactoring. In the domain of embedded systems, it is a common practice to have low-level libraries providing SPMD-compliant primitives providing core identification and synchronization [6,14,24].

In this work, we propose a novel approach based on the SPMD paradigm, leveraging the intuitive front-end of the OpenMP programming model to hide the increase in code complexity. Moreover, we present a comprehensive comparison to assess the benefits of the proposed approach. We compared two variants of the OpenMP runtimes: the first one (*OMP-base*) is a baseline implementation for an embedded MCU-class target, with the aim to reduce the code footprint and the execution time; the second one (*OMP-opt*) is fully optimized to take advantage of the PULP hardware support for core idling and synchronization. We considered a set of Digital Signal Processing (DSP) kernels and a full application that are highly representative of the embedded DSP domain and cover a wide range of typical parallelization schemes.

The main contributions of this paper are:

- the proposal of dedicated compile-time transformations to hide the increase in code complexity deriving by adopting the low-level SPMD runtime, using the OpenMP directives as a front-end (*OMP-SPMD*).
- a comprehensive comparison between the *OMP-base* runtime, a optimization of the OpenMP runtime (*OMP-opt*) for an embedded target yet preserving the fork/join behavior, and the proposed approach (*OMP-SPMD* - preserving the OpenMP syntax);

– a comparison between two different programming paradigms (fork/join and SPMD) in the domain of ULP parallel MCUs, revealing that the *OMP-SPMD* approach leads to performance improvement in terms of execution time and energy consumption of up to 178% compared to the native fork/join approach adopted for OpenMP.

We performed the experiments on a prototype implementation of the open-source PULP platform targeting a cycle-accurate FPGA emulator. Experimental evidence highlights that the *OMP-opt* runtime improves performance up to 69% w.r.t. to the baseline and up to 178% w.r.t. the proposed *OMP-SPMD* runtime.

2   Related Work

Parallel programming models provide abstractions to execute applications over multi- and many-core computing platforms [5]. They differ for many aspects (e.g., data organization, workload distribution, scheduling, communication, and synchronization), which imply a trade-off between full transparency for the programmer and rewriting the code from scratch. OpenMP is a widespread programming model for shared-memory platforms, and it has already been demonstrated in the context of embedded systems. In this domain, a common solution is to re-implement its semantics on top of resource-constrained middleware or even bare-metal [3,12]. The main programming models for general-purpose computing on graphics processing units (GPGPU) computing (i.e., CUDA [14] and OpenCL [6]) are based on the SPMD paradigm. While CUDA is specific for NVidia platforms, OpenCL has been adopted in the domain of heterogeneous embedded systems [25]. In the context of homogeneous multi-core systems, the adoption of SPMD over Multiple-Program Multiple-Data (MPMD) can be beneficial to increase the speed-ups on homogeneous multi-core systems due to factors such as the improved locality for code and data, the reduction of the memory footprint and synchronization overheads [4,23]. In this work, we compare the two paradigms to understand which one is more suitable for the multi-core MCU target, considering the main factors impacting this investigation.

The lowering of OpenMP directives consists of a set of code transformations that collect the affected code into new functions (outlining) and insert calls to runtime functions. In the typical case, this process is performed by compilers at an early stage of the front-end (e.g., GCC and clang/LLVM). This approach allows a runtime designer to map OpenMP directives into runtime calls, implementing other paradigms w.r.t. fork/join. Pereira *et al.* [16] describe a framework that automatically converts program sections annotated with OpenMP 4.x directives into OpenCL kernels. This design goes in the direction of our work, but we perform a step further, considering the severe constraints of the ULP MCUs, requiring specific optimizations.

The OpenMP specification includes a `simd` directive that can be applied to a loop with the intent to map multiple iterations on a set of instructions exposing SIMD semantics. For instance, this construct can be used to exploit the packed-SIMD instructions available on our target platform to perform operations on vectors with 8-bits or 16-bits elements. However, our approach based on the SPMD paradigm is more general as it is not limited to a program part (i.e., loops) but enables a global optimization of the whole program.

3   Background

3.1   PULP Platform

In this paper, we target a ULP multi-core MCU based on the open-source PULP platform. Using the open-source RTL, we instantiated a cycle-accurate emulation image of a multi-core cluster on a Xilinx VCU118 FPGA [19]. PULP is a multi-core programmable processor that features a RISC-V based core for control functions and a cluster (Fig. 1) of 8 RISC-V based cores for energy-efficient DSP. These cores, namely RI5CY [7], implement a 4 stage in-order single-issue pipeline, supporting the RV32IMC instruction set, plus extensions for optimized DSP and machine learning [18]. The platform features two memory levels, a 512 kB L2 memory (15 cycle latency for load/store operations) outside the cluster and a single cycle latency, multi-bank, 64 kB L1 memory inside the cluster, which enables shared-memory parallel programming. The cluster also includes four floating-point units (FPUs) shared among the cluster cores. The *event unit* (EU) is a hardware block introduced to support fine-grained parallelism with minimum overhead [8]. This unit accelerates the execution of data-parallel patterns (e.g., thread dispatching, barrier semantic, and critical regions) and enables power-saving policies to put the unused cores in idle state.

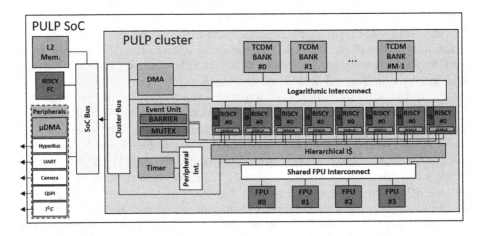

Fig. 1. Top-level view of the PULP architecture.

3.2   Parallel Programming Paradigms

OpenMP is one of the most adopted high-level programming models in different computing domains, from High-Performance Computing (HPC) to embedded systems. It makes use of directives (defined for C/C++ and Fortran languages), which are resolved at compile-time into low-level calls for a dedicated runtime library, such as GNU libgomp [9] or LLVM OpenMP library [10]. OpenMP relies on a fork/join parallel execution model. The execution of the program starts with a single thread (called *master*). When a parallel construct is encountered, $n - 1$ additional threads (*workers*) are recruited into a parallel team. *Work-sharing constructs* are employed to specify how the parallel workload is distributed among the threads. When the parallel region ends, all the threads reach a barrier for synchronization. Then, the master thread continues its execution sequentially.

The second approach considered in this paper adopts the SPMD paradigm, using a set of primitives for control flow handling and inter-core synchronization. In contrast to the fork/join paradigm adopted by OpenMP, where only the master core starts executing the program until the execution flow encounters a parallel region, all the cores start executing the same code. The cores follow the same execution flow unless the programmer explicitly indicates that a subset of cores must execute a specific region; parallel workloads are split among cores (based on the core number) and run concurrently on different data. Moreover, the synchronization points and the allocation of data variables in shared or private areas must be explicit. As the result of a preliminary analysis, the approach based on the SPMD runtime implies more programmer effort than OpenMP since it requires modifying the source code. Nevertheless, its adoption guarantees a higher control on the parallelization process and, in general, less overhead compared to a traditional OpenMP runtime. As introduced in Sect. 1, the adoption of compile-time code transformations can make this effort totally transparent to programmers. To enable automatic code transformations at compile-time, we need to introduce a set of *SPMD helper functions* that are described in the next section.

4   Deriving the SPMD-OMP Model

4.1   Low-Level Software Support for Parallel Computing

This work focuses on the work-sharing constructs that are more frequently used to parallelize code in the embedded DSP domain, illustrating the OpenMP directives, the SPMD helper functions, and their mapping. The presented runtimes are based on a common lightweight Hardware Abstraction Layer (HAL), which provides minimal access to platform features in the absence of a full-fledged operating system. This design choice enables a consistent reduction of the overhead and guarantees higher energy efficiency. Getting as much parallelism as possible out from an algorithm is not straightforward and usually requires a significant effort from programmers.

Table 1. List of the OpenMP directives and SPMD helper functions with a brief usage description.

OpenMP directives	SPMD helper functions	Description
#pragma omp for	SPMD_PARLOOP(start, end, from, to, step)	Worksharing construct to distribute Loop iterations among threads
#pragma omp for \ schedule(static, chunk)	SPMD_PARLOOP_SCHED(start, end, from, to, step, chunk) SPMD_PARLOOP_STEP(step, chunk)	Worksharing construct to distribute Loop iterations among threads
#pragma omp for \ reduction(op:var)	SPDM_PARLOOP_REDUCTION_OP(var, temp_vars) reduction_func(op_f);	Performs a reduction on variable With the operator (op)
#pragma omp master #pragma omp single	IS_CORE_0, ...	Identifies a portion of the code Executed only by a core
#pragma omp barrier	spmd_barrier();	All the threads wait the other for synchronization
#pragma omp critical	spmd_critical_enter(); spmd_critical_exit();	Critical section

4.2   Work-Sharing Constructs

Table 1 reports the OpenMP directives considered in this work and the equivalent SPMD helper functions. In OpenMP, the *#pragma omp for* directive is placed before a loop, informing the compiler that each loop iteration is independent of the others and, thus, executable concurrently. The workload is divided into equal chunks using the static scheduling (default option), where the chunk size is equal to the number of iterations over the number of cores involved in the parallel region. There is an implicit barrier at the end of the loop (unless a *nowait* clause is specified). In the SPMD programming model, the helper macro *SPMD_PARLOOP* computes the loop bounds (based on chunk size and core id) used to distribute the iterations on the available cores. In this case, barrier semantics must be explicit (e.g., calling *spmd_barrier*). The *#pragma omp for* directive also provides a *schedule(static, chunk)* clause to specify a custom chunk size. In SPMD, we can obtain the same behavior using the helper macros *SPMD_PARLOOP_SCHED* and *SPMD_PARLOOP_STEP* to compute the loop bounds (start and end) and the iteration step.

OpenMP supports loop reductions using the *reduction(op:var)* clause. A shared variable performs an accumulation based on a standard operator (i.e., $+, -, *$). In this case, OpenMP runtimes adopt a mechanism to avoid race conditions due to multiple accesses on the shared variable from multiple cores. In SPMD, a shared array must be explicitly declared before calling the helper function. In this way, each core can store the intermediate accumulation values into a dedicated array element (usually the one corresponding to the core id). At the end of the computation, the master core accumulates all the partial results in the target variable. A set of macros *SPMD_PARLOOP_REDUCTION_OP* perform the final reduction step based on the used operator.

Most of the algorithms are not fully parallel and, hence, include sequential code regions. The *#pragma omp master/single* directives allow executing the sequential code with a single core (the master or a generic one, respectively). This directive does not feature an implicit barrier; thus, a synchronization point must be added (when needed). In the SPMD approach, the code is enclosed in an *if* block that can be accessed only by one core (e.g., the core with the id equal to 0), while the others continue the execution or can be blocked on a barrier. The id of the executing core can be checked with a set of Boolean preprocessor macros (*IS_CORE_0, ...*).

The *#pragma omp critical* OpenMP directive specifies a portion of code that must be executed from one core at a time. This directive adds a total order constraint and, consequently, reduces the program speed-up. In SPMD, we can specify a critical section enclosing a region of code between the *spmd_critical_enter* and *spmd_critical_exit* helper functions. Finally, the *#pragma omp barrier* in OpenMP and *spmd_barrier()* in SPMD synchronize all the cores before proceeding with the rest of the execution. When a core reaches a barrier, it is blocked until all the other cores reach the barrier.

4.3 Event Unit Extensions for Overhead Reduction

The *OMP-opt* runtime makes use of the EU to reduce the overhead of the *OMP-base* directives. The EU design is based on 32 level-sensitive *event lines* (per core) correlated to *event sources*. Two EU extensions, namely *barrier* and *mutex*, contain the logic to handle core-to-core signaling. The *barrier* extension includes a register describing the status of each core. When the core reaches the *barrier*, the matching bit in the status register is set. The EU generates an event when all the cores reach the barrier, interpreted as a continuation condition for the idle cores. The *mutex* extension enables mutual exclusivity supporting synchronization primitives, being a resource that can only be owned by one core at a time. Tentative accesses (try-lock semantic) are signaled in a dedicated status register. The *mutex* extension keeps track of all pending requests.

The *OMP-opt* runtime leverages the EU to reduce the overhead associated with parallel regions and barrier constructs. Opening a parallel region, the *mutex* extension enables fast and mutually exclusive access to shared data structures, and the *barrier* extension simplifies the creation of a team of threads. When encountering a barrier construct, the *barrier* extension provides seamless support for the synchronization semantic. The benefits of hardware support are evident in OpenMP-based applications employing a higher amount of work-sharing and/or synchronization directives. Contrarily, the performance gain is still negligible for embarrassingly parallel kernels.

The introduction of a new runtime based on the SPMD paradigm is justified by the fact that reducing the overhead of the *OMP-base* version through hardware support is usually not enough to approach the ideal performance of a benchmark. The intuition for this effect is related to the granularity of parallel code regions. In the case of fine-grained parallelism, the overhead required to create multiple parallel teams can be significant. Also, the overhead for the loop bound computation in different parallel regions can be reduced by applying common subexpression elimination (CSE), which is a standard optimization

```
void kmeans()                          void kmeans()
{                                      {
  // ...                                 if(core_id == 0)
  do {                                   {
    delta = 0.0f;                          // ...
    #pragma omp parallel \               }
         num_threads(NUM_CORES) \
         shared(delta) private(index)    /* Compute loop bounds */
    {                                    SPMD_PARLOOP(start, end, 0, N_OBJECTS);
      /* main computation */             SPMD_PARLOOP(start2, end2, 0, N_CLUSTERS);
      #pragma omp for reduction(+: delta)
      for (i=0; i<N_OBJECTS; i++) {      do {
        // ...                             local_delta[core_id] = 0;
      }                                    /* main computation */
                                           for (i=start; i<end; i++) {
      /* array reduction */                  // ...
      #pragma omp for nowait               }
      for (i=0; i<N_CLUSTERS; i++) {       spmd_barrier();
        for (j=0; j<NUM_CORES; j++) {      /* Reduction on delta */
          // ...                           SPMD_PARLOOP_REDUCTION_SUM(delta,
        }                                                   local_delta);
      }                                    /* array reduction */
      // ...                               for (i=start2; i<end2; i++) {
    }                                        for (j=0; j<NUM_CORES; j++) {
  } while (delta > THRESH &&                   // ...
           loop < MAX_ITERS);                }
  // ...                                   }
}                                          // ...
                                         } while (delta > THRESH &&
                                                  loop < MAX_ITERS);

                                         if(core_id == 0)
                                         {
                                           // ...
                                         }
                                       }
```

Fig. 2. Code snippet that shows a simple use of OpenMP directives (left) and SPMD helper functions (right) applied to the K-MEANS kernel.

pass in compiler toolchains. However, the code outlining for different regions in a standard fork/join runtime can make its application harder.

4.4   Mapping OpenMP Directives on the SPMD Paradigm

As a motivating example to explain our approach, Fig. 2 shows the use of the OpenMP directives (left) and the SPMD helper functions (right) to parallelize the K-MEANS kernel, included in the benchmark suite described in Sect. 5. The OpenMP version is characterized by an overhead associated with opening parallel regions. State-of-the-art solutions provide a dedicated OpenMP runtime optimized for the embedded target, intending to reduce overheads as much as possible, even not supporting some features that are considered unnecessary. However, the overhead of parallel regions cannot be reduced under a few hundred cycles. Considering the example depicted in Fig. 2, a parallel directive inside a loop can incur a significant overhead.

In the SPDM version, the code outside parallel regions requires an additional check to force sequential execution, but the overhead of this operation is negligible (maximum 3 cycles). The additional code (highlighted in bold) is functionally equivalent to the code produced by the compiler for OpenMP, so it is not a source of overhead. Moreover, additional code optimizations are possible for the computation of static loop bounds because they are in the same code block. The SPMD interface requires to provide additional parameters (*start* and *end* indices), while OpenMP totally hides these details. The transformation from OpenMP-annotated code to its SPMD variant is syntactically well-defined; consequently, it can be performed as a source-to-source translation or a direct modification to the data structures in the compiler front-end. From this perspective, Table 1 provides a map to translate the OpenMP directives into an equivalent code adopting the SPMD helper functions. In addition to these guidelines, an additional requirement derives from the main difference between for/join and SPMD paradigms: the code outside an OpenMP parallel region must be executed by core 0. This behavior can be easily enforced by adding a conditional statement to the code regions that are not annotated.

In this work, we adopted a source-to-source approach. We prototyped our methodology using ROSE [20], an open-source tool developed at Lawrence Livermore National Laboratory to enable source-to-source program analysis and transformation. ROSE produces a high-level representation of the source code based on an abstract syntax tree (AST). It provides an API to analyze and modify the AST representation to derive a modified source code. We modified the standard ROSE flow for lowering OpenMP directives as follows:

- visiting the AST structure, the code outside a parallel region is enclosed by an if statement to ensure sequential execution;
- the computation of the loop bounds for the parallel loops is performed using the SPMD helper macros, which are placed at the beginning of the helper function to promote optimizations such as CSE;
- barriers and critical regions are mapped on the related SPMD functions, replacing the call to libgomp functions.

This transformation flow is automatically applied to the OpenMP program, and any additional modification is required to the programmer. The current prototype supports the OpenMP directives used by the benchmarks, which are reported in Table 2. Future extensions are discussed in Sect. 8.

5   Benchmarks

To compare the runtimes on the target multi-core architecture, we evaluate the performance of eight benchmarks that are commonly used in DSP for feature extraction, classification, and basic linear algebra functions. Table 2 reports the OpenMP directives used to parallelize the benchmarks, their application domains, and the percentage of parallelizable code.

The Principal Component Analysis (PCA) [1] is used for compression and feature extraction. It performs an orthogonal transformation, mapping possibly correlated variables into a set of linearly uncorrelated components. It requires a

Table 2. For each benchmark, this table reports the main application domain (Domain), the OpenMP directives applied (OpenMP Dir.) and the percentage of the parallelizable code (Par. Code[%]).

Application	Domain	OpenMP Dir.	Par. Code[%]
CONV	Audio, Image, ExG	#pragma omp for	100
DWT	Audio, Image, ExG	#pragma omp for	100
		#pragma omp for schedule(static, chunk)	
		#pragma omp barrier	
FFT	Audio, Image, ExG	#pragma omp for	100
		#pragma omp barrier	
MATMUL	Audio, Image, ExG	#pragma omp for	100
PCA	ExG	#pragma omp for	95
		#pragma omp for reduction(var:oper)	
		#pragma omp master	
		#pragma omp barrier	
SVM	ExG	#pragma omp for	99
		#pragma omp master	
		#pragma omp barrier	
K-MEANS	Audio, Image, ExG	#pragma omp for	97
		#pragma omp master	
		#pragma omp barrier	
M-NORM	Audio, Image, ExG	#pragma omp for	100
		#pragma omp for reduction(var:oper)	

mix of directives (Table 2), called multiple times, to exploit parallelism, resulting in a complex parallel scheme. Another common kernel used for feature extraction is the Discrete Wavelet Transform (DWT) [11], which decomposes a signal into a different level of frequency resolutions through a bank of Low Pass (LPF) and High Pass Filters (HPF), capturing both temporal and frequency information, easily parallelizable using *#pragma omp for* directives and explicit barriers. The Fast Fourier Transform (FFT) [2] transforms a signal from the time domain to the frequency domain. The cores of the cluster work on different data, enforcing consistency with synchronization barriers. There are several variants of this algorithm; in this paper, we consider decimation-in-frequency radix-2. The Support Vector Machine (SVM) [15] is a classifier that is widely used in machine learning embedded applications. Starting from a set of support vectors (SVs) that compose a hyper-plane, it classifies unknown samples into a known class, exploiting parallelism using *#pragma omp for* and barriers. We also include an unsupervised classifier named K-Means, which can inference an unknown outcome from input vectors. The parallel scheme includes *#pragma omp for*, reduction directives, and sequential sections. The Mean-Normalization (M-Norm) is a widespread operation in Machine Learning, and it is used to transform the data such that the new output vector has zero-mean. The parallelism is exploiting using *#pragma omp for* and reductions. The last two kernels are Basic Linear Algebra Subprograms (BLAS) commonly used in DSP: matrix multiplication (MatMul) and convolution (Conv), which is the most computing-intensive kernel in Convolutional Neural Network (CNN) workload. Both of them are fully parallel, requiring *#pragma omp for* directives to split the workload among the cores and synchronization barriers.

6   Experimental Results

In this section, we present an experimental assessment executing the benchmark suite on the FPGA emulator described in Sect. 3.1. We used the hardware performance counters available on the PULP cores, which provide accurate metrics on the core operation (clock cycles, executed instructions, instruction cache misses, memory contentions, pipeline stalls, and FPU contentions). We considered the clock cycles required for the benchmark execution, varying the number of cores involved in the computation (up to 8). To evaluate the single-core performance, we considered a version of the code without the overhead from the work-sharing constructs, which are not required for sequential execution. In parallel programs, there is a structural limit to the speed-up given by Amdahl's law. For each benchmark, we computed an *Amdahl limit* by measuring the percentage of parallelizable code (reported in Table 2) and supposing no parallelization overhead. A comparison between the measured speed-ups and the ideal ones provides a quantitative metric for code parallelization.

Figure 3 depicts a comparison between real speed-ups and Amdahl limits for all runtimes. As expected, *OMP-opt* is closer than *OMP-base* to the theoretical limit, thanks to the adoption of hardware support. To provide insight, Table 3 reports execution times (in cycles, for 1 and 8 cores), gains of the new runtimes over *OMP-base*, numbers of barriers and parallel regions, and the cycles lost for hardware stalls. The stalls derive from different hardware sources: contentions in accessing the TCDM by the cores, instruction cache misses, FPU contentions, and barriers. The stalls for the parallel case consider the *OMP-SPMD* runtime.

The overhead reduction is more evident in the kernels that require more barriers or parallel regions. The *OMP-SPMD* approach further reduces the overhead for two main reasons. First, it does not require the creation of a parallel team corresponding to a parallel construct. Second, a programmer can reduce checks on parallel loop intervals by combining the boundary computations over multiple loops. For the MatMul benchmark, the choice of a specific runtime does not bring to particular improvements, as the three approaches show similar performance (very close to the Amdahl limit). The benchmark that gains the most benefit from SPMD is DWT, which shows a reduction of 69% and 178%, passing from *OMP-base* to *OMP-opt* (i.e., optimized barriers and parallel regions), and finally to *OMP-SPMD* (i.e., optimized control flow), respectively. In DWT, we have reduced the parallelization overhead by unifying the logic to compute the bounds of two parallel loops; the compiler cannot apply the same transformation to the OpenMP version because the loops are in distinct modules of the control

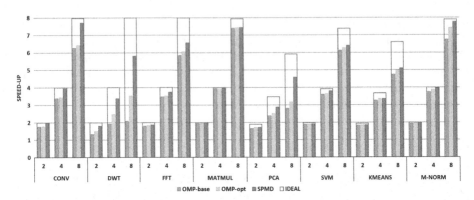

Fig. 3. Speed-ups from the parallel execution of the eight DPS benchmarks using the OMP-base, OMP-opt, and *OMP-SPMD* runtimes.

Table 3. ^a*OMP-base*, ^b*OMP-opt*, ^c*OMP-SPMD*, ^d[*OMP-base* over *OMP-opt*]/[*OMP-base* over *OMP-SPMD*] runtime (RT)[%], ^ebarriers (BR), ^fparallel regions (PR), ^g[1-core stalls (S)/8-core stalls] in kCycles.

Kernel	1 Core	8 Cores						
	kCycles	kCycles^a	kCycles^b	kCycles^c	RT[%]^d	BR^e	PR^f	S^g
CONV	136.9	21.8	21.3	17.7	2/23	1	1	0.69/0.70
DWT	24.9	11.9	7.0	4.3	69/178	27	9	0.28/0.55
FFT	228.0	39.0	37.6	34.7	4/12	13	1	3.39/3.53
MATMUL	959.3	130.4	129.0	127.5	1/2	1	1	8.40/8.41
PCA	1'173.8	417.4	321.3	255.0	30/64	206	262	33.64/35.70
SVM	29.6	4.9	4.4	4.3	11/14	1	1	3.13/3.14
K-MEANS	357.5	75.4	71.9	69.1	5/9	189	9	10.27/12.16
M-NORM	57.7	8.5	7.8	7.4	10/15	3	1	0.04/ 0.01
Application	kCycles	kCycles^a	kCycles^b	kCycles^c	RT[%]^d	BR^e	PR^f	S^g
SEIZURE DETECTION	1'230.9	459.6	390.7	256.6	18/79	450	344	31.44/35.93

flow graph (due to outlining). Consequently, the bounds are computed twice in OpenMP-based runtimes, doubling the overhead.

Varying the cores from 2 to 8, all the benchmarks (except for MatMul) approach the Amdhal limit with the 2-cores execution. For 4 and 8 cores, the speed-ups start saturating as a direct consequence of the overhead implied by the work-sharing constructs. The PCA kernel demonstrates a high benefit in using *OMP-opt* and *OMP-SPMD*. The main reason is that this kernel includes a consistent number of parallel regions and requires several barriers for synchronization. Reducing the overhead of *OMP-base* has a direct impact on performance (i.e., 30% and 64%, respectively). All the other benchmarks, including CONV, FFT, MATMUL, SVM, and M-NORM, show an improvement of up to 23%, 12%, 2%, 14%, and 15%, respectively, which is a direct consequence of the overhead reduction. The only exception is the K-MEANS kernel, which has a limited

Table 4. Energy consumption of 8-cores, based on real measurements on a silicon prototype of PULP (operative point: 110 MHz@0.8 V).

Kernel	OMP-base [μJ]	OMP-Opt [μJ]	SPMD [μJ]	Reduction [%]
Conv	3.54	3.49	3.20	1.44–9.60
DWT	1.40	1.09	0.77	22.50–45.00
FFT	6.61	6.54	6.26	1.06–5.30
MatMul	23.27	23.26	23.26	0.01–0.04
PCA	75.31	71.79	46.00	4.67–38.92
SVM	4.43	4.40	4.34	0.47–2.03
K-MEANS	12.99	12.57	12.47	3.20–4.00
M-NORM	1.43	1.37	1.34	4.09–6.29
Application	OMP-base [μJ]	OMP-Opt [μJ]	SPMD [μJ]	Reduction [%]
SEIZURE DETECTION	81.69	77.92	51.72	36.69–4.62

improvement even with many barriers and parallel regions (up to 9%). In this case, the number of hardware stalls (reported in Table 3) significantly increase with 8 cores, and this effect structurally limits the maximum speed-up. Moreover, the fine granularity of the parallel workload highly reduces the opportunities for optimizations.

Finally, we also evaluated the energy consumption of the DSP benchmarks. The estimation relies on power measurements on a fabricated prototype of Mr. Wolf [17], a PULP architecture with the same features of our FPGA emulator, running a typical high-utilization workload (matrix multiplication). Table 4 shows the results of the energy consumption for the 8-cores execution at the operating frequency of 110 MHz at 0.8 V, the optimal operating point to maximize energy efficiency. The results show a reduction of the energy consumption by up to 45% passing from *OMP-base* to *SPMD*, while the reduction from *OMP-base* to *Omp-Opt* is capped to 22.50%. The difference between the two gains provides a direct measure of the benefits of the SPMD approach w.r.t. an optimized runtime taking advantage of dedicated hardware units. There is no linear correlation between energy consumption and the variation in parallel speed-up due to the power-savings policy implied by optimizations (e.g., clock-gating).

7   Seizure Detection Application

To better evaluate the impact of our approach in a real scenario, we considered a full application taken from the biomedical field, the seizure detection processing chain [13], which aims at detecting the outcome of a seizure in subjects affected by epilepsy. This application contains three of the benchmarks included in this exploration, more precisely, PCA, DWT, and SVM. As shown in the previous section, these benchmarks demonstrate different parallel schemes and behaviors depending on the chosen runtime. Table 3 presents results in performance and speed-ups. In particular, passing from *OMP-base* to *OMP-opt*, we can see an improvement of 18%, further increased to 79% passing to *OMP-SPMD*, with a speed-up improvement from 2.7× to 4.8×. Table 4 also reports the total energy consumption of this application.

8   Conclusion

In this work, we propose a highly streamlined, low-overhead approach based on the SPMD paradigm as an alternative to the standard OpenMP approach (based on fork/join) to target the emerging ULP multi-core MCUs. We compared two alternative OpenMP runtimes, a baseline implementation suitable for a generic embedded target and a fully optimized version taking advantage of dedicated hardware support for core idling and synchronization, focusing on the most used work-sharing constructs. We evaluated the performance using a prototype implementation of the PULP platform on an FPGA emulator, using a set of benchmarks from the DSP domain and a full application. We demonstrated that the optimized OpenMP runtime improves performance by up to 69% compared to the baseline; the SPMD approach leads to a further improvement (up to 178%), approaching the maximum achievable speed-up envisioned by Amdahl's law, with an average distance of 18%. The benefits of the *OMP-SPMD* over the *OMP-base* programming model also emerge from the energy consumption, with a gain by up to 82%. To get the best of both worlds, we introduce compile-time source-to-source transformations to hide the increase in code complexity deriving by adopting the low-level *OMP-SPMD* runtime, using the OpenMP directives.

As future work, we will finalize the automatic lowering of the OpenMP directives into SPMD primitives, which is now at a prototype level and lacks support for a subset of OpenMP directives and clauses. We will also evaluate support for advanced directives included in 4.0 and 5.0 OpenMP specifications, even if the dynamic behavior of advanced constructs is generally not suitable for many embedded applications running on MCU-class devices.

Acknowledgments. This work has been partially supported by the European Union's Horizon 2020 research and innovation programme under grant agreement numbers 732631 (OPRECOMP), 863337 (WiPLASH), and 857191 (IOTWINS).

References

1. Abdi, H., Williams, L.J.: Principal component analysis. Wiley Interdisciplinary Rev. Comput. Stat. **2**(4), 433–459 (2010)
2. Brigham, E.O.: The Fast Fourier Transform and its Applications. Prentice-Hall Inc., Hoboken (1988)
3. Chapman, B., Huang, L., Biscondi, E., Stotzer, E., Shrivastava, A., Gatherer, A.: Implementing OpenMP on a high performance embedded multicore MPSoC. In: 2009 IEEE International Symposium on Parallel and Distributed Processing, pp. 1–8. IEEE (2009)
4. Chen, K.C., Chen, C.H.: Enabling SIMT execution model on homogeneous multi-core system. ACM Trans. Archit. Code Optim. (TACO) **15**(1), 1–26 (2018)

5. Diaz, J., Munoz-Caro, C., Nino, A.: A survey of parallel programming models and tools in the multi and many-core era. IEEE Trans. Parallel Distrib. Syst. **23**(8), 1369–1386 (2012)
6. Gaster, B., Howes, L., Kaeli, D.R., Mistry, P., Schaa, D.: Heterogeneous computing with OpenCL. Newnes (2012)
7. Gautschi, M., et al.: Near-threshold RISC-V core with DSP extensions for scalable IoT endpoint devices. IEEE Trans. Very Large Scale Integration (VLSI) Syst. **25**(10), 2700–2713 (2017)
8. Glaser, F., Tagliavini, G., Rossi, D., Haugou, G., Huang, Q., Benini, L.: Energy-efficient hardware-accelerated synchronization for shared-L1-memory multiprocessor clusters. IEEE Trans. Parallel Distrib. Syst. **32**(3), 633–648 (2021)
9. GNU Foundation: libgomp runtime. https://gcc.gnu.org/onlinedocs/libgomp/
10. LLVM Project: LLVM OpenMP runtime. https://openmp.llvm.org/Reference.pdf
11. Mallat, S.G.: A theory for multiresolution signal decomposition: the wavelet representation. IEEE Trans. Pattern Anal. Mach. Intell. **11**(7), 674–693 (1989)
12. Mitra, G., Stotzer, E., Jayaraj, A., Rendell, A.P.: Implementation and optimization of the OpenMP accelerator model for the TI keystone II architecture. In: DeRose, L., de Supinski, B.R., Olivier, S.L., Chapman, B.M., Müller, M.S. (eds.) IWOMP 2014. LNCS, vol. 8766, pp. 202–214. Springer, Cham (2014). https://doi.org/10.1007/978-3-319-11454-5_15
13. Montagna, F., Benatti, S., Rossi, D.: Flexible, scalable and energy efficient biosignals processing on the pulp platform: a case study on seizure detection. J. Low Power Electron. Appl. **7**(2), 16 (2017)
14. Nickolls, J., Buck, I., Garland, M., Skadron, K.: Scalable parallel programming with CUDA: Is CUDA the parallel programming model that application developers have been waiting for? Queue **6**(2), 40–53 (2008)
15. Noble, W.S.: What is a support vector machine? Nat. Biotechnol. **24**(12), 1565–1567 (2006)
16. Pereira, M.M., Sousa, R.C.F., Araujo, G.: Compiling and optimizing OpenMP 4.X programs to OpenCL and SPIR. In: de Supinski, B.R., Olivier, S.L., Terboven, C., Chapman, B.M., Müller, M.S. (eds.) IWOMP 2017. LNCS, vol. 10468, pp. 48–61. Springer, Cham (2017). https://doi.org/10.1007/978-3-319-65578-9_4
17. Pullini, A., Rossi, D., Loi, I., Tagliavini, G., Benini, L.: Mr. Wolf: an energy-precision scalable parallel ultra low power SoC for IoT edge processing. IEEE J. Solid-State Circuits **54**(7), 1970–1981 (2019)
18. PULP Project: RI5CY Manual. https://www.pulp-platform.org/docs/ri5cy_user_manual.pdf
19. PULP Project: Setup of Xilinx FPGA boards. https://github.com/pulp-platform/pulp/tree/master/fpga/pulpissimo-zcu104
20. Quinlan, D.: ROSE: compiler support for object-oriented frameworks. Parallel Process. Lett. **10**(02n03), 215–226 (2000)
21. Rossi, D., et al.: PULP: a parallel ultra low power platform for next generation IoT applications. In: 2015 IEEE Hot Chips 27 Symposium (HCS), pp. 1–39. IEEE (2015)
22. Sony Corporation: Sony Spresense multicore microcontroller. https://developer.sony.com/develop/spresense/
23. Stratton, J.A., et al.: Efficient compilation of fine-grained SPMD-threaded programs for multicore CPUs. In: Proceedings of the 8th Annual IEEE/ACM International Symposium on Code Generation and Optimization, pp. 111–119 (2010)

24. Tagliavini, G., Cesarini, D., Marongiu, A.: Unleashing fine-grained parallelism on embedded many-core accelerators with lightweight OpenMP tasking. IEEE Trans. Parallel Distrib. Syst. **29**(9), 2150–2163 (2018)
25. Taylor, B., Marco, V.S., Wang, Z.: Adaptive optimization for OpenCL programs on embedded heterogeneous systems. ACM SIGPLAN Notices **52**(5), 11–20 (2017)

Energy Efficient Power-Management for Out-of-Order Processors Using Cyclic Power-Gating

William Toms[(✉)] [iD], John Goodacre [iD], and Mikel Luján [iD]

Department of Computer Science, University of Manchester, Oxford Road,
Manchester M13 9PL, UK
{william.toms,john.goodacre,mikel.lujan}@manchester.ac.uk

Abstract. Dynamic Voltage and Frequency Scaling is the most commonly used power management technique in modern processors. However, the ability of an individual chip to operate under reduced supply voltage can no longer be predetermined at the design stage and may even change over time. This paper presents a dynamic power-management strategy for out-of-order CPUs using Cyclic Power Gating (CPG). CPG is an aggressive power-gating strategy where the CPU is powered on and off again at high frequency allowing the fine-grained control of frequency and power consumption without scaling the supply voltage. A key challenge with power-gating out-of-order CPUs is the serialization of memory accesses. The paper presents $CRIT_{CPG}$ a low-cost method to accurately predict serialized memory accesses that allows the impact of power-gating on performance to be determined. $CRIT_{CPG}$ is employed within a hardware governor that adapts the power-gating to CPU execution phases. Detailed simulations of the governor are carried out over a range of benchmarks, the CPG governor shows on average an 11% reduction in energy consumption and an 8% increase in energy efficiency over a state-of-the-art DVFS governor. Using these techniques, not only can CPG provide fine-grained power consumption control to rival DVFS, but it can also be used alongside DVFS to further increase the energy-efficiency of CPUs.

Keywords: Power-management · Superscalar-architecture · Power-gating

1 Introduction

The most commonly used power-management strategy in modern CPUs is Dynamic Voltage and Frequency Scaling (DVFS), where the supply voltage to and the clock frequency of a CPU are changed according to its execution profile: reducing power consumption during low-intensity (*memory-bound*) phases and increasing the performance during high intensity (*cpu-bound*) phases. When the supply voltage to a circuit is scaled by some value j, the clock frequency of

© Springer Nature Switzerland AG 2021
C. Hochberger et al. (Eds.): ARCS 2021, LNCS 12800, pp. 183–198, 2021.
https://doi.org/10.1007/978-3-030-81682-7_12

the CPU must be scaled by a corresponding value k to ensure that timing constraints of the circuit are upheld under the new voltage. The resulting voltage and frequency levels are called a *pair* or *node*.

However, voltage scaling is becoming challenging in deep sub-micron technologies:

- Over time, the ratio between supply voltage (V_{dd}) and threshold voltage (V_{th}) in deep sub-micron technologies has lowered to reduce power consumption [15] reducing the range of voltage scaling as a proportion of V_{dd}.
- With successive geometry shrinks, static power forms an increasing proportion of overall power consumption and although voltage scaling reduces dynamic power consumption quadratically, static power consumption scales linearly with V_{dd} [5]. The increase in execution time due to the corresponding frequency scaling severely limits static power energy savings.
- Process variability and wear-out cause variations in threshold voltages V_{th} not only across the area of a circuit but also throughout its lifetime, further reducing the range of voltage scaling. For example, in 10 nm finFETs, process variation has been shown to give a standard deviation in threshold voltages of around 33% (50 mV) of the mean threshold voltage (150 mV) [14].
- Increasing power densities increase the occurrence of transient voltage noise events [16], such as voltage droop, requiring frequency *guard-banding* around voltage levels, where the operating frequency is reduced to ensure timing constraints are met.

This paper investigates a novel power-management technique for out-of-order CPUs, which provides finer grained control of power consumption than DVFS with lower static power. Cyclic Power-Gating (CPG) [6] is a form of aggressive power-gating, where the CPU is powered-on and off over a small time period. The effective frequency of the processor and its power consumption can be controlled by changing the duty-cycle, the ratio between the on and off states of a power-gating period. The duty cycle may be set to any value between 0 and 1 and changed between periods with no discernible overhead. To minimize the impact of power-gating on performance, a state-retentive architecture is employed which saves the state of the CPU during power-gating. This paper investigates the use of CPG for energy-efficient power management of *out-of-order* CPUs. The paper makes the following contributions

- A hardware governor is introduced to apply CPG dynamically in response to CPU execution behaviour.
- A profitability model for CPG, that allows the energy-efficiency of CPG for any duty cycle to be determined for an execution period is presented.
- A low cost hardware mechanism is defined to detect serialization of memory accesses.

Using the techniques presented in this paper a CPG governor is compared to a state of the art DVFS governor and evaluated over a range of different benchmarks. The CPG governor exhibits energy savings of 11% and a 8% increase in energy efficiency over the DVFS governor. Furthermore, when operating under higher temperatures (consistent with a multi-core system under load) the CPG governor uses 15% less energy and is 13% more energy efficient than the DVFS governor. The results suggest that, not only can CPG provide fine-grained power consumption control to rival DVFS, but it can also be used alongside DVFS to further increase the energy-efficiency of CPUs.

2   Cyclic Power-Gating

A Cyclic Power Gating (CPG) scheme powers the CPU on and off over a fixed period, T_{CPG}. The effective operating frequency of the CPU is determined by the duty cycle ratio:

$$duty\_cycle = \frac{T_{CPG} - T_{off}}{T_{CPG}}. \tag{1}$$

where T_{off} is the powered-off time during each CPG period. T_{off} is controlled by a timer circuit in the CPG controller which is initialized at the start of each CPG period and so the duty-cycle (and hence the CPU frequency) can be changed between any CPG cycle with no overhead. The duty-cycle may be assigned to any value over the range [0..1] allowing for fine-grained power consumption control, without scaling the supply voltage. To minimize the performance overheads caused by power-gating, a state-retentive architecture is used to maintain the CPU state during T_{off}.

2.1   State-Retentive Architecture

In a conventional architecture, when a CPU is power-gated all of the state is lost. Before the power is switched off, issued instructions must be committed and the value of the registers written back to memory. When the CPU is powered-up the register values must be fetched and operation continues from the last committed instruction. To minimize this overhead in the CPG scheme, the state-retentive architecture shown in Fig. 1 is employed. In the state-retentive architecture all of the memory structures (except pipeline registers) within the CPU are implemented using SRAMs. The voltage supply to the cell-array of each SRAM is not gated and is maintained throughout the off-period. The L1 caches and TLBs (as well as the L2/L3 caches and corresponding memory-management hardware) are not power-gated, allowing any outstanding memory requests to be fulfilled while the CPU is asleep.

The micro-architectural units (Instruction Fetch Unit, Decode Unit etc.) of the CPU are internally pipelined. State-retentive registers are placed at the head of each unit. The remaining pipeline registers within each block are not state-retentive and so the internal pipelines of each unit must be drained when powering down and refilled when the CPU is powered up again. State-retention in the head pipeline stage allows the internal pipelines of all units to be drained and refilled in parallel. The drain and refill processes are each modelled by a 5 cycle delay which represents the maximum internal pipeline in a single unit.

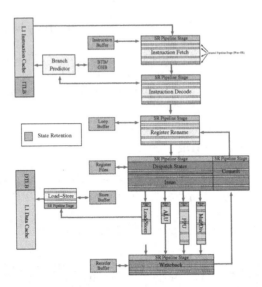

Fig. 1. State-Retentive architecture

Furthermore, there are additional overheads to clamp and retain data and initialize the registers and clocks (the exact penalty is design dependent so we have assumed an overhead of 5 clock-cycles).

State retention is a feature in most ARM Cortex CPUs, although the exact wake, sleep, preparation and initialization timings are implementation dependent and so difficult to ascertain. The ARM state-retention scheme applies to both the CPU and L1 caches and the CPU can only enter state-retention once any outstanding memory accesses are completed. The architecture presented here, suggests extensions to the state-retention to permit fine-grained power-gating, keeping the L1 Caches and the TLBs active to allow any outstanding memory accesses to be fulfilled.

A key value is the *break-even time*, T_{be}, which is the time below which power-gating consumes more energy than it saves. The break-even time of the state-retentive architecture is used to set a suitable time for the CPG period T_{cpg}. The overheads of power gating for the state-retentive architecture were determined by simulation and are detailed in Table 1 along with T_{cpg} for the CPG nodes.

3   Profitability Model for CPG

The power-management scheme presented in this paper is an energy-efficient hardware governor for cyclic power-gating, similar to existing governors presented for DVFS [13]. The DVFS hardware governor is periodic, with a period T. At the end of each period, the governor calculates, based on statistics collected during T, which power/frequency node *would have* executed the work carried out (instructions completed) during T the most efficiently. To calculate how energy-efficient each node will be, estimations of the time taken and the energy consumed by each node over period T must be made by the governor. The most energy-efficient node is then applied to the CPU, the statistics are recalculated at the end of period $T + 1$ and a further decision is made.

While CPG can be used to set the duty-cycle to any value between 0 and 1 (given a large enough period), to simplify the construction of the governor we limit the duty-cycles of the CPG-scheme to a set of nodes each with a different duty-cycle. To make a direct comparison with DVFS, the duty-cycles of these nodes correspond directly to the frequencies of the DVFS nodes of the target architecture shown in Table 1. In this section an interval model of CPG behaviour is introduced that can be used to estimate the time taken to execute the instructions of T under a given node.

3.1   DVFS Interval Models

To construct an energy efficient DVFS scheme it is important to predict the profitability of a DVFS node over a given period of time. Much of the research in this area has been in developing *interval models* of CPU behaviour which can be used to determine the execution time of a period when the CPU is running on a different DVFS node. The models partition execution time into two intervals (or phases) [12]:

- A *pipelined* (or cpu-bound) phase, whose execution time is dependent on the CPU clock frequency
- A *non-pipelined* (or memory-bound) phase whose execution time is unaffected by CPU clock frequency.

The non-pipelined phase is caused by events outside of the clock domain of the CPU, e.g. main-memory accesses. As the CPU clock frequency decreases, the number of cycles taken to execute the pipelined phase remains constant, but the number of cycles in the non-pipelined phase *decreases*. If the pipelined and non-pipelined phases of a period of execution are known, the time taken to execute the same amount of code by each of the DVFS nodes can be predicted:

For a given node n_k, whose frequency is given by kf_{typ}, where f_{typ} is the nominal clock frequency, the number of cycles, c_k, required to execute period T is given by:

$$c_k = (c_{typ} - c_n) + kc_n \qquad (2)$$

where c_{typ} is the number of cycles required to execute T at f_{typ} and c_n are the non-pipelined cycles of c_{typ}. The time T_k taken to execute on n_k can then be calculated by:

$$T_k = \frac{c_k}{kf_{typ}} \qquad (3)$$

Therefore, an efficient manner for determining the number of non-pipelined cycles is vital to ensure the correct DVFS node is selected.

The *Leading loads* model of non-pipelined execution [12] identified that, using CPU-stall time as a proxy for the non-pipelined execution phase underestimates the actual time spent in non-pipelined execution. The Leading-load model defines *loads* to be *non-speculative reads* (data loads and instruction fetches) and identifies them as the cause of stalls in out-of-order CPUs. After a load miss in the last-level cache (LLC), an out-of-order CPU continues to issue instructions until either the instruction-queue or reorder-buffer is full. If any further loads occur before the CPU stalls, then these subsequent loads will return a *fixed number of cycles* after the initial (*leading*) load (assuming a fixed memory latency). Therefore, the leading loads represent the start of non-pipelined execution phases and their latencies are the non-pipelined execution cycles, c_n. The arrival times of trailing loads are dependent on cycle time and so cycles after the leading load returns are considered pipelined execution. To determine c_n using the leading loads model, a LLC miss counter was proposed that counts LLC-misses caused by leading-loads and ignores any LLC misses that occur within M_{lat} cycles of another leading-load miss, where M_{lat} is a fixed value for the latency of a last level cache miss (ignoring any variation in the actual DRAM access time). The leading-load model is shown in Fig. 2, the leading loads in this example are A and C.

The leading-load model was further developed to accommodate variable memory latencies by the CRIT model [10]. The CRIT model states that the non-pipelined phases of execution can be determined by creating a *critical-path of dependent memory operations*. Dependent memory operations are *serialized*: each one must return its value before the next one can be issued, and so the chain of the dependent memory operations with the longest latencies represents an irreducible delay for any execution period.

The CRIT model is based on the following assumption:

$$If \; two \; memory \; requests \; are \; serialized, \atop the \; second \; one \; depends \; on \; the \; first \; one. \tag{4}$$

The assumption relies on the fact that an out-of-order CPU will attempt to issue all non-dependent operations as quickly as possible and so non-dependent loads will be issued by the processor before the leading-load returns its result. The critical path is calculated in hardware using a global critical path counter $CRIT_{global}$, which represents the total time of the current critical path:

- Each Miss Status Handling Register (MSHR) in the LLC has an associated local critical path counter $CRIT_i$.
- When an LLC-miss occurs due to a load, $Load_i$, it is assigned to $MSHR_i$ and $CRIT_{global}$ is copied into $CRIT_i$.
- When the load is fulfilled, the actual latency of the miss, M_{lat}^i, is added to $CRIT_i += M_{lat}^i$.
- If the new $CRIT_i$ is longer than the current $CRIT_{global}$, then the value of $CRIT_{global}$ is updated to $CRIT_i$: $CRIT_{global} = CRIT_i$
- Any serialized memory operations will occur after $CRIT_{global}$ has been updated, and the associated MSHR will use new value of $CRIT_{global}$.

– If a concurrent memory operation $Load_j$ with a longer latency occurs after $Load_i$ then $CRIT_{global}$ will be set to the $CRIT_j$ and the latency of $Load_i$ will no longer be on the critical path.

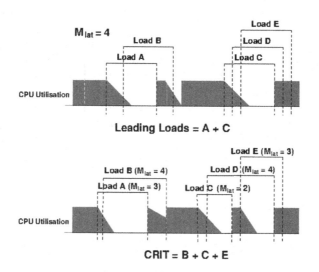

Fig. 2. DVFS interval models: i. Leading loads, ii. CRIT memory critical path

An example of the CRIT model is shown in Fig. 2.ii. Initially $CRIT_{global} = 0$

– *Load A* has a latency of 3, and so when it is completed $CRIT_{global}$ is updated to include *Load A* ($CRIT_{global} = 3 \ (A)$).
– As *Load B* is initiated before *Load A* is completed, *Load A* and *Load B* are not serialized and hence not dependent. When *Load B* is completed $CRIT_{global}$ is updated to include *Load B* and *Load A* is removed ($CRIT_{global} = 4 \ (B)$).
– When *Load C* misses in the LLC, it takes the current value of $CRIT_{global} = CRIT_C = 4 \ (B)$. When it completes, $CRIT_{global}$ is updated to include *Load C* ($CRIT_{global} = 6 \ (B + C)$).
– As *Load D* was initiated before *Load C* completed $CRIT_D = 4 \ (B)$, and when *Load D* completes, $CRIT_{global}$ is updated to include *Load D*, removing *Load C* ($CRIT_{global} = 8(B + D)$).
– *Load E* was initiated before *Load D* completed, but after *Load C* and so initially $CRIT_E = 6 \ (B + C)$. When *Load E* returns, although it had a lower latency than *Load D*, its critical path is higher and so $CRIT_{global}$ is updated to include *Load E*, ($CRIT_{global} = 9 \ (B + C + E)$).

It should be noted that in the example in Fig. 2.i, if $M_{lat} = 4$ for all Loads, then both Leading Loads and CRIT, have the same value: $CRIT_{global} = 8 \ (A + C)$. However, applying the leading load model to Fig. 2.ii assuming a fixed latency of 4 still gives *Leading Loads* = 8 $(A + C)$.

3.2   Interval Model for CPG

To determine the CPG-node which provides the most energy-efficient execution, an interval model for CPG must be defined. In CPG, the frequency is not scaled, but rather power-off time is distributed throughout the execution time according to the CPG period. The effect on the execution time of the period varies depending on whether each power-gate occurs during the pipelined or non-pipelined phases. In the pipelined phase the power-gating will prevent the CPU from doing useful work and the increase in the execution time is inversely proportional to the duty-cycle. In the non-pipelined phase, the CPU is waiting for external events and so power-gating will have no effect on the execution time. On average we assume that the likelihood of the CPU being power-gated in either phase is proportional to the size of the phases. Therefore, for CPG node n_k, with duty-cycle k, the number of cycles required to execute period T is:

$$c_k = \frac{(c_{typ} - c_n)}{k} + c_n \tag{5}$$

As the clock-period in CPG scheme does not change:

$$T_k = \frac{c_k}{f_{typ}} \tag{6}$$

and Eqs. 3 and 6 are equivalent. However, power-gating affects the behaviour of the CPU and the execution phases need to be redefined to fit the CPG model. The biggest problem with power-gating out-of-order CPUs is that it can *serialize non-dependent memory accesses* that could have taken place in parallel, as no instructions can be issued while the CPU is power-gated. This makes techniques such as Memory-Access Power-Gating [8] difficult to execute on out-of-order CPUs, as the execution time (and even energy consumption) is often increased. The CRIT dependent memory critical path is based on the assumption (4) that serialized memory accesses are dependent. Under a CPG scheme assumption 4 is no longer valid and so we must create a new algorithm to determine *CPG-CRIT*, the dependent memory critical path for CPG schemes.

In the original CRIT algorithm, concurrent misses, i and j, will both take the same value of $CRIT_{global}$ and the longest latency miss will overwrite the other in the new $CRIT_{global}$. Any subsequent miss, k, will copy this new $CRIT_{global}$ and add its own latency to it. When two concurrent LLC misses, i and j, are serialized by power-gating, i will update $CRIT_{global}$ before j takes a copy and so $CRIT_{global}$ will contain the latencies of both i and j. Under normal operation, however, only one of the latencies would appear in the global path. This results in an overly large non-pipelined execution fraction, which will affect the selection of the next CPG node and hence the energy-efficiency of the governor.

Although the serialization of memory accesses, affects the performance of the CPU and changes the timing of subsequent memory accesses, CRIT is an aggregate of dependent memory accesses and the time between accesses is not recorded. Therefore, we only need to check for serialized memory accesses in a *serialization window* after each power-gate (The length of the serialization window is equivalent to the length of the power-gate). Loads that are issued during this window need to be checked to see if they were dependent on any instructions that were executed after the power-gating or if they could have been issued while the CPU was power-gated. To do this we assign a *colour* to each CPG-cycle. To correctly determine the serialization of memory accesses, the colours of the CPG cycles that occur during a memory access must be unique. For the experiments presented in this paper colours were represented by a 5-bit value which allows for 32 distinct colours.

1. Before the CPU is power-gated, a copy, $CRIT_{CPG}$, of $CRIT_{global}$ is taken and kept until the CPU is power-gated in the next CPG cycle.
2. When a register is written to by an instruction, the colour of the current CPG-cycle is added to the register allocation table entry associated with the register. Each instruction has an associated colour, it is assigned an initial colour based on the colour of CPG-cycle the instruction was fetched in (subject to exceptions, see below).
3. When the source registers of an instruction are allocated, their colours are compared with the initial instruction colour and the instruction is assigned the most recently issued colour out of its initial colour and the colours of its source registers.
4. When an LLC miss occurs, the load is assigned a $CRIT$ value. The $CRIT$-CPG algorithm uses instructions' colour to determine whether to take a copy of the current $CRIT_{global}$ or (if the load has been serialized) to use the value from before the CPU was power-gated $CRIT_{CPG}$ (discussed in more detail below).
5. If the load results in an LLC miss and the resulting critical path is greater than the existing one, $CRIT_{global}$ is updated as per the original $CRIT$ algorithm.
6. Any loads that occur outside the serialization-window are not checked for serialization, and $CRIT_i = CRIT_{global}$. The CPG colour is added to the register allocation table for every register write throughout the entire execution to ensure the values are consistent.

The assignment of colours to registers and instructions (step 2) is subject to two exceptions:

i) Loads that were completed while the CPU was power-gated are treated as if they occurred in the previous CPG cycle. For Data Loads, the target register is assigned the colour of the previous CPG-cycle. For Instruction Fetches, the initial colour of the resulting instruction is the previous CPG cycle colour.
ii) If a *serialized* instruction fetch is *completed* within the serialization window, the fetched instruction is assigned the colour of the previous CPG-cycle, as the instruction would have been fetched in the previous cycle if the fetch had not been serialized.

To select which initial $CRIT$ value to assign to a Load upon an LLC miss, the $CRIT$-CPG algorithm must determine whether the Load has been serialized. As with existing interval models, Loads are defined as data-loads and instruction fetches, the rules for detecting serialization (and hence selecting between $CRIT$ values) are slightly different for each:

- **Data Loads.** Serialized loads are load instructions whose source operands were all available in an earlier CPG-cycle. If a load is issued during the serialization window, its instruction colour is checked with the colour of current CPG cycle. If the colour is the same, the instruction is dependent on instructions that have executed since the power-gating and the load is **not** serialized. A copy is taken of the current global $CRIT_i = CRIT_{global}$. If the colour is different, the instruction is independent and therefore has been serialized by the power-gating and $CRIT_{CPG}$ is used.

- **Instruction Fetches.** Any instruction fetch that occurs during the serialization window is considered *independent* (and hence serialized) unless it is caused by the misprediction of a branch whose value was resolved in the current CPG-cycle. Independent instruction fetches that occur in the serialization window take a copy of $CRIT_{CPG}$. If a branch instruction causes a misprediction, the colour of the branch instruction is compared to the current CPG colour. If the colour is different, the instruction fetch succeeding the branch is independent and a copy of $CRIT_{CPG}$ is taken. If the colour is the same, the branch is dependent on instructions in the current CPG-cycle and a copy of the $CRIT_{global}$ is taken.

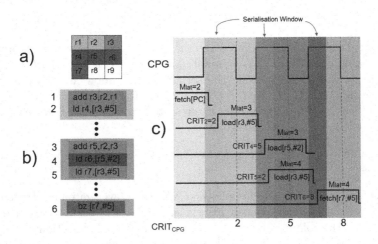

Fig. 3. CPG-CRIT example a) Register colours, b) Instruction colours, c) LLC cache misses (Color figure online)

An example of the *CRIT-CPG* algorithm is shown in Fig. 3. It shows four CPG periods coloured yellow, green, red and blue. The figure shows a sequence of instructions and the resulting register and instruction coloring's. Registers r1 and r2 were assigned by instructions (not shown) in the yellow CPG cycle.

1. An LLC miss occurs fetching instruction 1 and the global critical path is updated to include the memory latency of the fetch. Although the fetch was independent of the current green CPG-cycle, it was not serialized and so instruction 1 is initially assigned the green colour. When instruction 1 is issued, colour of the source registers (r1 and r2) are checked, but as they are less than instruction's existing colour it is not changed. The instruction writes to r3 in the green CPG-cycle, so the r3 entry in the allocation table is updated to green.

2. Instruction 2 takes the green colour from its r3 source register and issues a load. As the load is dependent on instructions in the current CPG-cycle the load is assigned with $CRIT_{global}$.

3. Instruction 3 is assigned the green colour, but writes to register 5 in the red CPG-cycle, meaning r5 is assigned the red colour.

4. Instruction 4 is assigned the red colour from r5 and so takes the value of $CRIT_{global}$ when it issues its load ($CRIT_4 = 5$). The load is completed by memory while the CPU is power-gated and so the value will not actually be written back to register 6 until the CPG wakes up and enters the blue CPG cycle. However, register 6 is assigned the red colour as this register write is considered to be serialized (see exception i)).

5. Instruction 5, is independent of any instructions in the red CPG cycle and, because it is issued in the serialization window, it is considered a serialized instruction. The load takes a copy of $CRIT\text{-}CPG$ from the previous CPG-cycle ($CRIT_5 = 2$). Even though the memory latency of instruction 5 is greater than instruction 4 and it arrives after instruction 4 its latency is not added to the critical path, this is because it was serialized from the green CPG-cycle and would have arrive early if the CPU had not been power-gated.

6. The final instruction, 6, is a branch that causes a branch misprediction and an LLC miss on the corresponding instruction fetch. Although it was issued in the serialization window, the instruction was dependent on r6 which was not written until the blue CPG-cycle. Therefore the instruction was not serialized and a copy of the global CRIT is assigned to the miss ($CRIT_6 = 8$).

The final CRIT value is 12, and includes all the LLC misses except for instruction 5, which was serialized from a previous CPG window and would have been completed ahead of instruction 4. The $CRIT\text{-}CPG$ algorithm ensures that any serialization that occurs due to the power-gating of CPG is not reflected within the critical path of memory operations and therefore the $CRIT\text{-}CPG$ can be used to accurately determine the non-pipelined execution of a period and hence by the governor to select the correct CPG node.

4   Simulation Infrastructure and Target Architecture

To evaluate the energy trade-offs and overheads of CPG, the gem5 system simulator was enhanced with a custom statistics package that allows the simulator to interface with a variety of modelling tools. Energy estimation (along with power-gating wake-up and sleep times) was performed using the McPAT power

Table 1. Simulation parameters

Parameter	Configuration
Architectural parameters	
Processor	ARMv8
Machine width	3-wide (up to 8 micro-ops)
L1 instruction cache	48 KB 3-Way Set-Associative
L1 data cache	32 KB 2-Way Set-Associative
L2 private cache	2 MB 16-Way Set-Associative
Memory Size	8 GB
Physical Register File	128-Entry Integer, 192-Entry Float
Load/Store Queue	16-Entry
Reorder buffer	40-Entry
Issue Queue	32-Entry
Physical Parameters	
Area	2.2 mm^2
TDP	3W
C_D	17.3 nF
Wake-up Energy	7.98 nJ
Wake-up Time	5.27 ns
Sleep Time	8.3 ns
Break-Even Time	20.7ns

Voltages (V)	1.1	1.09	1.05	1.01	0.97	0.93	0.87	0.84
Frequencies (GHz)	2.00	1.8	1.60	1.40	1.20	1.0	0.7	0.5
Equivalent Duty Cycle	1.00	0.91	0.81	0.71	0.61	0.50	0.35	0.25

estimation tool, temperature modelling was performed using Hotspot [7] and the power-delivery network was modelled with the Voltspot PDN modeller [16].

The McPat power estimator was used as it provided detailed models of SRAM components and CPU capacitances not available in instruction-level empirical power models. The target architecture was based on an Cortex A72 out-of-order CPU implementing the ARMv8 instruction set [1] with 2 MB L2 cache and 8GB memory. The architecture details are shown in Table 1. The DVFS nodes were taken from the cpu-freq values for Mediatek's MT8173 A72 implementation [3].

5   Results

The CPG governor described in this paper was evaluated over a set of benchmarks running on the target architecture. The benchmarks include 11 SPEC CPU 2006 benchmarks (xalan, gobmk, tonto, gcc, lbm, astar, perlbench, povray, h264, hmmer, and mcf), a graph500 [2] benchmark running a breadth-first search

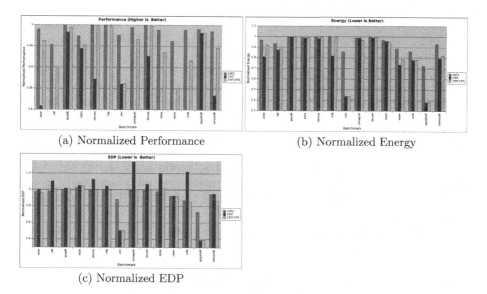

(a) Normalized Performance   (b) Normalized Energy

(c) Normalized EDP

Fig. 4. Normalized performance, energy and EDP of CPG and DVFS governors

over a large graph with 2^{23} nodes and an aggregation of queries from TPC-H database benchmark, using a 5.2 GB data-set (generated with TPC-H scale factor 5) running on the MonetDBLite database server [4]. The benchmarks were selected to cover a range of behaviours, with a mix of both CPU-bound and memory-bound applications. Figures 4a, 4b and 4c show the performance, energy and EDP of the CPG governor normalized to the CPU running at the nominal operating frequency (2 GHz). The figures show four different governor implementations:

- *DVFS:* A DVFS governor using the using the standard CRIT interval mode with the voltage/frequency scaling pairs defined in Table 1. The DVFS implementation doesn't employ the state-retentive architecture and operates with a period of 500us (500× the *transition latency* defined by the Mediatek's cpufreq governor [3]).
- *CRIT:* A CPG governor implementation using the standard CRIT interval model to determine the non-pipelined execution cycles and select the CPG node for the next governor period. As the frequency of a CPG scheme can be changed with zero overhead, all the CPG governors have a period of 500ns.
- *CRIT-CPG:* A CPG governor implementation using the CRIT-CPG interval model defined in this paper.

Overall, the CRIT CPG governor reduces energy by 18% and Energy Delay Product by 14% over the nominal operating frequency. Amongst the four most memory-bound benchmarks (mcf, lbm, TPC-H and graph500) the average energy reduction is 40% and the EDP reduction 36%.

The efficacy of the CRIT-CPG interval model can be determined by comparing the CRIT-CPG governor with the CRIT governor. The CRIT CPG has a 14% improvement in performance and a 8% improvement in EDP. The performance (and EDP) improvements are due to the improved accuracy of the CRIT-CPG model by accounting for serialized memory-accesses within the interval CRIT interval model. The CRIT-CPG governor reduces energy by 11% and EDP by 8% compared to the DVFS governor. In particular the CPG governors exhibit very large energy savings (27% and 42%) for the benchmarks graph500 and mcf where a significant amount of the execution time is spent stalled waiting for memory accesses. As the CPU is (frequently) power-gated during the stalls, significant savings are made in both leakage power and idle clock power. Averaged across all benchmarks, the performance of the CPG-CRIT governor is 4% worse than the DVFS governor, this is because the enforced power-gating does not necessarily coincide with CPU stalls and so the CPU may be power-gated during normal execution or not woken immediately when a dependent memory access returns. However, in almost all benchmarks, the benefits of reduced energy outweigh the performance decreases providing EDP reductions.

These results show that the CRIT-CPG governor allows for fine grained control of the power consumption of a CPU that rivals, and even outperforms, a state-of-the art DVFS governor without scaling the supply voltage. However, DVFS and CPG need not be mutually-exclusive and can actually be applied together to exploit the best properties of each scheme. The development of a hybrid CPG/DVFS governor is the subject of on-going work.

6   Related Work

Memory-Accessed Power-Gating [8] introduced a state-retentive architecture to facilitate low-overhead power-gating during memory accesses on an in-order core. This was extended by Token-based Adaptive Power-gating (TAP) [9] to multiple, out-of-order, CPUs. In TAP, power-gating occurs only once the CPU has stalled and the length of time the CPU is power-gated is determined by the time of any outstanding memory requests. As described in Sect. 3, stall-time is not a good proxy for the non-pipelined execution in out-of-order CPUs and in TAP the power-gated time is reduced further by the need to determine approximate latency of outstanding cache misses before power-gating. Furthermore, the TAP model does not take into account the effects of memory serialization caused by power-gating. Unlike TAP, the CPG power management scheme is predictive rather than responsive and accurately calculates the non-pipelined execution of a period. The $CRIT_{CPG}$ performance model determines memory serialization caused by power-gating and uses it to set the power-gating scheme.

IQG+MAG [11], is a method of tracking dependencies within out-of-order pipelines for power-gating execution units. This scheme adds *snooze bits* to each instruction in the instruction queue, to determine the dependencies between each instruction and the load instructions that cause last level cache misses. Execution Units can be power-gated if the instructions issued to it are dependent on stalled load instructions. To track dependencies of an instruction, IGQ+MAP requires an entry in the allocation table for each Load Queue Entry, which in this architecture requires 32 bits per instruction. $CRIT_{CPG}$ tracks dependencies using colours of CPG phases which requires only 5 bits per instruction entry.

7 Conclusions

This paper introduced a dynamic power-management scheme for out-of-order CPUs based on Cyclic Power-Gating. By power-gating the CPU at high-frequencies, CPG can provide fine-grained control of operating frequency and power consumption without scaling the supply voltage. A governor was developed to match the CPG operation to the execution phases of the CPU. A key challenge with fine-grained power-gating of out-of-order cores is the serialization of memory accesses and a low cost hardware mechanism to detect this was proposed. The CPG governor was evaluated on a range of benchmarks showing average energy reductions of 18% and EDP reductions of 14%. Furthermore, the governor has 11% energy and 8% EDP savings over a state-of-the-art DVFS governor. The serialized memory access detection hardware increases the performance of the CPG governor by 14% and reduces EDP by 8%.

Acknowledgements. This work was supported by EPSRC grants DOME EP/J016330/1 and PAMELA EP/K008730/1, and also the EuroEXA project funded by the EU's Horizon 2020 Programme (grant agreement no. 754337). Mikel Luján is funded by an Arm/RAEng Research Chair award and a Royal Society Wolfson Fellowship.

References

1. Arm cortex-a72 technical reference manual. https://tinyurl.com/cortexa72
2. Graph 500. http://graph500.org
3. Mediatek mt8173 cpufreq driver. https://tinyurl.com/mediatekcpufreq
4. Monetdb lite. https://github.com/hannesmuehleisen/MonetDBLite
5. Butts, J.A., Sohi, G.S.: A static power model for architects. In: International Symposium on Microarchitecture, pp. 191–201. IEEE (2000)
6. Cakmaki, Y., Toms, W., Navaridas, J., Lujan, M.: Cyclic power-gating as an alternative to voltage and frequency scaling. IEEE Comput. Archit. Lett. **15**(2), 77–80 (2016)
7. Huang, W., Ghosh, S., Velusamy, S., Sankaranarayanan, K., Skadron, K., Stan, M.: HotSpot: a compact thermal modeling methodology for early-stage VLSI design. IEEE Trans. VLSI **14**(5), 501–513 (2006)
8. Jeong, K., Kahng, A.B., Kang, S., Rosing, T.S., Strong, R.: MAPG: memory access power gating. In: DATE (2012)
9. Kahng, A.B., Kang, S., Rosing, T., Strong, R.: TAP: token-based adaptive power gating. In: ISLPED, pp. 203–208. ACM (2012)
10. Miftakhutdinov, R., Ebrahimi, E., Patt, Y.N.: Predicting performance impact of DVFS for realistic memory systems. In: MICRO (2012)

11. Ozen, E., Orailoglu, A.: The return of power gating: smart leakage energy reductions in modern out-of-order processor architectures. In: ARCS (2019)
12. Rountree, B., Lowenthal, D.K., Schulz, M., de Supinski, B.R.: Practical performance prediction under dynamic voltage frequency scaling. In: IGCC (2011)
13. Spiliopoulos, V., Kaxiras, S., Keramidas, G.: Green governors: a framework for continuously adaptive DVFS. In: IGCC. IEEE (2011)
14. Wang, X., Brown, A., Cheng, B., Asenov, A.: Statistical variability and reliability in nanoscale finfets. In: IEEE International Electron Devices Meeting (2011)
15. Weste, N.H., Harris, D.M.: CMOS VLSI Design: A Circuits and Systems Perspective, 4th edn. Pearson Education, London (2010)
16. Zhang, R., Wang, K., Meyer, B., Stan, M., Skadron, K.: Architecture implications of pads as a scarce resource. In: ISCA (2014)

VEFRE Workshop

BCH 2-Bit and 3-Bit Error Correction with Fast Multi-Bit Error Detection

Christian Schulz-Hanke$^{(\boxtimes)}$

Institute of Computer Science, University of Potsdam, Potsdam, Germany
christian.schulz-hanke@cs.uni-potsdam.de

Abstract. In this paper an new approach combining 2-bit and 3-bit BCH error correction with fast and simple error detection for errors of higher order is presented. Under the assumption that a 2-bit error or 3-bit error occurred, the corresponding correction bits are determined using the syndrome components s_1, s_3 for 2-bit errors and s_1, s_3, s_5 for 3-bit errors. These correction bits are used to calculate higher syndrome components up to s_{2T-1}, which are compared to the actual corresponding syndrome components. If the syndrome components match, a 2-bit error or 3-bit error was detected. In the case of a syndrome mismatch, an error other than a 2-bit error or 3-bit error occurred and was detected. The proposed method provides a simple way to differentiate between 2-bit errors (3-bit errors) and errors of higher order.

Keywords: BCH code · Error detection · Error correction

1 Introduction

Applications with high security standards may require a guaranteed error detection up to a certain number of erroneous bits. Using a BCH code allows to detect or correct errors up to a given number of erroneous bits. The number of errors that are guaranteed to be detected/corrected are set by construction.

Given a T-bit error correcting BCH code ($T > 3$), all up to T-bit errors can be corrected or all up to $2T$-bit errors can be detected. We present an approach that allows to use such a BCH code to correct all 1-bit, 2-bit and 3-bit arrors while also detecting 100% of all up to $(2T - 3)$-bit errors.

The classic approach [3] computes determinants corresponding to the number of errors in descending size. The first non-zero determinant identifies the number of erroneous bits. In [5], we proposed a simplified detection step combined with 1-bit error correction. This detection step checks for errors higher than a 1-bit in ascending order and reduces the previous determinants into simple equations of the form $s_1^X \stackrel{?}{=} s_X$. In this paper, we combine a BCH 2-bit error correction and a 3-bit error correction with additional error detection. The 1-bit error case has been covered in our previous work [5].

© Springer Nature Switzerland AG 2021
C. Hochberger et al. (Eds.): ARCS 2021, LNCS 12800, pp. 201–212, 2021.
https://doi.org/10.1007/978-3-030-81682-7_13

2   BCH Code and Error Correction

A binary T-bit error correcting BCH code (code distance $2T + 1$) of length $n \leq 2^m - 1$ has a H-matrix of the form

$$H = \begin{bmatrix} \alpha^0, & \alpha^1, & \alpha^2, & \cdots & \alpha^{n-1} \\ \alpha^0, & \alpha^3, & \alpha^6, & \cdots & \alpha^{(n-1)\times 3} \\ \vdots & \vdots & \vdots & \ddots & \vdots \\ \alpha^0, & \alpha^{2T-1}, & \alpha^{2\times(2T-1)}, & \cdots & \alpha^{(n-1)\times(2T-1)} \end{bmatrix}$$

$$= \begin{bmatrix} H_1 \\ H_3 \\ \vdots \\ H_{2T-1} \end{bmatrix} \tag{1}$$

where $\alpha^0, ..., \alpha^i \in GF(2^m)$ and all exponents are modulo $2^m - 1$.

Multiplying the check matrix H with an erroneous word w (of length n) yields the syndrome $S = H \times w$. The syndrome consists of syndrome components $S = [s_1, s_3, s_5, \ldots, s_{2T-1}]^T$ where $H_x \times w = s_x$ and $x \in [1, 3, 5, ..., 2T - 1]$. Only odd syndrome components $(s_1, s_3, ...)$ have to be calculated for binary BCH codes, since $(s_x^2 = s_{2x}) \forall x \in \mathbf{N}^+$. Multiplying the check matrix with a code word c results in a zero vector $H \times c = 0$.

The BCH error correction approach presented in [3] contains two steps: Identifying the number of erroneous bits and identifying the error positions. Assume that T is the maximal number of errors taken into account. The number of erroneous bits is identified by calculating a sequence of determinants in descending order starting at $T + 1$ where T is the number of errors to correct: $det(M(T + 1)), det(M(T)), ..., det(M(2))$. The first non-zero determinant $det(M(x))$ in descending order identifies the number of erroneous bits as $x - 1$. For example, if $det(M(4))$ is the first non-zero determinant, then the error is identified as a 3-Bit error. To demonstrate the complexity of this approach, the matrizes and determinants are shown from $det(M(2))$ up to $det(M(9))$:

$$M(2) = \begin{bmatrix} 1, & 0 \\ s_1^2, & s_1 \end{bmatrix}$$

$$det(M(2)) = s_1$$

$$M(3) = \begin{bmatrix} 1, & 0, & 0 \\ s_1^2, & s_1, & 1 \\ s_1^4, & s_3, & s_1^2 \end{bmatrix}$$

$$det(M(3)) = s_1^3 + s_3$$

$$M(4) = \begin{bmatrix} 1, & 0, & 0, & 0 \\ s_1^2, & s_1, & 1, & 0 \\ s_1^4, & s_3, & s_1^2, & s_1 \\ s_3^2, & s_5, & s_1^4, & s_3 \end{bmatrix}$$

$$det(M(4)) = s_1^3 s_3 + s_1^6 + s_3^2 + s_1 s_5$$

$$M(5) = \begin{bmatrix} 1, & 0, & 0, & 0, & 0 \\ s_1^2, & s_1, & 1, & 0, & 0 \\ s_1^4, & s_3, & s_1^2, & s_1, & 1 \\ s_3^2, & s_5, & s_1^4, & s_3, & s_1^2 \\ s_1^8, & s_7, & s_3^2, & s_5, & s_1^4 \end{bmatrix}$$

$$det(M(5)) = s_1^7 s_3 + s_1^{10} + s_1 s_3^3 + s_1^2 s_3 s_5$$
$$+ s_1^5 s_5 + s_1^3 s_7 + s_5^2 + s_3 s_7$$

$$M(6) = \begin{bmatrix} 1, & 0, & 0, & 0, & 0, & 0 \\ s_1^2, & s_1, & 1, & 0, & 0, & 0 \\ s_1^4, & s_3, & s_1^2, & s_1, & 1, & 0 \\ s_3^2, & s_5, & s_1^4, & s_3, & s_1^2, & s_1 \\ s_1^8, & s_7, & s_3^2, & s_5, & s_1^4, & s_3 \\ s_5^2, & s_9, & s_1^8, & s_7, & s_3^2, & s_5 \end{bmatrix}$$

$$det(M(6)) = s_1^7 s_3 s_5 + s_1^8 s_7 + s_1^6 s_3^3 + s_1^{12} s_3 + s_1^{15}$$
$$+ s_1 s_3^3 s_5 + s_1^9 s_3^2 + s_1^2 s_3^2 s_7 + s_1^4 s_3^2 s_5 + s_3^5$$
$$+ s_1^2 s_3 s_5^2 + s_1^5 s_3 s_7 + s_1^5 s_5^2 + s_1^3 s_5 s_7 + s_1^3 s_3 s_9$$
$$+ s_1^6 s_9 + s_5^3 + s_3^2 s_9 + s_1 s_7^2 + s_1 s_5 s_9$$

$$M(7) = \begin{bmatrix} 1, & 0, & 0, & 0, & 0, & 0, & 0 \\ s_1^2, & s_1, & 1, & 0, & 0, & 0, & 0 \\ s_1^4, & s_3, & s_1^2, & s_1, & 1, & 0, & 0 \\ s_3^2, & s_5, & s_1^4, & s_3, & s_1^2, & s_1, & 1 \\ s_1^8, & s_7, & s_3^2, & s_5, & s_1^4, & s_3, & s_1^2 \\ s_5^2, & s_9, & s_1^8, & s_7, & s_3^2, & s_5, & s_1^4 \\ s_3^4, & s_1 1, & s_5^2, & s_9, & s_1^8, & s_7, & s_3^2 \end{bmatrix}$$

$$det(M(7)) = s_1^7 s_3^3 s_5 + s_1^{15} s_3^2 + s_1^{13} s_3 s_5 + s_1^9 s_5 s_7$$
$$+ s_1^9 s_3 s_9 + s_1^8 s_3^2 s_7 + s_1^3 s_3^2 s_5 s_7 + s_1^3 s_3^3 s_9$$
$$+ s_1^6 s_3^5 + s_1^{21} + s_1^7 s_5 s_9 + s_1 s_3^5 s_5 + s_1^9 s_3^4$$
$$+ s_1^3 s_3 s_5^3 + s_1^6 s_5^3 + s_1 s_3^2 s_7^2 + s_1 s_5^4 + s_1 s_3 s_5^2 s_7$$
$$+ s_1^4 s_3^4 s_5 + s_3^7 + s_1^6 s_3 s_5 s_7 + s_1^5 s_3^3 s_7 + s_3^3 s_5 s_7$$
$$+ s_1^5 s_3^2 s_5^2 + s_1^{11} s_5^2 + s_1^7 s_3 s_{11} + s_1^2 s_3^4 s_7 + s_1^{14} s_7$$
$$+ s_1^{10} s_{11} + s_1^{12} s_9 + s_1 s_3^3 s_{11} + s_3^2 s_5^3 + s_1^4 s_3 s_5 s_9$$
$$+ s_1^2 s_5 s_7^2 + s_1^2 s_5^2 s_9 + s_1^4 s_3 s_7^2 + s_1^2 s_3 s_7 s_9$$
$$+ s_1^2 s_3 s_5 s_{11} + s_1^5 s_7 s_9 + s_1^5 s_5 s_{11} + s_3^3 s_9^2$$
$$+ s_1^3 s_7 s_{11} + s_7^3 + s_5^2 s_{11} + s_3 s_9^2 + s_3 s_7 s_{11}$$

$$M(8) = \begin{bmatrix} 1, & 0, & 0, & 0, & 0, & 0, & 0, & 0 \\ s_1^2, & s_1, & 1, & 0, & 0, & 0, & 0, & 0 \\ s_1^4, & s_3, & s_1^2, & s_1, & 1, & 0, & 0, & 0 \\ s_3^2, & s_5, & s_1^4, & s_3, & s_1^2, & s_1, & 1, & 0 \\ s_1^8, & s_7, & s_3^2, & s_5, & s_1^4, & s_3, & s_1^2, & s_1 \\ s_5^2, & s_9, & s_1^8, & s_7, & s_3^2, & s_5, & s_1^4, & s_3 \\ s_3^4, & s_11, & s_5^2, & s_9, & s_1^8, & s_7, & s_3^2, & s_5 \\ s_7^2, & s_13, & s_3^4, & s_11, & s_5^2, & s_9, & s_1^8, & s_7 \end{bmatrix}$$

$det(M(8)) = s_1^7 s_3^3 s_5 s_7 + s_1^3 s_3^6 s_7 + s_1^7 s_3^2 s_3^3 + s_1^{13} s_3 s_5 s_7$

$+ s_1^{12} s_3^3 s_7 + s_1^8 s_3 s_5^2 s_7 + s_1^9 s_5 s_7^2 + s_1^9 s_3 s_7 s_9 + s_1^9 s_3 s_5 s_{11}$

$+ s_1^{10} s_9^2 + s_1^{10} s_7 s_{11} + s_1^8 s_3^3 s_{11} + s_1^{14} s_3 s_{11} + s_1^{21} s_7 + s_1^{17} s_{11}$

$+ s_1^3 s_3^2 s_5 s_7^2 + s_1^3 s_3^3 s_7 s_9 + s_1^3 s_3^3 s_5 s_{11} + s_1^4 s_3^2 s_7 s_{11} + s_1^4 s_5^3 s_9$

$+ s_1^{14} s_3^3 s_5 + s_1^{22} s_3^2 + s_1^{16} s_5 s_7 + s_1^{16} s_3 s_9 + s_1^{15} s_3^2 s_7 + s_1^{20} s_3 s_5$

$+ s_1^7 s_3^7 + s_1^{13} s_3^5 + s_1^{28} + s_1^2 s_3^7 s_5 + s_1^{10} s_3^6 + s_1^{13} s_3^2 s_9$

$+ s_1^7 s_3 s_7 s_{11} + s_1^{14} s_5 s_9 + s_1 s_3^5 s_5 s_7 + s_1^5 s_3^6 s_5 + s_1 s_3^9$

$+ s_1^3 s_3 s_3^3 s_7 + s_1^3 s_3^5 s_5^2 + s_1^2 s_5^5 s_{11} + s_1^{12} s_7 s_9 + s_1^4 s_3 s_5^2 s_{11}$

$+ s_1^{11} s_5^2 s_7 + s_1^7 s_3^4 s_9 + s_1 s_3^2 s_7^3 + s_1 s_3^3 s_9^2 + s_1 s_3 s_5^3 s_9$

$+ s_1 s_3 s_5^2 s_7^2 + s_1^2 s_3^3 s_{11} + s_3^7 s_7 + s_1^4 s_3^3 s_5^3 + s_3^6 s_5^2 + s_1^{10} s_3^2 s_5 s_7$

$+ s_1 s_3^6 s_9 + s_1^{10} s_3 s_5^3 + s_1^6 s_3 s_5 s_7^2 + s_1^6 s_3^2 s_5 s_{11} + s_1^5 s_3^3 s_7^2$

$+ s_1^3 s_3^2 s_5^2 s_9 + s_1^{11} s_3^2 s_{11} + s_1^{10} s_3^3 s_9 + s_3^3 s_5 s_7^2 + s_3 s_5^5 + s_3^4 s_7 s_9$

$+ s_1^{13} s_5^3 + s_1^5 s_3 s_5 s_9 + s_1^3 s_5^5 + s_1^2 s_3^4 s_5 s_9 + s_1^{18} s_5^2 + s_1^7 s_5 s_7 s_9$

$+ s_1^7 s_3 s_5 s_{13} + s_1^8 s_9 s_{11} + s_1^8 s_7 s_{13} + s_1^{14} s_7^2 + s_1^6 s_3^3 s_{13}$

$+ s_1^{12} s_3 s_{13} + s_1^7 s_5^2 s_{11} + s_1^{15} s_{13} + s_1 s_3 s_5 s_7 s_9 + s_1 s_3^3 s_5 s_{13}$

$+ s_1^9 s_3^2 s_{13} + s_1^2 s_3^2 s_9 s_{11} + s_1^2 s_3^2 s_7 s_{13} + s_3^2 s_5^3 s_7 + s_1^4 s_5^2 s_7^2$

$+ s_3^3 s_5^2 s_9 + s_1^2 s_5 s_7^3 + s_1^5 s_5 s_9^2 + s_1^5 s_5 s_7 s_{11} + s_1^4 s_3 s_7^3$

$+ s_1^4 s_3^2 s_5 s_{13} + s_3^5 s_{13} + s_1^2 s_3 s_7^2 s_9 + s_1^2 s_3 s_5^2 s_{13} + s_1^5 s_3 s_9 s_{11}$

$+ s_1^5 s_3 s_7 s_{13} + s_1^5 s_7^2 s_9 + s_1^5 s_5^2 s_{13} + s_1^3 s_7 s_9^2 + s_1^3 s_5 s_9 s_{11}$

$+ s_1^3 s_7^2 s_{11} + s_1^3 s_5 s_7 s_{13} + s_1^3 s_3 s_{11}^2 + s_1^3 s_3 s_9 s_{13} + s_1^6 s_{11}^2$

$+ s_1^6 s_9 s_{13} + s_7^4 + s_5 s_7^2 s_9 + s_5^2 s_9^2 + s_5^3 s_{13} + s_3^2 s_{11}^2 + s_3^2 s_9 s_{13}$

$+ s_1 s_9^3 + s_1 s_7^2 s_{13} + s_1 s_5 s_{11}^2 + s_1 s_5 s_9 s_{13}$

$$M(9) = \begin{bmatrix}
1, & 0, & 0, & 0, & 0, & 0, & 0, & 0, & 0 \\
s_1^2, & s_1, & 1, & 0, & 0, & 0, & 0, & 0, & 0 \\
s_1^4, & s_3, & s_1^2, & s_1, & 1, & 0, & 0, & 0, & 0 \\
s_3^2, & s_5, & s_1^4, & s_3, & s_1^2, & s_1, & 1, & 0, & 0 \\
s_1^8, & s_7, & s_3^2, & s_5, & s_1^4, & s_3, & s_1^2, & s_1, & 1 \\
s_5^2, & s_9, & s_1^8, & s_7, & s_3^2, & s_5, & s_1^4, & s_3, & s_1^2 \\
s_3^4, & s_11, & s_5^2, & s_9, & s_1^8, & s_7, & s_3^2, & s_5, & s_1^4 \\
s_7^2, & s_13, & s_3^4, & s_11, & s_5^2, & s_9, & s_1^8, & s_7, & s_3^2 \\
s_1^16, & s_15, & s_7^2, & s_13, & s_3^4, & s_11, & s_5^2, & s_9, & s_1^8
\end{bmatrix}$$

$$det(M(9)) = s_1^{15}s_3^3s_5s_7 + s_1^{17}s_3s_7s_9 + s_1^{17}s_3s_5s_{11} + s_1^{15}s_3^2s_5^3$$
$$+ s_1^3s_3^{11} + s_1^{15}s_3^7 + s_1^{21}s_3s_5s_7 + s_1^{20}s_3^3s_7 + s_1^{16}s_3s_5^2s_7 + s_1^3s_3^7s_5s_7$$
$$+ s_1^{17}s_5s_7^2 + s_1^9s_3^2s_5s_7s_9 + s_1^9s_3s_5^3s_9 + s_1^9s_3^3s_5s_{13} + s_1^{10}s_3^2s_9s_{11}$$
$$+ s_1^{10}s_3^2s_7s_{13} + s_1^5s_3^2s_7^2s_{11} + s_1^5s_3^2s_5s_9s_{11} + s_1^5s_3^2s_5s_7s_{13}$$
$$+ s_1^5s_3^3s_9s_{13} + s_1^{16}s_3^3s_{11} + s_1^{29}s_7 + s_1^{25}s_{11} + s_1^5s_5^3s_7s_9$$
$$+ s_1^{15}s_3s_7s_{11} + s_1^{11}s_3^4s_{13} + s_1^5s_3s_5^3s_{13} + s_1^{12}s_5^2s_7^2 + s_1^8s_5^3s_{13}$$
$$+ s_1^6s_5^2s_9s_{11} + s_1^3s_5^4s_{13} + s_1^{18}s_3^3s_9 + s_1^{22}s_3^3s_5 + s_1^{30}s_3^2$$
$$+ s_1^{24}s_5s_7 + s_1^{23}s_3^2s_7 + s_1^{28}s_3s_5 + s_1^{24}s_3s_9 + s_1^6s_3^7s_9$$
$$+ s_1^{21}s_3^2s_9 + s_1^4s_3^2s_5s_7 + s_1^{21}s_3^5 + s_1^9s_3s_5^2s_7^2 + s_1^{36}$$
$$+ s_1^6s_3^4s_7s_{11} + s_1^{12}s_3^2s_7s_{11} + s_1^4s_3^6s_7^2 + s_1^{22}s_5s_9 + s_1^8s_5s_7^2s_9$$
$$+ s_1^6s_3^{10} + s_1^{15}s_5^2s_{11} + s_1^5s_5^4s_{11} + s_1^{13}s_3^4s_{11} + s_1^2s_3^2s_5^2s_9$$
$$+ s_1^2s_3^2s_7^4 + s_1^2s_5^5s_9 + s_1^2s_3^4s_5^3s_7 + s_1^2s_3^8s_5^2 + s_1^2s_3s_5^2s_7^3$$
$$+ s_1^{13}s_3^2s_5^2s_7 + s_1^5s_3^2s_5^5 + s_1^7s_3^3s_7^2 + s_1^{14}s_3^3s_7s_9 + s_1^8s_3^2s_{11}^2$$
$$+ s_1^5s_3^3s_5^3s_7 + s_1^3s_3^5s_7s_{11} + s_1^5s_3^7s_5^2 + s_1^{11}s_3^2s_5s_7^2 + s_1^{11}s_3s_5^3s_7$$
$$+ s_1^{11}s_5^5s_5^2 + s_1^7s_3s_5s_7^3 + s_1^7s_5^6s_{11} + s_1^{22}s_3s_{11} + s_1^6s_3^6s_7^3$$
$$+ s_1^4s_3^7s_{11} + s_1s_3s_5^5s_7 + s_1s_3^5s_5s_7^3 + s_1s_3^3s_5^5 + s_1^4s_3^2s_5^3s_{11}$$
$$+ s_1^{12}s_3^3s_9 + s_1^{20}s_5s_{11} + s_1^{12}s_5^3s_9 + s_1^8s_3s_7^2s_{11} + s_1^{11}s_3^2s_5^3s_9$$
$$+ s_1^{19}s_3^2s_{11} + s_1^{19}s_5^2s_7 + s_1^2s_3^3s_7^2s_{11} + s_1s_3^3s_5^3s_{11} + s_1^5s_3s_5s_7^2s_9$$
$$+ s_1^3s_5s_7^4 + s_1s_3^3s_5^2s_7s_9 + s_1^5s_3s_5^4 + s_1^3s_3s_7^3s_9 + s_1^3s_3s_5s_7^2s_{11}$$
$$+ s_1^{18}s_9^2 + s_1^{18}s_7s_{11} + s_1^6s_7^3s_9 + s_1^2s_3^2s_5^3s_{13} + s_1^6s_3^4s_5s_{13}$$
$$+ s_1^4s_5^2s_{11}^2 + s_1^4s_5^2s_9s_{13} + s_1s_5^2s_7s_9^2 + s_1s_7^5 + s_1s_3s_5^2s_{11}^2$$
$$+ s_1s_3s_7^2s_9^2 + s_1s_3s_7^3s_{11} + s_1^{12}s_3^4s_5s_7 + s_1^{20}s_3^2s_5^2 + s_1^{16}s_3^5s_5$$
$$+ s_1^{24}s_3^4 + s_3^{12} + s_1^{12}s_3^8 + s_1^{18}s_3^2s_5s_7 + s_1^6s_3^6s_5s_7 + s_1^{17}s_3^4s_7$$
$$+ s_1s_3^6s_5^2s_7 + s_3^8s_5s_7 + s_3^5s_5^2s_{11} + s_1^{18}s_3s_5^3 + s_1^6s_3^3s_5s_7s_9$$

$$+ s_1^6 s_3^2 s_5^3 s_9 + s_1^{12} s_3 s_5 s_7 s_9 + s_1^6 s_3^4 s_9^2 + s_1^8 s_3 s_7 s_9^2$$

$$+ s_1^8 s_3 s_5 s_9 s_{11} + s_1^8 s_3 s_5 s_7 s_{13} + s_1^{11} s_3^3 s_7 s_9 + s_1^7 s_3^3 s_7 s_{13}$$

$$+ s_1^2 s_3^3 s_7 s_9^2 + s_1^2 s_3^3 s_5 s_9 s_{11} + s_1^2 s_3^3 s_5 s_7 s_{13} + s_1^{13} s_3^3 s_7$$

$$+ s_1^7 s_3^5 s_7^2 + s_1^7 s_3^2 s_5^2 s_{13} + s_1 s_3^2 s_5^4 s_9 + s_3^5 s_5 s_7 s_9 + s_1^2 s_3 s_5^3 s_7 s_9$$

$$+ s_1^2 s_3 s_5^5 s_9 + s_1^6 s_3 s_7^2 s_{13} + s_1^6 s_3 s_5 s_9 s_{13} + s_3^9 s_9 + s_1^2 s_3 s_5^6 s_{11}$$

$$+ s_3^5 s_7^3 + s_3 s_5^3 s_7 s_{11} + s_3^3 s_9^3 + s_3^3 s_5 s_{11}^2 + s_3 s_5^3 s_9^2 + s_3^2 s_5^2 s_9 s_{11} + \cdots$$

$$\cdots + s_1^{21} s_3^3 + s_1^{13} s_3^3 s_5 s_9 + s_1^{15} s_5 s_7 s_9 + s_1 s_3^{10} s_5 + s_1^{13} s_3^6 s_5$$

$$+ s_1^{11} s_5^5 + s_1^3 s_3^6 s_5^3 + s_1^{11} s_3^3 s_5 s_{11} + s_1^{26} s_5^2 + s_1 s_5^7 + s_1^9 s_3^4 s_5^3$$

$$+ s_1^5 s_3^4 s_5^2 s_9 + s_1^{15} s_3^3 + s_1^7 s_3^2 s_5 s_7 s_{11} + s_1^{15} s_3 s_5 s_{13} + s_1^7 s_3^3 s_5 s_{15}$$

$$+ s_1^{15} s_3^2 s_{15} + s_1^{13} s_3 s_5 s_{15} + s_1^9 s_9^3 + s_1^9 s_7 s_9 s_{11} + s_1^9 s_5 s_9 s_{13}$$

$$+ s_1^9 s_5 s_7 s_{15} + s_1^9 s_3 s_{11} s_{13} + s_1^9 s_3 s_9 s_{15} + s_1^{16} s_7 s_{13}$$

$$+ s_1^8 s_3^2 s_7 s_{15} + s_1^3 s_3^2 s_7 s_9 s_{11} + s_1^3 s_3^2 s_5 s_7 s_{15} + s_1^{11} s_3 s_{11}^2$$

$$+ s_1^3 s_3^3 s_{11} s_{13} + s_1^3 s_3 s_9 s_{15} + s_1^6 s_3^2 s_5^2 s_7^2 + s_1^6 s_5^3 s_{15}$$

$$+ s_1^{16} s_9 s_{11} + s_1^8 s_5^2 s_7 s_{11} + s_1^8 s_3^4 s_7 s_9 + s_1^3 s_3^8 s_9 + s_1^{15} s_3^4 s_9$$

$$+ s_1^{23} s_{13} + s_1^{21} s_{15} + s_1^{14} s_9 s_{13} + s_1^2 s_3^7 s_{13} + s_1^9 s_5^4 s_7$$

$$+ s_1^5 s_3^4 s_5 s_7^2 + s_1^{11} s_7 s_9^2 + s_1^3 s_3^4 s_7^3 + s_1^3 s_3^4 s_5 s_7 s_9 + s_1^{13} s_5 s_9^2$$

$$+ s_1^{13} s_5^2 s_{13} + s_1^{13} s_3 s_9 s_{11} + s_1^7 s_7 s_{11}^2 + s_1^7 s_7 s_9 s_{13}$$

$$+ s_1^7 s_5 s_{11} s_{13} + s_1^7 s_5 s_9 s_{15} + s_1 s_3^7 s_5 s_9 + s_1 s_3^5 s_5 s_{15} + s_1 s_3^8 s_{11}$$

$$+ s_1^{17} s_3^2 s_{13} + s_1^9 s_3^4 s_{15} + s_1^3 s_3^5 s_5 s_{13} + s_1^3 s_3 s_5^3 s_{15}$$

$$+ s_1^6 s_5^3 s_{15} + s_1^4 s_3^4 s_7 s_{13} + s_1 s_3^2 s_9^2 s_{11} + s_1 s_3^2 s_7^2 s_{15} + s_1 s_5^4 s_{15}$$

$$+ s_1 s_3 s_5^2 s_7 s_{15} + s_1^{16} s_5^4 + s_1^{10} s_5^2 s_7 s_9 + s_1^2 s_5^4 s_7^2 + s_1^4 s_3^3 s_5 s_9^2$$

$$+ s_1^8 s_3^4 s_5 s_{11} + s_1^2 s_3^2 s_5 s_7^2 s_9 + s_1^6 s_5 s_7 s_9^2 + s_1^9 s_3^2 s_5^2 s_{11}$$

$$+ s_1^{11} s_5 s_9 s_{11} + s_1^3 s_5^2 s_7 s_{11} + s_1^{11} s_5 s_7 s_{13} + s_1^3 s_3^2 s_5 s_{11}^2 + s_3^3 s_5^3 s_7$$

$$+ s_3^2 s_5 s_7 s_9^2 + s_5^5 s_{11} + s_1^{12} s_3 s_7^3 + s_1^4 s_3^3 s_5 s_7 s_{11} + s_1^{16} s_3^2 s_7^2$$

$$+ s_3^6 s_7 s_{11} + s_3^4 s_5^3 s_9 + s_1^{12} s_3^2 s_9^2 + s_1^4 s_3^4 s_5 s_{15} + s_1^8 s_3^5 s_{13}$$

$$+ s_3^7 s_{15} + s_1^6 s_3 s_7 s_9 s_{11} + s_1^6 s_3 s_5 s_7 s_{15} + s_1^2 s_3^4 s_{11}^2 + s_1^9 s_3^3 s_9^2$$

$$+ s_1 s_3^5 s_9 s_{11} + s_1^5 s_3^3 s_7 s_{15} + s_1^3 s_3 s_5^2 s_7 s_{13} + s_3^3 s_7 s_9 s_{11}$$

$$+ s_3^3 s_5 s_7 s_{15} + s_1 s_3^4 s_7^2 s_9 + s_1^5 s_3 s_5^2 s_7 s_{11} + s_1^3 s_5^2 s_7 s_9$$

$$+ s_1^{14} s_7 s_{15} + s_1^{10} s_{13}^2 + s_1^{10} s_{11} s_{15} + s_1^{12} s_{11} s_{13} + s_1^{12} s_9 s_{15}$$

$$+ s_1 s_5^2 s_7^2 s_{11} + s_1 s_3^3 s_{13}^2 + s_1 s_3^3 s_{11} s_{15} + s_1^8 s_7^4 + s_3^2 s_7^3 s_9$$

$$+ s_1^4 s_5 s_7^2 s_{13} + s_1^4 s_3 s_7 s_{11}^2 + s_1^4 s_3 s_7 s_9 s_{13} + s_1^2 s_7 s_9^3 + s_1^2 s_3^3 s_{13}$$

$$+ s_1^4 s_5 s_9^3 + s_3^2 s_5^3 s_{15} + s_1^4 s_3 s_5 s_{11} s_{13} + s_1^4 s_3 s_5 s_9 s_{15}$$

$$+ s_1^2 s_5 s_9^2 s_{11} + s_1^2 s_5 s_7^2 s_{15} + s_1^2 s_5^2 s_{11} s_{13} + s_1^2 s_5^2 s_9 s_{15}$$

$$+ s_1^4 s_3 s_9^2 s_{11} + s_1^4 s_3 s_7^2 s_{15} + s_1^2 s_3 s_9 s_{11}^2 + s_1^2 s_3 s_7 s_{11} s_{13}$$

$$+ s_1^2 s_3 s_9^2 s_{13} + s_1^2 s_3 s_7 s_9 s_{15} + s_1^2 s_3 s_5 s_{13}^2 + s_1^2 s_3 s_5 s_{11} s_{15}$$

$$+ s_1^5 s_9 s_{11}^2 + s_1^5 s_9^2 s_{13} + s_1^5 s_7 s_{11} s_{13} + s_1^5 s_7 s_9 s_{15} + s_1^5 s_5 s_{13}^2$$

$$+ s_1^5 s_5 s_{11} s_{15} + s_1^3 s_{11}^3 + s_1^3 s_9^2 s_{15} + s_1^3 s_7 s_{13}^2 + s_1^3 s_7 s_{11} s_{15}$$

$$+ s_9^4 + s_7 s_9^2 s_{11} + s_7^2 s_{11}^2 + s_7^3 s_{15} + s_5^2 s_{13}^2 + s_5^2 s_{11} s_{15} + s_3 s_3 s_{11}^3$$

$$+ s_3 s_3 s_9^2 s_{15} + s_3 s_3 s_7 s_{13}^2 + s_3 s_3 s_7 s_{11} s_{15}$$

The number of products added in the determinant $det(M(x))$ has an upper bound of $x \times (x-1) \times (x-2) \times ... \times 1 = x!$. Therefore identifying the number of errors is slower for a higher multiplicity.

After determining the number n_e of erroneous bits, the error positions $i_1, i_2, i_3, ..., i_{n_e}$ are identified as solutions of the following equations:

$$s_1 = \alpha^{i_1} + \alpha^{i_2} + ... + \alpha^{i_{n_e}}$$

$$s_3 = \alpha^{3i_1} + \alpha^{3i_2} + ... + \alpha^{3i_{n_e}}$$

$$s_5 = \alpha^{5i_1} + \alpha^{5i_2} + ... + \alpha^{5i_{n_e}}$$

$$\vdots$$

$$s_{2T-1} = \alpha^{(2T-1) \times i_1} + \alpha^{(2T-1) \times i_2} + ... + \alpha^{(2T-1) \times i_{n_e}}$$

For details, see [3].

3   BCH Code with Additional Detection

In this section, we present a general explanation on how the presented approach works. Our approach can be summarized as follows:

In order to perform a 2-bit (3-bit) error correction with additional detection, we propose a speculative calculation (assuming that a 2-bit (3-bit) error occurred) of the 2-bit (3-bit) error positions given a correction approach and comparing the resulting syndrome components.

The speculative part is the assumption that a 2-bit (3-bit) error occurred. Under this assumption, the 2 error positions of a 2-bit error are determined using the syndrome components s_1, s_3. For the 3-bit error case, s_1, s_3, s_5 are used instead to determine the 3 error positions. The correctness of the assumption that a 2-bit (3-bit) error occurred is checked by use of the higher syndrome components. For this purpose, the (expected) higher syndrome components are calculated from the 2 (3) error positions and compared to the (actual) higher syndrome components determined by multiplying the check matrix H by the transferred word w. For the speculative calculation, any existing approach that identifies the error positions under the assumption that a 2-bit (3-bit) error occurred can be used.

Given an erroneous word $w = c + e$ based on code word c ($H \times c = 0$) and an error vector $e \neq 0$, the syndrome $S \neq 0$ can be calculated using $H \times w = S$. Since

$H \times c = 0$ for each code word c, the syndrome only depends on the error vector e. Speculative calculation of the 2-bit and 3-bit error vectors e_2, e_3 using any applicable approach allows to generate expected syndrome components S_{e_2}, S_{e_3} by $H \times e_2 = S_{e_2}$, $H \times e_3 = S_{e_3}$. If the calculation of the 2-bit error fails, no 2-bit error can have occurred. The same is true for the calculation of the 3-bit error. By construction of a T-bit ($T > 3$) error correcting BCH code, all 3-bit errors can be differentiated from 2-bit errors by their corresponding syndromes. Therefore $S_{e_2} \neq S_{e_3}$. If $S_{e_2} = S$ then a 2-bit error with error vector e_2 was detected, if instead $S_{e_3} = S$ then a 3-bit error with error vector e_3 was detected. Otherwise a detectable error occurred that is not a 2-bit and not a 3-bit error.

In comparison, the known approach presented in [3] computes determinants in descending order until the first determinant is non-zero. The first non-zero determinant identifies the number of erroneous bits. The presented approach verifies the number of occurred errors in a simpler and faster way by comparing syndrome components instead of calculating determinants.

As another example, instead of using the Berlekamp-Massey algorithm [2] to identify the locator polynomial and then applying chien search, a locator polynomial for a 2-bit (3-bit) error can be assumed and chien search can be used for a speculative identification of the error positions. The correctness of the error positions is then checked by comparing expected syndrome S_{e_2} (S_{e_3}) against the actual syndrome S.

In the following sections, we present the specific approaches for the 2-bit error correction, 3-bit error correction and correction for errors with more than 4 bits in detail.

4   2-Bit Correction with Additional Detection

The proposed 2-bit correction process performs a speculative 2-bit correction and verifies the error locations using the syndrome components. Given a T-bit error correcting BCH code of length n described by H and a transferred word w (of length n), the following steps are performed:

1. Calculate the syndrome components s_i using $H \times w = \{s_1, s_3, s_5, \ldots, s_{2T-1}\}$. If $S = 0$, then no detectable error occurred.
2. Use a known approach to calculate both error positions i, j with $i \neq j$ using only the syndrome components s_1 and s_3. E.g. the approach shown by Okano and Imai [4]:
The 2-bit error locator polynomial

$$0 = (x + \alpha^i) \times (x + \alpha^j)$$
$$= x^2 + x \times s_1 + \frac{s_1^3 + s_3}{s_1}. \tag{2}$$

can be transformed using $x = s_1 \times z$.

$$(z + 1) \times z = (1 + \frac{s_3}{s_1^3}) \tag{3}$$

Using this equation, a precomputed table t can be created assigning each $C = \frac{s_3}{s_1^3}$ as input to a solution $t(C) = z_1$ for z as output. The second solution is $z_2 = z_1 + 1$. In order to caluclate the error positions, calculate $C = \frac{s_3}{s_1^3}$, then use the table to determine $z_1 = t(C)$. The values i and j indicate the error positions, where $\alpha^i = z_1 \times s_1$ and $\alpha^j = (z_1 + 1) \times s_1$. If the calculation fails (e.g. $s_1 = 0$), then no 2-bit error can have occurred.

3. Calculate expected error syndromes for the identified positions i, j:

$$s_{5_e} = \alpha^{5i} + \alpha^{5j}$$
$$s_{7_e} = \alpha^{7i} + \alpha^{7j}$$
$$\vdots \tag{4}$$
$$s_{(2T-1)_e} = \alpha^{(2T-1)i} + \alpha^{(2T-1)j}$$

4. Compare the remaining error syndrome components to the expected error syndromes. The syndrome components used to calculate the error positions (s_1, s_3) do not have to be checked.

$$s_5 \overset{?}{=} s_{5_e}$$
$$s_7 \overset{?}{=} s_{7_e}$$
$$\vdots \tag{5}$$
$$s_{(2T-1)} \overset{?}{=} s_{(2T-1)_e}$$

If the equations hold for all syndrome components, then a 2-bit error at the identified positions (or an undetectable error) occurred. Since a T-bit error correcting BCH code has a code distance of $2T + 1$ and given a 2-bit error correction, an undetectable error must be at least a $(2T - 1)$-bit error. Up to $(2T - 2)$-bit errors are covered by the code distance and can be detected by the syndrome components by construction of the BCH code. $(2T - 1)$-bit errors can be 2 bit away from another codeword. In such a case, a $(2T-1)$-bit error could be incorrectly identified as a 2-bit error instead. Therefore only all up to $(2T - 2)$-bit errors are guaranteed to be detected correctly in the case of a 2-bit error correction.

5. If a 2-bit error occurred, correct the erroneous positions i, j. Otherwise return that an error other than a 2-bit error occurred.

Using the presented approach allows to identify and correct 2-bit errors using equations (constant length equations independent of T) instead of calculating the determinants (matrix size increases with higher T) the known approach in [3].

5   3-Bit Correction with Additional Detection

The approach for the 3-bit correction works similar to the approach of the 2-bit correction. Given a T-bit error correcting BCH code of length n described by H and a transferred word w (of length n), the following steps are performed:

1. Calculate the syndrome components s_i using $H \times w = \{s_1, s_3, s_5, \ldots, s_{2T-1}\}$. If $S = 0$, then no detectable error occurred.
2. Use a known approach to calculate the 3 error positions i, j, k with $i \neq j \neq k \neq i$ using only the syndrome components s_1, s_3 and s_5. E.g. the 3-bit error correction also shown by Okano and Imai [4]:
   The 3-bit error locator polynomial is

$$0 = (x + \alpha^i) \times (x + \alpha^j) \times (x + \alpha^k)$$
$$= x^3 + \sigma_1 \times x^2 + \sigma_2 \times x + \sigma_3$$

$$\text{where } \sigma_1 = s_1, \quad \sigma_2 = \frac{s_1^2 \times s_3 + s_5}{s_1^3 + s_3}, \tag{6}$$

$$\sigma_3 = s_1^3 + s_3 + \frac{s_1 \times (s_1^2 \times s_3 + s_5)}{s_1^3 + s_3}$$

Using $x = y + \sigma_1$, the equation can be transformed to

$$0 = y^3 + \eta \times y + \delta$$
$$\text{where } \eta = \sigma_2 + \sigma_1^2, \quad \delta = \sigma_2 \sigma_1 + \sigma_3 \tag{7}$$

The equation can now be brought into the form

$$0 = z^3 + z + C$$
$$\text{where } z = \frac{y}{\eta^{\frac{1}{2}}}, \quad C = \frac{\delta}{\eta^{\frac{3}{2}}} \tag{8}$$

In the special case $\eta = 0$, the equation can be simplified to $x = \sqrt[3]{\sigma_2 \sigma_1 + \sigma_3} + \sigma_1$. Otherwise, a precomputed table t' can be used assigning C as input to the three roots z_1, z_2, z_3 of $z^3 + z = C$ as output. The solutions $x_1 = \alpha^i, x_2 = \alpha^j, x_3 = \alpha^k$ can be calculated using the equation $x = \eta^{\frac{1}{2}} \times z + \sigma_1$. The exponents i, j and k are the positions of the errors. If the calculation fails $(s_1^3 + s_3 = 0)$, then no 3-bit error can have occurred.
3. Calculate expected error syndromes for the identified positions i, j:

$$s_{7_e} = \alpha^{7i} + \alpha^{7j} + \alpha^{7k}$$
$$s_{9_e} = \alpha^{9i} + \alpha^{9j} + \alpha^{9k}$$
$$\vdots$$
$$s_{(2T-1)_e} = \alpha^{(2T-1)i} + \alpha^{(2T-1)j} + \alpha^{(2T-1)k} \tag{9}$$

4. Compare the remaining error syndrome components to the expected error syndromes. The syndrome components used to calculate the error positions (s_1, s_3, s_5) do not have to be checked.

$$s_7 \stackrel{?}{=} s_{7_e}$$

$$s_9 \stackrel{?}{=} s_{9_e}$$

$$\vdots$$

$$s_{(2T-1)} \stackrel{?}{=} s_{(2T-1)_e} \tag{10}$$

If the equations hold for all syndrome components, then a 3-bit error at the identified positions (or an undetectable error) occurred. Since a T-bit error correcting BCH code has a code distance of $2T + 1$, given a 3-bit error correction an undetectable error must be at least a $(2T - 2)$-bit error.

5. If a 3-bit error occurred, correct the identified erroneous bits at i, j, k. Otherwise return that a error other than a 3-bit error occurred.

Using the presented approach allows to identify and correct 3-bit errors using equations (constant length equations independent of T) instead of calculating the determinants (matrix size increases with higher T) the known approach in [3].

6   General Approach for Errors Higher Than 3-Bit

The proposed approach can be applied to 4-bit and higher errors. For 5-bit or higher errors, there is no general way of solving the error locator polynomial (5th degree and higher equations), therefore a different way of identifying the error locations has to be used. One example would be the algorithm proposed by Berlekamp et al. [2].

Our approach can be generalized as follows. Given a T-bit error correcting BCH code of length n described by H and a transfered word w (of length n), a number of erroneous bits m to be corrected and an approach to identify the error locations, the following steps are performed:

1. Calculate the syndrome components s_i using $H \times w = \{s_1, s_3, s_5, \ldots, s_{2T-1}\}$. If $S = 0$, then no detectable error occurred.
2. Use the given approach to identify all m error positions $i_1, \ldots, i_m$ (the error positions have to be different: $\forall j, k \in \{i_1, i_2, \ldots i_m\} : j \neq k$). We assume that identifying the error positions will fail if no m-bit error corresponds to the syndrome components $s_1, \ldots, s_{2m-1}$.
3. Calculate expected error syndromes for the identified positions i, j:

$$s_{(2m+1)_e} = \sum_{x=1}^{m} \left(\alpha^{i_x (2m+1)} \right)$$

$$s_{(2m+3)_e} = \sum_{x=1}^{m} \left(\alpha^{i_x (2m+3)} \right)$$

$$\vdots$$

$$s_{(2T-1)_e} = \sum_{x=1}^{m} \left(\alpha^{i_x (2T-1)} \right) \tag{11}$$

4. Compare the error syndrome components to the expected error syndromes.

$$s_{(2m+1)} \stackrel{?}{=} s_{(2m+1)_e}$$

$$s_{(2m+3)} \stackrel{?}{=} s_{(2m+3)_e} \tag{12}$$

$$\vdots$$

$$s_{(2T-1)} \stackrel{?}{=} s_{2T-1_e}$$

If the equations hold for all syndrome components, then a m-bit error at the identified positions (or an undetectable error) occurred. Given the $2T + 1$ bit code distance of a T-bit error correcting BCH code, an undetectable error must have at least $(2T + 1 - m)$ bit.

5. If an m-bit error was detected, correct the erroneous bits at $i_1, \ldots, i_m$. Otherwise return that a error other than a m-bit error occurred.

Summary

In this paper, we presented an approach combining BCH 2-bit and 3-bit error correction with additional error detection. We showed that the approach can also be generalized to errors with more than 3 bit. Under the speculative assumption that a 2-bit (3-bit) error occurred, the positions of the expected errors are determined. These expected errors are used to compute expected higher syndrome components which are then compared to the actual error syndrome components. A mismatch indicates an error higher than 2-bit (3-bit). The expected errors can be determined either in parallel as described or by any other error correction approach.

The presented approach allows a fast and simple 2-bit, 3-bit or higher error correction combined with additional detection of higher errors. Compared to known approaches, the number of erroneous bits does not need to be identified before the correction approach. Therefore calculating large determinants is not necessary compared to the known approach as described in [3].

Acknowledgment. I would like to thank Prof. Michael Gössel from the University of Potsdam for his stimulating discussions and remarks.

References

1. Berlekamp, E.R.: Algebraic Coding Theory. Mcgraw-Hall, New York (1968)
2. Massey, J.: Shift-register synthesis and BCH decoding. IEEE Trans. Inf. Theory **15**, 122–127 (1969)
3. Peterson, W.W., Weldon, E.J.: Error-Correcting Codes. MIT Press, Cambridge (1972)
4. Okano, H., Imai, H.: A construction method of high-speed decoders using ROM. IEEE Trans. Comput. **10**, 1165–1171 (1987)
5. Schulz-Hanke, C.: Fast BCH 1-bit error correction combined with fast multi-bit error detection. In: 2020 IEEE 26th International Symposium on On-Line Testing and Robust System Design (IOLTS), pp. 1–5 (2020)

Evaluating Soft Error Mitigation Trade-offs During Early Design Stages

Hao Qiu[1]($\boxtimes$), Bor-Tyng Lin[1], Semiu A. Olowogemo[1],
William H. Robinson[1], and Daniel B. Limbrick[2]

[1] Vanderbilt University, Nashville, TN, USA
hao.qiu@vanderbilt.edu
[2] North Carolina A&T State University, Greensboro, NC, USA

Abstract. Protecting computation systems against soft errors is expensive. Unoptimized soft error mitigation schemes can cause area, power, and performance overheads. Therefore, efficient fault-tolerant design should be guided by assessing the cost of developing reliable systems. We present a method to quantify and evaluate trade-offs to protect the system. Using gem5Panalyzer, the toolset we developed to estimate vulnerability factors of microprocessors, we conducted sweeps of Program Vulnerability Factor (PVF) masking to collect the PVF responses to instruction-level masking. We evaluated the confidence in PVF estimations made by gem5Panalyzer with multiple benchmarks from the MiBench suite. Then, we analyzed PVF-masking sweep results. The sensitivity of vulnerability improvement to mitigation techniques varies with the types of applications. When the instruction-level masking effect is 90%, time-averaged PVF reductions of selected benchmarks range from a high of 67% to a low of 10%. The differences in PVF reduction inform designers whether it is worth improving the masking level. As the masking factor is correlated with the efforts to implement mitigations, our method can help to optimize system design choices.

Keywords: Design trade-offs · Fault-masking metrics · Program vulnerability factors · Soft error sensitivity · Error resilience

1 Introduction

Aggressive technology scaling has led modern microprocessors to be more susceptible to faults. Numerous factors introduce faults in electronic components, such as radiation effects, temperature or process variations, and voltage fluctuations [1]. Fault mitigation has been a key challenge in advanced technology nodes. Faults propagate through the system stack to create erroneous outputs and behaviors. Errors can be classified as Silent Data Corruption (SDC), Detected Unrecoverable Error (DUE), and control flow failures (e.g., crashes and hangs)

This material is based upon work supported by the National Science Foundation (NSF) under Grant No. CNS-1629853 and CNS-1629839.

[2,3]. For life-critical and mission-critical systems, countermeasures against soft errors have been an essential concern for system designers.

The reliability community has proposed many soft error mitigation techniques spanning across the system stack. Protection schemes deployed at device or circuit layers significantly improve system resilience, but they are also likely to suffer from a high penalty of area, power, and budget. Implementing resilience techniques at higher abstraction layers, like architectural or software layers, may have little impact on hardware constraints. Conversely, higher layer hardening can hurt the execution time considerably [4,5]. Therefore, deploying soft error resilience techniques in every component of the system is prohibitively expensive.

Various effects residing in the computing system stack usually mask many faults in the underlying hardware. Therefore, not all faults are causing a system failure. The system vulnerability to lower-level faults can vary drastically across workloads. Meanwhile, many trending computing tasks do not need perfectly accurate outputs. Such applications, including recognition, data mining, digital signal processing, allow less reliable but more efficient protection schemes as long as system outputs are "acceptable" [6]. Take YOLO object detection for example; SDCs can lead to inaccurate class probabilities but may not affect the correctness of classification. In this work, we investigate an indirect, efficient, and dependable method to evaluate the effectiveness of mitigation techniques. Using gem5Panalyzer [7], a light-weight tool to assess architectural reliability, we conducted instruction-level masking sweeps on selected benchmarks from MiBench [8]. Since masking factors usually correlate with costs of resilience solutions, the Program Vulnerability Factor (PVF) [9] responses to masking levels provide insights into system hardening effectiveness. Though instruction-level masking is affected by many lower-layer mechanisms, we limit this work's scope on architectural and program vulnerability.

The rest of this paper is organized as follows. Section 2 describes some system reliability research, including relevant tools and frameworks. Section 3 introduces the implementation of gem5Panalyzer, the toolset we developed to evaluate system vulnerability. Section 4 presents the results to validate gem5Panalyzer. In Sect. 5, PVF responses to different masking levels are discussed and characterized. We also examine results with two higher-level error mitigation techniques. Section 6 summarizes the paper.

2 Related Work

Efficient error mitigation requires designers to take a holistic perspective to determine cost-resilience trade-offs. The difference in tolerance to errors for computing tasks can help set a reasonable goal of accuracy. Also, system vulnerability is dependent on workload and hardware architecture. Spatial and temporal variations can further help minimize the cost of fault-tolerant design [10]. The soft error rate (SER) of different physical microarchitectural components varies (i.e., spatial), which guides selective hardening. SER also differs over time (i.e., temporal), which is helpful to achieve adaptive protection. A combination of selective and adaptive protection is preferred to get a specified reliability level with lower costs. Since protections at different abstraction layers have diverse impacts on costs for system reliability, early-stage reliability assessment is essential. It is conducive to locate highly vulnerable hardware components and code segments at early design stages. Similarly, estimating the resilience improvement can guide more cost-effective system hardening strategies.

2.1 Methods and Metrics to Model System Reliability

There are two main categories of methods to evaluate the microprocessor vulnerability: (1) Architecturally Correct Execution (ACE) analysis [11] and (2) testing/simulation-based approaches like fault injection (FI). Metrics derived from AVF are usually estimated using ACE and ACE-like analysis in one or several fault-free runs. Radiation tests or FI campaigns execute workloads repeatedly to get statistically significant results. These approaches measure system error reports error rates with outcomes breakdowns [12]. ACE analyses are typically more efficient, whereas radiation tests or FI merit higher accuracy but tend to be more expensive for budget and time.

Mukherjee et al. proposed the metric of AVF [11]. AVF of a structure refers to the probability that a fault will result in an error. Typically, the ACE analysis identifies the total number of bits that will not affect outputs, i.e., the un-ACE bits. Unless proven to be un-ACE, all other bits are considered ACE. Therefore, the original ACE analysis method provides a pessimistic system vulnerability estimate. Many researchers presented metrics derived from AVF. Biswas et al. presented Quantized AVF (Q-AVF) [13]. Instead of averaging AVF across the application, this method computes AVF over many short intervals to address system vulnerability's runtime variations. PVF, which was proposed by Sridharan and Kaeli [9], extracts the software-dependent part from AVF. PVF models the effect of architectural level faults on various workloads to assist software engineers in getting insights into system vulnerability. Apart from ACE analysis, Vulnerability Factors (VF) can also be estimated at runtime. Runtime VF estimations can be achieved by adding additional logic or via Machine Learning models. The primary drawback of VFs computed by ACE-like analysis is overestimation problems, which leads to overprotection and increases the costs to harden the system. Conversely, testing/simulation-based techniques can quantify system resilience very accurately. Radiation hardness tests measure failure in time (FIT) of the actual hardware directly. Test results will provide a golden reference for future simulation-based research. However, FI is not suitable for guiding the early design. Also, lower-level simulations are time-consuming. High-performance microprocessors and large workloads make the fault space grow exponentially on both spatial and temporal dimensions. Therefore, trade-offs also exist when choosing appropriate methods to characterize system resilience. Speed and accuracy are usually contradictory.

2.2 Early Stage Resilience Evaluation Frameworks

Many researchers combined ACE analysis and fault injection to accelerate archi-
tectural/microarchitectural level fault injection to optimize the accuracy and
efficiency when characterizing system vulnerability. Kaliorakis et al. presented
MeRLiN [14], a framework that allows more efficient AVF measurements with
high accuracy. Using ACE-like analysis and fault grouping, MeRLiN reduces the
fault space significantly. Similarly, Gem5-Approxilizer [15] performs fault injec-
tions at operand registers in dynamic instructions. The fault injection campaign
is also accelerated by pruning the fault space. This tool predicts the software level
vulnerability and the distribution of fault outcomes. Some studies have proposed
methods to provide finer-grained Vulnerability Factors. Enhanced PVF (ePVF)
[3] distinguishes crash-causing bits from the original PVF. In addition to ACE
analysis, ePVF utilizes algorithms to determine the memory accesses that will
trigger segment faults, which is the dominant source of crashes. A probabilistic graphical model presented in [16] provides more accurate soft error rates
estimation by reducing the overestimation of AVF.

2.3 Design for Reliability Cost and Returns

Successful soft error mitigation solutions should achieve the specified resilience
target with minimal costs. The prominent overheads of hardening techniques
vary with abstraction layers and mitigation strategies. Faults in sequential logic
circuits, including flip-flops and memory cells, are the primary contributor to
the overall soft error rate. While circuit-level protection schemes reduce the
structure's inherent vulnerability to transient and upset faults with the minimal
performance penalty, it also introduces area and power overheads. For example, DICE flip-flops are virtually immune to single-node hits but nearly double
the area and power [5]. Redundancy techniques, such as triple modular redundancy (TMR), parity, and Error Correction Codes (ECC), are classical ways
for hardware-level hardening, which enable error detection or correction. Apart
from the drawbacks similar to circuit-level mitigation, they need additional logic
components. A modified microarchitecture can throttle the clock frequency then
degrade the performance. Architectural and software level hardening approaches
usually do not require modifications on hardware, thus the penalty on the area
and power will be minimal. However, higher-level mitigations often incur performance loss or increased code size. Naïve instruction rearranging suffers from
the code size and runtime overheads of more than 40% [17]. Optimized solutions
can reduce such overheads with efforts at the compilation time [18].

Several metrics are presented to quantify the return of hardening to evaluate
the return of system hardening. A more straightforward definition is computing the improvement of error rates. If the system vulnerability is evaluated using
AVF-like metrics, then VF reduction is usually equivalent to reducing error rates
[5]. In addition to the enhancements of reliability metrics, more complex metrics may consider the overheads brought by protection; such metrics reflect the
"profit" of system hardening.

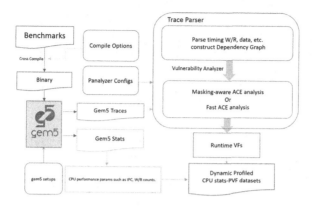

Fig. 1. Gem5Panalyzer structure. Gem5 provides program traces and statistics; gem5Panalyzer computes and profiles PVFs

3   Gem5Panalyzer Implementation

Gem5Panalyzer is a light-weight tool we developed to evaluate embedded microprocessor resilience at early design stages. This section will introduce the toolset's structures, input/outputs, and the method of PVF computation.

Gem5Panalyzer estimates architectural level resilience and measures microprocessor parameters. A unique feature of this tool is that all reported results are dynamically profiled. Vulnerability Factors with timestamps provide users with the temporal variance of system vulnerability to explore adaptive protection schemes.

We implemented gem5Panalyzer on top of the gem5 simulator, a cycle-level computer architecture simulator. Our tool consists of three stages: gem5 trace parser, VF computation, and VF dataset constructor. The structure of the gem5Panalyzer is shown in Fig. 1. Trace parser extracts information such as timing, dependency, architectural structure occupancy, and dataflow from gem5 dynamic instruction traces. VF computation modules evaluate the vulnerability of microarchitecture structures. The last stage profiles previous results and constructs a dataset from VFs and concerned CPU runtime performance parameters. In this work, we configured gem5Panalyzer to explore the behaviors of PVFs.

To compute PVFs, we collect dynamic instruction traces to conduct ACE analysis. The offline ACE analysis relies on the "execute-in-execute" feature of gem5 EXEC debugging. This feature means EXEC flag will be triggered only when all dependencies of executed instructions have been resolved [19]. Gem5's "execute-in-execute" feature assures a dominant portion of the traced dynamic instructions impacts program execution, then ACE analysis could be more efficient. The ACE analysis to estimate PVFs follows the steps proposed in [11]. NOP, performance-enhancing, and predicated false instructions can be filtered using flags in the instruction trace. For address-based structures, Dynamically Dead instructions can be located using lifetime analysis. ACE intervals can be found using the data accesses pattern [2]: W(Write)-R(Read) intervals and R-R intervals after a W operation are ACE. Others are Idle or un-ACE; usually Idle intervals are not counted as ACE. Furthermore, we implemented probabilistic models similar to [16] to compute both first-level and transitive masking effects. If we denote the instruction-level masking factor of instruction i as M_i, then the equation to estimate PVF of architectural register with N entries can be written as:

$$PVF_{RF} = \frac{\sum_{i=0}^{(N-1)} \sum ACE \ cycles_i \times (1 - M_i)}{Total \ Execution \ Cycles} \tag{1}$$

Gem5Panalyzer provides the following user-defined inputs: 1) The minimum depth of data dependency graph, i.e., the "quanta" proposed in [13]. This parameter represents the size of the dependency analyzing window. Analyzing the data dependency of large workloads suffers prohibitive RAM overheads in most host machines. Our experiment indicates that when the window size is greater than ten thousand instructions, reported PVF could be treated as the averaged PVF over runtime. Splitting the trace file with a small min-depth lets users measure Quantized-PVFs. 2) The depth of PVF samples N: Gem5Panalyzer will sample N PVF values. These samples are distributed uniformly throughout the entire lifetime of the program. In this way, users can control the length of dynamically profiled PVFs. 3) Overall instruction-level masking factor: Gem5Panalyzer can compute each instruction's masking effects when its operands are being read. The computation of fine-grained masking suffers from runtime overheads. Users may set an overall masking factor to accelerate for efficiency. The average masking factor is the key variable for efficient hardening explorations in Sect. 5.

4   Gem5Panalyzer Evaluation

This section evaluates the accuracy of vulnerability estimation made by gem5Panalyzer. We compared the relative vulnerability assessment from Paralyzer with FIT results in [20]. Though some preliminary results are presented in [7], this section provides a more comprehensive evaluation of the proposed tool. We examined representative behavioral characteristics of PVF with studies presented in [9,13].

4.1   Benchmarks and Experiment Setups

In this work, we deployed gem5Panalyzer on the gem5 simulator (version 20.0). In-stock Gem5 configurations are modified to support customized ROB size, Physical register size using simulation command. Table 1 shows some major microarchitectural configurations in this experiment. Unless otherwise specified, all other microarchitectural parameters are consistent with the default gem5 configuration. DerivO3 and HPI models are used in the simulation to model Out-of-order and In-Order CPUs, respectively. We set the simulator on System-Call Emulation (SE) mode to make the PVF computation is conducted over the entire program lifespan.

Table 1. Table captions should be placed above the tables.

Parameter	ARM32IO	ARM32O3	ARM64O3
Frequency	4 GHz	2 GHz	2 GHz
Arch registers	15	15	32
Int physical RF	15	128	128
ROB	128	128	128
Memory	2 GB	2 GB	2 GB

All experiments are performed on a host machine with an Intel i7-8700K CPU running at 4.7 GHz. The simulated systems are ARM-like in-order or out-of-order machines. We compiled source codes to ARMv7 and ARMv8 binaries with consistent compilation options. We selected more than ten benchmarks from MiBench suite [8] and Matrix Multiply (M × M) benchmark from [12]. Selected programs attribute a wide range of embedded applications with diverse instruction distributions and control flow. Unless otherwise noted, we use the small inputs option for all tests. The minimum dependency graph depth is configured dynamically for each application. The depth ranges from 26 thousand to 1162 thousand instructions. Each Dynamically profiled resilience report includes 6,000 uniformly distributed PVFs throughout the program's lifetime.

4.2   Discussion of Results

Figure 2 shows the time averaged PVF of baseline benchmarks under two system setups: ARMv7a and ARMv8a ISAs, i.e., AArch32 and AArch64. The out-of-order CPU models are the same. For most benchmarks, A32 PVFs are approximately 1.5× or 2× as large as the A64 PVFs at the same phase of the program runtime. PVF is a ratio of the total number of ACE bits to all bits in the concerned structure. A64 has 32 general-purpose registers. Comparing with A32, the available architectural register doubles in A64. More architectural resources mean more bits in the architectural register file. If we only consider the program's execution and ignore instruction related to the operating system, then the number of register accesses should be in the same order of magnitude. Therefore, an approximate ratio of 2 between these two ISAs is a natural outcome of PVF computation methodology. Susan_S and String Search benchmarks are two special cases; ratios between A32 and A64 are 1.25 and 2.32. This diversion could be a result of different PVF responses to masking. The factors that may affect PVF response include register accesses, instruction-level logic masking, algorithms, or data structures in higher-level codes. The first half of FFT execution phases also differed with other workloads: PVF of A64 is higher than A32. One reason could be FFT has a few floating-point operations, yet PVF computation only considered integer registers in this work.

Despite the apparent variance in PVF values, the shapes of A32 and A64 PVFs are similar for most benchmarks. The average correlation coefficient

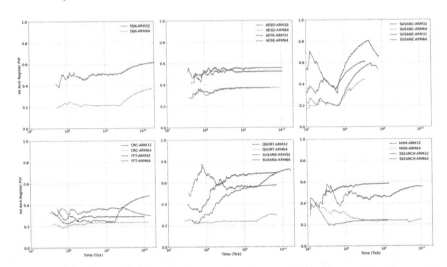

Fig. 2. Time-averaged PVFs of different ISAs (A32 and A64) estimated by gem5Panalyzer. Note the horizontal axis (time) is on a logarithm scale. PVF of A32 is usually two times larger than A64. Though special cases exist, such as SUSAN_S, StringSearch, and FFT

between A32 and A64 PVFs of all test benches is 0.69. This correlation indicates though A32 and A64 are different ISAs, they still share some similarities. It is predictable that an ISA other than ARM, such as X86 and RISC, will behave differently. Note that ARM64 is usually faster than ARM32 systems under the same microarchitectural configuration. AES encryption benchmark running in 64-bit gets a more than 2× speedup over the 32-bit. These results show advanced architectures tend to be efficient and may have a lower PVF.

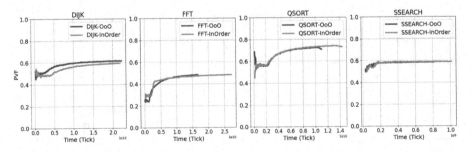

Fig. 3. Time averaged PVFs of AArch32 for in-order (InOrder) and out-of-order (OoO) systems. Except for DIJK (Dijkstra), other benchmarks run faster on O3 CPUs. The horizontal axis is on a linear scale to highlight that the OoO microarchitecture usually has better performance

Figure 3 shows the PVFs of 32-bit in-order and out-of-order systems (a subset of 15 benchmarks). The in-order CPU typically requires a much longer time to run the same program than the out-of-order model. There is little difference between the PVF values for in-order and out-of-order microarchitectures. The PVFs of the in-order system behave like a delayed out-of-order system. If the execution time is normalized to the same scale, then the PVF curves and values will be identical. For all A32 applications, the average correlation coefficient of PVFs between in-order and out-of-order reaches 0.98. The high correlation and the small PVF difference show computed PVF is microarchitectural independent.

Figure 4 presents the comparison between PVF estimations made by gem5Panalyzer with the beam-test results published in [20]. The beam test experiments are conducted on an ARM Cortex-A9 CPU embedded in the Xilinx Zynq board. ACE bits in architectural resources may cause SDC, a crash, or hanging, depending on where they are in the instruction flow. As a result, PVFs are relevant to the vulnerabilities of lower levels in the system stack. By summing up all types of error rates in the beam test, a comparison between PVF and beam test will be more rational. The experimental results show a correlation between A32 PVFs and beam test results on the Cortex-A9 CPU, and its correlation coefficient reached 0.71. Gem5Panalyzer provides a quick lower bound estimation of software vulnerability though some mismatches exist.

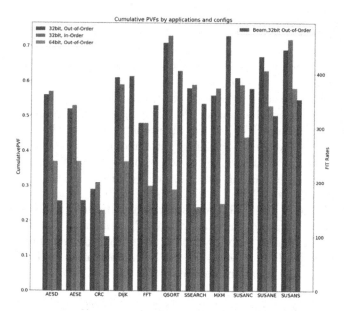

Fig. 4. PVF-masking sweep results of selected benchmarks. PVFs of GSM, AESD are more sensitive to masking, whereas the PVF SUSAN_S Note M × M shows a noticeable temporal variance in PVF response to masking.

4.3 Summary of Toolset Evaluation

In this section, we validated gem5Panayzer in the following characteristics of PVF: 1) PVF calculations made by gem5Panalyzer can provide a conservative estimation of the system vulnerability. Compared with total FIT rates from beam tests in [20], gem5Panalyzer provides a reasonable assessment of systems' vulnerability running various workloads. 2) PVF computations from gem5Panalyzer matched PVF behaviors described in [9, 13]. Computed PVFs are only dependent on binaries associated with an ISA. When the program implementation, compiler options, and associated inputs are constant, PVF does not vary with different microarchitectures.

5 PVF Responses to Masking Effects

Instruction level masking reflects mitigation techniques deployed at its underlying abstraction layers. Typically, a higher masking factor leads to a lower system error rate. Meanwhile, the cost of resiliency design will increase. In this section, we analyzed the PVF response to masking. Instruction-level masking sweep is a more abstract but efficient way to guide trade-offs for system resilience.

5.1 Masking Sweep Methodology and Metrics

Recall the methodology we applied to estimate PVF: apart from computing the fine-grained masking factor, users can directly set the average instruction-level masking. The overall masking level is set to step from 0.0 to 0.9. A 0.0 masking factor indicates all bits during the ACE interval may lead to incorrect outputs. Conversely, when masking equals 1.0, all instruction level faults are masked, then PVF will be zero. The runtime PVF is computed for each step of masking level sweep to catch the PVF improvements at resiliency when hardening the design. Improving the overall masking factor requires additional efforts, which can grow drastically when a high masking level is needed. The return of the efforts to increase the masking factor is defined in Eqs. (2) and (3). Reduction means the reduction of PVF of increased masking levels to the PVF when the masking level is zero. The PVF drop is normalized from 0 to 1 range. We define the terminology "Return of Investment (ROI)" to quantify benefits of investing area, power, performance for applying various mitigation techniques to improve system masking level. ROI equals to the harmonic mean of PVF reductions throughout the entire program lifetime.

$$Reduction = \frac{|PVF_{original} - PVF_{improved}|}{PVF_{original}} \tag{2}$$

$$ROI = \frac{n \times \prod_{i-1}^{n} Reduction_i}{\sum_{n=1}^{n} [\frac{1}{Reduction_i} \times \prod_{i-1}^{n} Reduction_i]} \tag{3}$$

5.2   ROIs of Selected Benchmarks

Figure 5 shows the masking level sweep results of selected benchmarks. The PVFs of the GSM, Sha, and AES decryption are sensitive to masking factor changes. For AES decryption, increasing the masking level to 0.9 can reduce the cumulative PVF from 0.56 to 0.18. When GSM is the workload, PVF will go from 0.67 to 0.23 if the masking factor rises to 0.9. On the other hand, the PVF Dijkstra and Susan smoothing applications are robust to escalated masking. When the masking factor is less than 0.7, the PVF of SUSAN_S remains nearly fixed and ranges from 0.65 to 0.7. A 0.9 masking help reduce PVF from 0.70 to 0.53. Matrix Multiplication behaves like a mix of the previous two workloads. The first half of M × M performs element-wise matrix multiplications, and the PVF response is similar to SUSAN_S. In the second half of the program lifetime, it returns computed results. PVF becomes more sensitive to changes in the masking level. This finding is worthy to note, as the temporal variance of PVF sensitivity will help design dynamic and adaptive system hardening schemes. Using Eq. (3), we extracted the ROIs (time-averaged PVF reductions) from deploying mitigation techniques to improve the masking factor. ROIs of several applications are grouped and shown in Fig. 6. For the SUSAN application set to perform edge detection or corner detection, program resilience will benefit from the improved masking. However, the ROI of SUSAN smoothing workload is limited. When masking is 0.9, corner detection can achieve a 0.53 PVF reduction, whereas the ROI of smoothing is only 0.23. The ROI of M × M benchmarks is also confined to up to 0.31. Improving the masking level can provide significant ROI for AES_D and FFT applications; the maximum ROI can reach 0.68 and 0.61, respectively. Figure 7 also shows when the masking is at a lower level, like 0 0.3. ROIs are close for most workloads except for M × M, Dijkstra, and SUSAN_S.

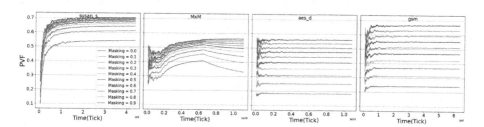

Fig. 5. PVF-masking sweep results of selected benchmarks. PVFs of GSM, AESD are more sensitive to masking, whereas PVFs of SUSAN_S and M × M are robust to masking. Note M × M shows a noticeable temporal variance in PVF response to masking

5.3   Factors Affect the ROI

As shown in Fig. 5 and Fig. 6, improving masking levels cannot provide noticeable PVF reduction when the system runs workloads, including M × M and SUSAN_S.

One common attribute of these two applications is extensive operations interact with arrays or matrices. M × M multiplies two randomly initialized matrices with pre-defined dimensions. SUSAN_S performs image smoothing, which also invokes Gaussian filtering. Applying Gaussian filtering on images is equivalent to carrying convolution operations using the Gaussian Kernel and the image pixels.

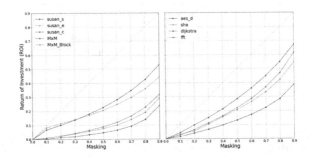

Fig. 6. ROI of selected benchmarks, responses of SUSAN_S, Dijkstra, and M × M are less sensitive to masking

To examine the possible correlations between extensive array operations and insensitivity response, we modified Qsort and SUSAN_S to control the intensity of array operations. A series of redundant array operations are added to Qsort_small source code in MiBench. For each call of the compare function between two strings, the original returned value is used to fill an array with specified lengths. Instead of returning the comparison result directly, the modified compare function retrieves results from the redundant array. When the length of the redundant array increases, the intensity of the array operation grows. Similarly, SUSAN_S can control the intensity by increase the size of the Gaussian Kernel. Increasing the kernel size is equivalent to performing more element multiplications between elements in matrices. Figure 7 shows the ROI response when the intensity of array operations grows. Qsort with redundant vector operations shows the overall PVF reduction decreases with increased redundant array size. SUSAN smoothing shows a similar trend. When kernel size increases from 3 to 10, the ROI is reduced by more than 50% (from 0.23 to 0.09, masking = 0.9). Figure 7 also shows adverse effects of array-like operations can be alleviated if the masking level is low. Comparing with higher masking levels, The ROI at a 0.3 masking factor remains stable.

5.4   Optimize the ROI

Different algorithms for the same functionality differ in performance and system vulnerability. The algorithm may affect the ROI as well. We examined Qsort and M × M benchmarks with alternative algorithm implementations. Original

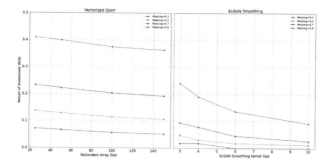

Fig. 7. ROI response to the intensity of array operations. Redundant array size and kernel size are positively correlated with array ops intensity

M × M uses element-wise multiplication, whereas the modified M × M multiplies by block (blocksize = 16). Vanilla Qsort calls the qsort function in Cstdlib, which uses insertion the PVF of M × M_block is higher than M × M for all masking levels. As shown in Fig. 8, the difference between ROI is comparable though the ROI of M × M is slightly higher. The PVF or Qsort_iter is lower than the original Qsort. Besides, Qsort_iter shows a better ROI response than Qsort when the masking level is higher than 0.6. Therefore, algorithm optimization for specific programs not only helps improve system resilience but can improve the ROI to implement system hardening.

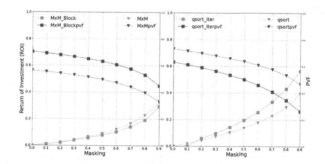

Fig. 8. Algorithm impact on ROIs of M × M and Qsort. Blue curves represent PVFs, and red ones means ROI responses., dashed lines are vanilla programs and solid lines represents alternated algorithms. Modified Qsort program improves both PVF and ROI response (Color figure online)

Rescheduling instructions to shorten Write-Read and Read-Read intervals but lengthen the Read-Write intervals is a trending approach to reduce PVF. Previous publications such as [9,18] show that appropriate loop unrolling may reduce vulnerable periods and improve PVF. Figure 9 shows loop unrolling also helps to optimize the return-cost trade-offs if used correctly. The PVFs of

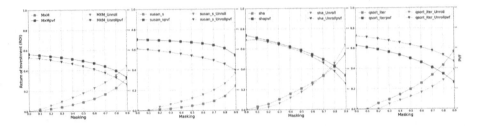

Fig. 9. Impact of loop unrolling on PVFs and ROIs of selected workloads. Unguided loop unrolling can be either beneficial (SUSAN_S and M × M), harmful (Qsort), or nonobvious (SHA)

SUSAN_S and M × M are reduced after loop unrolling, and ROI also increased slightly. At a masking level of 0.5, the ROI of SUSAN_S increases by 140% compared to the original binary. However, inappropriate loop unrolling can be harmful to system reliability. We use the SHA application to show less efficient instruction rescheduling. The PVFs of loop-unrolled SHA and the vanilla one is analogous with little differences at most masking levels. When masking level is smaller than 0.7, the ROI of vanilla SHA is slightly higher than the loop-unrolled one. For Qsort_iter application, unguided loop unrolling leads to increased PVFs and diminishes ROIs. In this example, we show instruction rescheduling hurts the PVF reduction from system hardening.

6   Summary

We examined PVF estimations of gem5Panalyzer, a light-weight architectural reliability evaluation tool, with the discussions in relevant publications. An efficient approach to evaluate trade-offs of system hardening was discussed. The efforts of implementing protections below the architectural layer are modeled as the instruction-level masking factor. We use the metric: The Return of the investment to improving the masking (ROI) to quantify the efficiency of lower layer hardening, i.e., the average PVF reduction is expected to get when deploying lower-layer protections. We also provide examples to show how software and software-layer optimization affect the ROI of hardening. Results suggest that appropriate higher-layer optimization can help improve system resilience and the return of lower-layer protections.

References

1. Chatzidimitriou, A., Gizopoulos, D.: rACE: reverse-order processor reliability analysis. In: 2020 Design, Automation & Test in Europe Conference & Exhibition (DATE), pp. 1115–1120. IEEE (2020)
2. Biswas, A., et al.: Computing architectural vulnerability factors for address-based structures. In: 32nd International Symposium on Computer Architecture (ISCA 2005), pp. 532–543. IEEE (2005)

3. Fang, B., et al.: ePVF: an enhanced program vulnerability factor methodology for cross-layer resilience analysis. In: 2016 Proceedings of the 46th Annual IEEE/IFIP International Conference on Dependable Systems and Networks, pp. 168–179. IEEE (2016)
4. Shafique, M., Rehman, S., Aceituno, P.V., Henkel, J.: Exploiting program-level masking and error propagation for constrained reliability optimization. In: Proceedings of the 50th Annual Design Automation Conference, pp. 1–9 (2013)
5. Cheng, E., et al.: Tolerating soft errors in processor cores using clear (cross-layer exploration for architecting resilience). IEEE Trans. Comput. Aided Des. Integr. Circ. Syst. **37**(9), 1839–1852 (2017)
6. Leem, L., et al.: ERSA: error resilient system architecture for probabilistic applications. In: 2010 Design, Automation & Test in Europe Conference & Exhibition (DATE 2010), pp. 1560–1565. IEEE (2010)
7. Qiu, H., et al.: Gem5Panalyzer: a light-weight tool for early-stage architectural reliability evaluation & prediction. In: 2020 IEEE 63rd International Midwest Symposium on Circuits and Systems (MWSCAS), pp. 482–485. IEEE (2020)
8. Guthaus, M.R., et al.: MiBench: a free, commercially representative embedded benchmark suite. In: Proceedings of the Fourth Annual IEEE International Workshop on Workload Characterization, pp. 3–14. IEEE (2001)
9. Sridharan, V., Kaeli, D.R.: Eliminating microarchitectural dependency from architectural vulnerability. In: 2009 IEEE 15th International Symposium on High Performance Computer Architecture, pp. 117–128. IEEE (2009)
10. Henkel, J., et al.: Reliable on-chip systems in the nano-era: lessons learnt and future trends. In: 2013 50th ACM/EDAC/IEEE Design Automation Conference (DAC), pp. 1–10. IEEE (2013)
11. Mukherjee, S.S., et al.: A systematic methodology to compute the architectural vulnerability factors for a high-performance microprocessor. In: 2003 Proceedings of the 36th Annual IEEE/ACM International Symposium on Microarchitecture, MICRO-36, pp. 29–40. IEEE (2003)
12. Quinn, H., et al.: Using benchmarks for radiation testing of microprocessors and FPGAs. IEEE Trans. Nucl. Sci. **62**(6), 2547–2554 (2015)
13. Biswas, A., Soundararajan, N., Mukherjee, S.S., Gurumurthi, S.: Quantized AVF: a means of capturing vulnerability variations over small windows of time. In: IEEE Workshop on Silicon Errors in Logic-System Effects (2009)
14. Kaliorakis, M., Gizopoulos, D., Canal, R., Gonzalez, A.: MeRLiN: exploiting dynamic instruction behavior for fast and accurate microarchitecture level reliability assessment. In: Proceedings of the 44th Annual International Symposium on Computer Architecture, pp. 241–254 (2017)
15. Venkatagiri, R., et al.: Gem5-Approxilyzer: an open-source tool for application-level soft error analysis. In: Proceedings of the 49th Annual IEEE/IFIP International Conference on Dependable Systems and Networks, pp. 214–221. IEEE (2019)
16. Jiao, J., Juan, D.-C., Marculescu, D., Fu, Y.: Exploiting component dependency for accurate and efficient soft error analysis via Probabilistic Graphical Models. Microelectron. Reliab. **55**(1), 251–263 (2015)
17. Lee, J., Shrivastava, A.: A compiler optimization to reduce soft errors in register files. ACM Sigplan Not. **44**(7), 41–49 (2009)
18. Rehman, S., Shafique, M., Kriebel, F., Henkel, J.: Reliable software for unreliable hardware: embedded code generation aiming at reliability. In: Proceedings of the International Conference on Hardware/Software Codesign and System Synthesis, pp. 237–246. IEEE (2011)

19. Binkert, N., et al.: The gem5 simulator. SIGARCH Comput. Archit. News **39**(2), 1–7 (2011)
20. Chatzidimitriou, A., et al.: Demystifying soft error assessment strategies on arm CPUs: microarchitectural fault injection vs. neutron beam experiments. In: Proceedings of the 49th Annual IEEE/IFIP International Conference on Dependable Systems and Networks, pp. 26–38. IEEE (2019)

Author Index

Printed in the United States
by Baker & Taylor Publisher Services